◇

European Cases in Retailing

◇

Edited by

MARC DUPUIS AND JOHN DAWSON

BLACKWELL
Business

Copyright © Blackwell Publishers Ltd 1999

Editorial selection, arrangement and
apparatus copyright © Marc Dupuis and John Dawson 1999

First published 1999

2 4 6 8 10 9 7 5 3 1

Blackwell Publishers Ltd
108 Cowley Road
Oxford OX4 1JF
UK

Blackwell Publishers Inc.
350 Main Street
Malden, Massachusetts 02148
USA

British Library Cataloguing in Publication Data
A CIP catalogue record for this book is available from the British Library

Library of Congress Cataloging-in-Publication Data

European cases in retailing / edited by Marc Dupuis and John Dawson.
p.   cm.
Includes bibliographical references and index.
ISBN 0-631-20730-9 (alk. paper)
1. Retail trade–Europe–Case studies. I. Dupuis, Marc.
II. Dawson, John A.
HF5429.6 E9E868 1999
381'.1'094–dc21   98-27031
CIP

Typeset in 10½ on 12½ pt Times Roman by Wearset, Boldon, Tyne and Wear.
Printed in Great Britain by TJ International, Padstow, Cornwall.

This book is printed on acid-free paper

Contents

List of Contributors

Marc Benoun, Université Paris IX-Dauphine, place du Maréchal de Lattre de Tassigny, 75775 Paris Cedex 16, tel: +33 1 44 05 44 26, fax: +33 1 44 05 44 49, E-mail: benoun@dauphine.fr.

David Bennison, Department of Retailing and Marketing, Faculty of Management and Business, Manchester Metropolitan University, Aytoun Street, Manchester M1 3GH, tel: +44 161 2473858, fax: +44 161 2476305, E-mail: D.Bennison@mmu.ac.uk.

Christina Boutsouki, Management Centre, University of Leicester, University Road, Leicester LE1 7RH, tel: +44 116 2525647, fax: +44 116 2523949, E-mail: CB37@le.ac.uk.

Enrico Colla, University of Lyon, 24 rue Louis Blanc, 75010 Paris, E-mail: ecolla@schamp.ccip.1.

John Dawson, School of Management, University of Edinburgh, 50 George Square, Edinburgh EH8 9JY, tel: +44 131 650 3828, fax: +44 131 668 3053, E-mail: John.Dawson@ed.ac.uk.

Tomás Drtina, INCOMA Praha, Benesovská 21, Prague 10, CZ 10100, tel: +42 2 67311300, fax: +42 2 67311401.

Marc Dupuis, Groupe École Supérieure de Commerce de Paris, 79, avenue de la République, 75011 Paris, tel: +33 1 49 23 22 47, fax: +33 1 49 23 22 48, E-mail: dupuis@escp.fr.

Paul Freathy, Institute for Retail Studies, University of Stirling, Stirling FK9 4LA, tel: +44 1786 467410, fax: +44 1786 465290, E-mail: j.p.freathy@stirling.ac.uk.

Frédéric Fréry, Groupe École Supérieure de Commerce de Paris, 79, avenue de la République, 75543 Paris Cedex 11, tel: +33 1 49 23 22 62, fax: +33 1 43 55 99 63, E-mail frery@escp.fr.

Jacqui Gush, School of Service Industries, Bournemouth University, Poole,

Dorset BH21 2UJ, tel: +44 1202 59 5097, fax: +44 1202 515707,
E-mail: jgush@bournemouth.ac.uk.
Evert Helfferich, Retail Management School Leeuwarden, P.O. Box 1298,
8900 CG Leeuwarden, tel: +31 58 2330381 or 2330533,
fax: +31 58 2330430.
Marjolein Hinfelaar, Retail Management School Leeuwarden, P.O. Box
1298, 8900 CG Leeuwarden, tel: +31 58 2330381 or 2330533,
fax: +31 58 2330430.
Frédéric Jallat, Groupe École Supérieure de Commerce de Paris, 79,
avenue de la République, 75543 Paris cedex 11, tel: +33 1 49 23 22 51,
fax: +33 1 43 55 99 63, E-mail: jallat@escp.fr.
Tomás Krásny, INCOMA Praha, Benesovská 21, Prague 10, CZ 10100,
tel: +42 2 67311300, fax: +42 2 67311401.
Malcolm Lochhead, Department of Consumer Studies, Glasgow
Caledonian University, Park Campus, 1 Park Drive, Glasgow G3 6LP,
tel: +44 141 337 4382, fax: +44 141 337 4420.
Lluís Martínez-Ribes, ESADE, Av. Pedralbes, 60–62, 08034 Barcelona,
tel: +34 93 280 61 62, fax: +34 93 204 81 05,
E-mail: lluis@martinez-ribes.com.
Christopher M. Moore, Department of Consumer Studies, Glasgow
Caledonian University, Park Campus, 1 Park Drive, Glasgow G3 6LP,
tel: +44 141 337 4382, fax: +44 141 337 4420.
Edmund O'Callaghan, School of Distribution, Dublin Institute of
Technology, Mountjoy Square, Dublin 1, tel: +353 1 4024201,
fax: +353 1 4024296, E-mail: eocallag@comad.dit.ie.
Gilles Paché, Centre de Recherche sur le Transport et la Logistique,
Université de la Méditerranée (Aix-Marseille II), CRET-LOG, avenue
Gaston Berger, 13625 Aix-en-Provence Cedex 1, tel: +33 42 93 90 51,
fax: +33 42 93 90 40.
Nathalie Prime, Groupe École Supérieure de Commerce de Paris, 79,
avenue de la République, 75011 Paris, tel: +33 1 49 23 22 44,
fax: +33 1 49 23 22 48, E-mail: prime@escp.fr.
Léon Salto, Deputy Chief Operating Officer, Promodès.
Lynn Stainsby, Leicester University Management Centre, University Road,
Leicester LE1 7RH, tel: +44 116 2525638, fax: +44 116 2525638,
E-mail: LS13@Le.ac.uk.
Élisabeth Tissier-Desbordes, Groupe École Supérieure de Commerce de
Paris, 79, avenue de la République, 75011 Paris, tel: +33 1 49 23 22 47,
fax: +33 1 49 23 22 48, E-mail: tissier@escp.fr.
María Dolores De Juan Vigaray, Facultad de Ciencias Económicas y
Empresariles, Universidad de Alicante, San Vicente, E-03080, Alicante,

tel: +34 96 590 3400, fax: +34 96 590 3621, E-mail: mayo@ua.es.

Paul Whysall, Nottingham Business School, Nottingham Trent University, Burton Street, Nottingham NG1 4BU, tel: +44 (0)115 9418418, fax: +44 (0)115 9416512, E-mail: smm3whysapt@ntu.ac.uk.

Mary Wilcox, School of Distribution, Dublin Institute of Technology, Mountjoy Square, Dublin 1, tel: +353 1 4024218, fax: +353 1 4024296, E-mail: mwilcox@comad.dit.ie.

$\Diamond$

Preface

Retailing within the European economy is one of the success stories of the late twentieth century. The sector has expanded in volume and variety of activity; productivity of labour and capital has risen; retailers have responded positively to the challenges of new information and communication technologies; and the sector has been instrumental in governmental policies to restrain inflationary processes within the economy. Whilst many of the traditional manufacturing sectors have suffered decline, the very long-established and traditional sector of retailing has been restructured and has prospered. The large firms, exemplified by Metro, Marks & Spencer, Ahold, Tesco and Promodès have become benchmark companies for others wishing to measure their own performance against the best in Europe. At the same time, the sector has seen the birth of many small firms which are successful at a local and family level. In looking for an economic sector where good management practice can be viewed through all sizes of firm, then the retail sector is particularly prominent.

The reasons for the success of the retail sector and of firms within it relate to its responsiveness to consumer demand and behaviour which imbues in the sector a need to be generally responsive to the environment in which it operates. This environment goes beyond the consumer issues to include responsiveness to suppliers and competitors, responsiveness to market opportunities, responsiveness to governmental policy or to technology. By its nature, retailing is concerned with responding to change and, in so doing, shaping the same environment to which it also responds.

In considering the changes, we see as particularly important the changes in consumer demand and behaviour. Retailers have to monitor, respond to and shape consumer demand in all its forms. In Europe, there are strong processes of convergence in consumer patterns with European-wide branding of products and stores, European-wide store formats, European-wide fashion and food trends and other moves to generate a Euro-consumer. At the same time, however, there are similarly strong trends to divergence with consumers seeking individuality in products and stores, a greater wish by consumers to relate to their local or regional cultures and the emergence of highly distinctive regional consumer lifestyles and culture. The tension between convergence and divergence in consumer patterns is a key factor in understanding the success of European retailing.

A second key factor is the tension between centralization and decentralization of management. This can be seen in respect of the retail firm and of the public sector management of the economy more generally. Retailing is an industry in which large firms have to grapple with the issues of decentralization because the large firms in store-based retailing have a spatially dispersed and, in consequence, managerially decentralized, to some extent, network of decision points, namely a chain of shops. The challenges faced by retailers focus on managing a dispersed network of managers who respond to local conditions and at the same time having sufficient centralization of transaction costs to benefit from scale economies in the organization. That the best of the large companies have found ways of achieving this balance is impressive but the equilibrium they have achieved is a dynamic one.

A third factor in understanding why retailing has been so successful is the change in the role that retailing has taken for itself in the economy. From a situation in which retailers were passive conduits for the distribution of goods, the role has changed dramatically across Europe in the last 30 years. Retailers now increasingly pull products from retailers. Retailers have become more active in interpreting consumer demand. With this knowledge the retailers can influence product design, development and delivery by the manufacturers. Negotiating power has thus moved from manufacturer to retailer. Retailers have become, as a consequence, a more decisive force within the European economy.

The dynamism of retailing is reflected in the cases proved in this book. The cases originally were presented at a conference of the European Association for Research and Education in Commercial Distribution. The Association is a network of university-based scholars from across Europe. The Association saw a need for good case studies to enhance the teaching of retail management and the conference was the result. The cases are not simply stories of how particular firms undertook particular activities. Each of the cases addresses a particular set of issues and the case is written to enable the exploration of the issues. Some of the cases deal with specific conditions which no longer concern the particular firm but the case illustrates a general issue applicable to retail management. The cases are drawn from across

Europe and illustrate some of the similarities and differences in the issues facing retailers from different countries.

The cases are divided into two groups and are presented as Parts I and II in this book. The first group considers issues about the internationalization of retailing and the second group considers various aspects of the retail mix.

The editors acknowledge with thanks the work of the advisory group for the conference. This comprised: Barry Davies (Manchester Metropolitan University, UK), Marjolein Hinfelaar (Retail Management School, Leeuwarden, the Netherlands), Luca Pellegrini (Bocconi University, Milano, Italy), Lluís Martínez-Ribes (ESADE, Barcelona, Spain) and Leigh Sparks (University of Stirling, UK)

Professor Marc Dupuis
Professor John Dawson

Part I
The Internationalization of Retailing

$\diamondsuit$

Introduction to Part I

The internationalization of retailing presents some very particular managerial problems for retailers. Unlike the internationalization of manufacturing where often a small number of large economic units such as factories, are involved, the internationalization of retailing often involves the management of a large number of relatively small economic units such as shops. Issues of communication, consistency, control and responsibility are very different in the case of retailing.

The contact between retailers and consumers, which is the core of retail activity, is profoundly influenced as retailers establish stores in different countries with their different cultures. Not only do consumers from different countries expect different product ranges but also store layout, design, employee relations, and many other operational aspects become influenced by the society and culture in which the store operates.

The case studies in Part I illustrate some key themes and provide opportunities for exploration of these issues through case discussion. Chapter 1 is an introductory presentation which provides an overview for the internationalization process and explores its rationale. It examines the case of Promodès as reported by Léon Salto, the firm's Deputy Operating Officer. The issues raised are those of the strategies available in the growth of the large firm – can a successful large firm in Europe have a strategy which does not involve operating outside its domestic market? He explores why he believes the answer to this question is a resounding 'No'.

Five case studies follow, each of which explores different approaches to internationalization. They each explore retailing in a different product area. Christopher Moore considers fashion clothes and explores the franchise approach to international operation. The case of IKEA illustrates a firm which is internationalizing a design concept through the home furnishing market. In many ways, as Nathalie Prime points out, IKEA is an exporter with the export being Swedish design and Swedish managerial style. Few concessions are made to local culture in such an exercise. Mary Wilcox and Edmund O'Callaghan explore a very specific form of retailing within a very controlled shopping environment, albeit an international one. Their case study deals with Aer Rianta, an international duty-free shop. Again, there are limited concessions to local culture but as the firm has moved up its learning curve so more local adaptation occurs. The Free Record Shop explores how an entrepreneurial managerial style can be the mechanism for international expansion. Evert Helffreich and Marjolein Hifelaar consider the options for a relatively small firm with a very tightly defined store format and consider how consumers in a different country react to such a tightly constrained retail offer. The final case study of the sequence on different approaches to internationalization again addresses franchising with the case of Body Shop. Paul Freathy also explores the extent to which strength of retail concept and franchising interact with stronger issues of corporate culture.

A second group of case studies in Part I considers the impact of international retailers on domestic competition. Case studies from contrasting sectors and situations are explored. Christina Boutsouki explores the transfer of management know-how which results from international joint ventures. The conflict in such activities are well recorded but the specific managerial benefits are often less well recorded. The case study considers the emergent market of Greece whilst the following case study also considers an emergent market, namely the Czech Republic. Tomás Drtina and Tomás Krásny consider the Interkontakt group which has responded aggressively to foreign competition by building up its own chain of stores.

The key questions raised by the case studies in Part I are:

1   What are the benefits of going international, and what are the costs?
2   To what extent is a retail concept exportable and to what extent has it to be modified to the local consumer?
3   When is franchising an appropriate mechanism for international expansion?
4   What are the alternative mechanisms for market entry and what considerations do retailers have in making a choice of entry mechanism?
5   How can local retailers co-operate or compete with foreign entrants?

The internationalization of retailing in Europe is a process which is not well understood by academics and by retailers alike. There are some exceptional successes but equally there are some dramatic failures. In the next few years, as more firms succeed and more fail then perhaps we will gain a better understanding of the factors behind success.

1

Towards Global Retailing: The Promodès Case

LÉON SALTO

For the major food producers, internationalization is already well under way: Nestlé was already in Japan in 1904 and had established itself in nearly every country of Latin America before the Second World War. Specialist retailers like McDonald's, Toys 'R' Us, Marks & Spencer and IKEA started going international more recently but have already made up a lot of ground. On the other hand, internationalization is a relatively recent strategy for non-specialist mass retailers, and a number of experts argue against it, making the valid point that, unlike manufacturing, selling has to be a localized activity because consumers in Seville do not have the same tastes as shoppers in Berlin, Liverpool or Paris, to say nothing of Taipai, Dubai or Casablanca.

It is true that national markets are generally dominated by regional or national companies. It is also true that numerous unsuccessful attempts at internationalization, notably by US or Canadian companies in Europe in the 1960s and by French companies in the United States more recently, have strengthened the idea that it is difficult to export non-specialist retailing skills.

Despite all this, however, it is clear that internationalization has accelerated in our sector over the past 20 years. A growing number of companies, for example Metro, Makro, Lidl, Aldi, Delhaize, Carrefour, Ahold, Auchan, Tengelman and, more recently, Wal-Mart, KMart, Price-Costco, Tesco and Sainsbury, have been developing very successful strategies for going international.

At Promodès our first moves into international markets came about by chance, and it was only later that they became a necessity. The chance was a matter of unforeseen events and meetings, and unexpected opportunities. The necessity followed from the fact that internationalization then became part and parcel of our growth strategy, which has always made geographical diversification a major objective. Promodès is now present, in one form or another, in seven European countries outside France: Spain, Portugal, Italy, Germany, Greece, Turkey and Belgium. We have also signed agreements with local groups to develop in Taiwan, Morocco and in the Gulf region at Dubai. In addition, of course, we have Continent stores in the Canary Islands, the Antilles, Tahiti, Noumea, Réunion and Mauritius.

WHY WE NEED TO INTERNATIONALIZE

No matter how it may have started, our move into international markets after 1974 was as determined as it was cautious. At that time, if we wanted to assure our future by becoming one of the leaders of our sector, we needed to identify better paths to growth than our much bigger competitors. International development was such a path on both strategic grounds, and economic and political grounds

The strategic reasons for pursuing international development

Starting from the assumption that one is as competent as one's rivals, we think competition makes internationalization a necessity for a retailing group. The reasons for this view are twofold:

1 so that the retail group can be of a comparable size to its main rivals and not suffer from a lack of economies of scale;
2 so that the retail group can invest wherever it finds good expansion opportunities, such as a less competitive market or a behind-the-times retail sector, offering both superior growth potential and a faster return on investment.

On the first point, I want to stress that achieving sufficient size relative to one's rivals, and the speed at which one needs to grow in order to achieve and then keep this size, have become key issues in today's commercial world. For a long time, people thought that pursuing size as such was a mistake, and that once one had achieved 'critical mass', for example sufficient to purchase on the best terms, growth need no longer be a primary objective. In fact, critical mass is not a question of absolute but of relative size. Relative, that is, to one's partners and one's competitors. This is why it is so important to identify carefully one's potential rivals, whose number is not necessarily limited to those one is facing today; Wal-Mart offers a good example. As long as your partners and rivals are growing you must grow too, and sometimes faster than them if you have started too small or too late in a given market.

I see five main areas in which a group's relative size can either create an advantage or be a handicap in a competitive market.

Purchasing

Let us take the example of Aldi, because its arrival in France opened our eyes on this point. What Aldi made us realize is that, even where there is limited scope for increasing productivity in a specific type of store, we can uncover a big reserve of productivity upstream by rationalizing our purchasing and distribution systems in partnership with our industrial suppliers. All that Aldi had succeeded in doing was to keep overheads at the same percentage level for 40 years. But this performance was none the less better than anyone else in the sector, with the exception of Wal-Mart.

The volume of orders that Aldi is able to pass to a single supplier allows it to buy much more cheaply, while maintaining both the quality of the product and the manufacturer's profitability. This is because the manufacturer can afford to invest in the latest technology to meet Aldi's requirements, and has time to familiarize itself fully with the product. The presumption is that the relationship between Aldi and a particular supplier will be relatively long term and to the benefit of both parties.

Thus, by channelling a growing volume of orders towards a particular manufacturer, the retailer allows the latter to reduce the added costs of production and to spread his investment in research and development over a bigger turnover. The fact that the retailer contracts to take a guaranteed quantity for a guaranteed period reduces the manufacturer's level of risk on the contract, and therefore the level of profit needed to cover it.

This is why it is essential, particularly at the international level, to seek to turn manufacturers into partners, on the basis of at least three fundamental principles:

1 Respect for the terms of the contract on both sides.
2 Partnership in the development of retailers' own brands.
3 Partnership in looking for ways of cutting costs right down the chain from production to distribution.

This is also why Promodès has set up the two international purchasing centres, P.W.T. for food and CIM for general merchandise.

As a general rule, a manufacturer's added costs of production fall by

20 per cent every time output doubles. This shows the tremendous leverage effect of volume in a partnership based on the three principles listed above. Where purchases are sourced world-wide rather than country-wide or continent-wide, as is increasingly the case with mass consumer goods, particularly non-food lines, one can readily see the difference between the prices faced by a company like Wal-Mart, with a turnover of $85bn and a world-wide buying organization, and a local business competing against it with, for example, similar stores in Arkansas or Canada, in Argentina or Brazil. And this is true whether for an electric drill, a TV set, a shirt, a pair of shoes or a tin of dog or cat food. You can ask a lot of your colleagues, but to ask them to satisfy consumers despite a big disadvantage in purchasing costs is really to set them an almost impossible task.

Efficient logistics

As sourcing becomes more and more a world-wide exercise it is essential to organize the distribution of products, whatever their source and destination, at the lowest cost possible. Here, again, the stakes are high, and concentrating volumes by large continental area will be a key tool in optimizing flows at the national or regional level. In addition, one must try to make use of a logistics network carrying the biggest volume per square kilometre relative to one's competitors. This must be achieved even if it means sharing a network with several retail chains, as long as their commercial policy and thus their sourcing are well coordinated. In this case, the links between Champion and Continent are a good example.

Efficient management

Sourcing, logistics, merchandising and check-out registration, to cite just a few steps in the movement of a product, now require *high performance, adaptable and reasonably priced data-processing networks* which are all efficiently managed. All this is possible, but the right choices must be made about the goals one wants to attain and what software to buy, all the more so if sourcing is going to be conducted on a world-wide basis.

Experience

I must not fail to mention *accumulated experience* as a strategic factor because to achieve your targets, apart from making the right strategic choices, you must have people with the knowledge and skills to implement strategy rapidly and well. Internationalization and competition are not happening in a vacuum, and while you are moving so your major competitors are themselves running faster and faster. Here, again, big groups that know how to accumulate and then transfer experience in a shorter and shorter time have a decisive advantage.

Advertising and promotion

This is the fifth strategic factor linked with absolute size. Communication is still mainly regional or national, but it is already clear that the world-wide recognition of names like McDonald's, Toys 'R' Us, IKEA and Marks & Spencer makes it easier for them to grow, to gain a foothold in a local market and to develop a loyal clientele.

We must not forget that we are selling personal items and household equipment that consumers have long bought by mail order. Who is to say that, with interactive TV, buying from home will not become more common, at least for these types of products? If it does, do you imagine that satellite TV will respect frontiers? This new kind of retailing will require a sizeable investment to cover the world, but much smaller than that needed to set up networks of shops on the ground, and it will be investment of a different type, with more soft goods and fewer hard goods. All they will then need to deliver goods such as shirts, electric drills, shoes or TV sets is a very high-performance logistics system, such as Federal Express, UPS, DHL and others which have developed in recent years. It is certain that part of the attraction of these new competitors will depend on their ability to communicate, and on their having the necessary means at an acceptable cost to get their message across. Here, again, size will be decisive at the global level.

The economic and political reasons for pursuing international development

As we have just seen, competition imposes a strategy of pursuing size, and therefore growth, and therefore internationalization. I now want to look at four reasons for internationalization that are more economic and political.

1   As a result of urbanization and the development of mass communications, the lifestyles and the behaviour of consumers is becoming more homogeneous throughout the world. By the beginning of the twenty-first century, more than half of the world's population will live in towns.

2   The elimination of frontiers in Europe and, progressively, in other parts of the world, will lead to the creation of very big homogeneous markets.

3 The relative maturity of domestic markets, i.e. their saturation with consumer goods, in Western countries and Japan, where today's big retail groups started.
4 Concentration in the sector.

Let me illustrate this last factor. Over the past century, the geographical area in which a shopkeeper could operate has grown continuously. When the founder of our company set up his business in Cherbourg, in 1900, there were 80 wholesalers in this town of 50,000 inhabitants. None of them delivered to clients who could not be reached by a horse going there and back in the same day. That was, not more than 10 kilometres distant. Today, Promodès covers the whole of France, supplying 80 Continent hypermarkets and 500 Champion supermarkets, with six distribution centres, and the country now has only a dozen wholesalers, the second biggest of which generates less than 10 per cent of Promodès' wholesale turnover.

The same trend which has affected Promodès is to be seen everywhere in the world, and it is accelerating. For all the reasons discussed above, mergers and acquisitions are one way to achieve critical mass and to rationalize global organization. What is new is that this phenomenon of concentration, which at the beginning (after the Second World War) had a purely regional justification, became a national phenomenon as of the 1960s, before turning at the end of the century into a continental, and in the near future a world-wide, phenomenon.

If one looks at the competitive situation in a number of Western countries, one sees that retailing is gradually organizing itself on the British or Canadian model. That is, depending on their size, whether there are fewer than or more than 20 million inhabitants, three leaders in the smaller countries and five or six in the larger ones hold more than 60 per cent of the total market. Increasingly, there is the common characteristic of the legal or regulatory impossibility of increasing individual market share either through opening new sites or through acquiring competitors. The large firms are thus more or less condemned to internationalize if they want to use their human and financial resources in the same sector of commerce. This is one explanation of why internationalization has accelerated.

THE CONSEQUENCES

If you agree with the above analysis, what are the alternatives today for groups that are not of the size of Wal-Mart, Metro or Carrefour and are not able on their own to develop rapidly a totally integrated world-wide strategy?

The first alternative is the model of the English retailers, who accumulate cash surplus above their national requirements, in a market that has already been rationalized, and then start making foreign acquisitions that they try to fit into their existing organizational and commercial structure.

The second alternative is mergers. Up to now they have primarily occurred inside individual countries, but a number of bigger projects are in progress at the moment, and I think one can say with confidence that we will see international mergers in retailing before the end of the century, which is a bit later than in the industrial sector.

The third alternative is to form strategic alliances via various forms of partnership. There seems to be no limit to what might be done under this heading because, fortunately, the human imagination is very fertile when it comes to assuring commercial survival. Many successful solutions have already been tried in North America and Europe over the last several decades.

Some of these alliances met the needs of an era, then lost relevance and became marginal. Examples are the regional and national purchasing groups set up by wholesalers, retailers and franchisers and the voluntary national retail chains in Europe and North America.

There were two main types of reason for their decline. The first was their inability to pool those functions that needed to be centralized if they were really to benefit from the economies of scale that I have mentioned. The second was that they took too static, too limited, too conservative a view of development. Many of their members sought above all to protect their own local market, which prevented any geographical dynamism from developing. This in turn led members to leave the organization, which retained only companies without a growth strategy, and this inexorably brought about their decline.

Today we can see the same thing happening, not nationally this time but at the continental level. Purchasing groups are being created without the pooling of know-how, of product marketing, of commercial policies, of store concepts which are the elements on which the major integrated groups build their lasting success. Personally, I believe that history will repeat itself for these latest attempts, and that we will see these alliances go the same way as the national alliances over the last few decades.

The strategic problem for the head of a company who wants to remain in charge of the enterprise is to find an answer to a two-pronged question: how can I gain the same advantages as the big integrated groups and still keep control of management, of strategy, of the medium and long-term development of my company?

THE CONSTRAINTS AND LIMITATIONS OF INTERNATIONALIZATION

I have tried to demonstrate why the pursuit of relative size must be a strategic aim, and why this leads, among other things, to internationalization. I would now like to look at the constraints and limits on size and internationalization for a retailer.

Retailers sell between 50 and more than 100,000 products as illustrated by McDonald's and Wal-Mart respectively. The more products one sells, the larger the sales surface needed, and therefore the bigger the investment. The investment can only be justified if there is a big potential local market, and this means that site costs will be high and that in some countries it will take a long time to obtain the necessary planning permission. Winning significant market share thus takes time and enormous financial resources. What are the limits to size of investment?

A single factory can produce for many tens of millions of customers, whereas it takes hundreds or even thousands of shops to hold 10 per cent of a national market like the United States, which means billions of dollars of investment. Wal-Mart, for example, has 2,400 outlets, with a share of a little more than 10 per cent of the US market for general goods and less than 5 per cent in food. Is there a limit to the number of shops which can be managed effectively in a market?

The same condition necessitates the employment of hundreds of thousands of people. Wal-Mart employs more than half a million people, although it is active in only three countries. Is there any limit to the number of employees a single enterprise can manage? If Wal-Mart wanted to go world-wide and hold a similar market share, it would have to employ several million people. Would this cause social, political or management problems? Can such businesses remain sufficiently flexible to evolve, or will they suffer from the dinosaur syndrome?

In between retailing 50 products and retailing over 100,000 there is room for dozens of different formulas and formats corresponding to more or less precise market segmentation. In how many segments can a retailer be successful at the same time?

These are just a few of the questions that need thinking about, but even more, it seems to me, they need testing before anyone can affirm the limits of retailing size and internationalization. However, I do think that a group of companies linked by a strategy of alliances may have advantages that allow it to give a more positive answer to some of these questions than a big integrated group.

In the management field, in particular, a group of allied companies is much more decentralized from the beginning, and therefore more flexible, with managers who are closer to local people and local markets and therefore better placed to decide on necessary adaptations to local conditions. Equally, individual companies can carry out carefully controlled experiments that, if successful, could benefit all group members. Raising pertinent questions is also more natural in such a group than in one organized on hierarchical lines. Faults become known faster, and information about them reaches top management more quickly and without window dressing.

As in everything else, identifying the problem is half the solution. Used with trust and openness, a tradition of positive criticism of alliance operations could avoid reactions which are too late or inadequate for the problem. I would also add that, as a result of their history and the characteristics of their market, companies in an alliance often develop their own diversifications that, apart from spreading their risks, may one day offer new opportunities to another alliance member.

$$\diamond$$

Conclusion

I believe that the internationalization of retailing is as unavoidable as it has proved to be in manufacturing industry. It is a strategic response to the way the world and competitive conditions are evolving. Internationalization allows a company to increase its growth opportunities and to diminish its risks by widening its portfolio of national markets, so long as it knows how to develop all the potential synergies. There does not appear to be any alternative to internationalization today, whether undertaken by an integrated group or via alliances. It seems certain that by the end of this decade the retailing of mass consumer goods will be more and more international. It will not be only washing powders, chocolate bars, jeans, drinks and hamburgers that will be able to take on the world market. Already, groups, for example C&A, Toys 'R' Us, Virgin, Marks & Spencer, IKEA and Aldi, and other companies like Norma, Lidl and Gap, are developing in France in their own specific niches. Today the big American groups have discovered the necessary ingredients for international success, for example Wal-Mart in Mexico and Canada, and Price-Costco in the same two countries as well as in England. We have also seen big chains specializing in textiles, toys and office supplies arriving in Europe with their world-wide organization and their technological strength.

Just one example helps us realize that the world is at our doorstep: 'Every evening a cargo aircraft leaves Canton, chartered by the chain The Limited. American customs officials carry out customs formalities during the flight over the Pacific. The aircraft lands at the nearest airport to The Limited's central warehouse, and within 48 hours the merchandise is being distributed all over the United States at unbeatable prices.' The delay between a store's order and the sale to a customer has fallen from several months to just a few days.

Why is all this possible today? First, for mass consumption products it is broadly true to say that there are fewer and fewer technological barriers to getting them manufactured anywhere in the world; secondly, for many of these products the cost of transport is marginal; thirdly, consumers' needs are becoming more homogeneous while global information is becoming almost instantaneous; and finally, GATT and its successor the World Trade Organization, added to the European Union, to NAFTA, to Mercosur and to other treaties, are gradually transforming the world into one enormous free trade area.

In these conditions, it seems to me more dangerous to pretend that retailing should remain local, so as to be better adapted to its markets, than to try to cross frontiers.

The limit I see is more in the managerial capacity of retailers, because the real challenge, the real competition, is as much at this level as at the level of strategic choice. Internationalization of our group has given my colleagues and myself a different view of our problems and of the context in which we must deal with them. No matter how open to outside influences one may be, nothing replaces direct contact and almost daily experience of the world's diversity. The explosion of one's accustomed frame of reference, the approach to new cultural environments, to new ways of thinking, the dialogue with heads of businesses or with people in charge of economic policy from very different backgrounds, all these elements put one's own experience in perspective and allow one to see things in a new light.

In conclusion, I would suggest that whilst world-wide internationalization may not come about by tomorrow for retailing, in the way that industry already sees it, retailing has nevertheless made a good start down the road. Many major players are already on the stage, and to succeed they will have to try to take account of some of the conditions I have described above, as well as others, while not forgetting the need for speed of execution in strategic decisions. In our business, when a company has taken a good position in the market the cost is high to dislodge it without having recourse to major innovation. Self-service was invented nearly 70 years ago. Are we now on the eve of a new innovation followed by a new revolution that would allow the small players to become big ones? This seems to me a good subject for reflection, for those who believe that trees cannot grow up to the sky.

2

The Internationalization of Prêt-à-Porter – the Case of Kookai and Morgan's Entry into the UK Fashion Market

CHRISTOPHER M. MOORE

OVERVIEW

This case study examines the internationalization of fashion retailing and is based upon the entry of French fashion retailers, Kookai and Morgan, into the UK. The case considers their motives for entry into the UK and explores, in particular, the associated push, pull and enabling factors. Methods of fashion internationalization are also investigated, as is the contribution of wholesaling as a first stage of fashion retailing market entry. The case compares and contrasts the respective approaches to franchise management adopted by Kookai and Morgan and considers the respective advantages of each. The case concludes with an assessment of the potential barriers that exist in respect of successful fashion retail internationalization and seeks to identify the internal competencies of Kookai and Morgan, which appear to have enabled both fashion retailers quickly to replicate their success, both in the UK and in other parts of the world.

———— KEY WORDS ————

Fashion retail internationalization, Motivations for expansions, Methods of internationalization, Internal competencies, Barriers to internationalization

YOUR COMMISSION

Assume you are a researcher for a Marketing Research Agency that specializes in international fashion retailing research. You have just received this letter from the client, the British Fashion Institute who are responsible for protecting British retailers from 'foreign' fashion retailer competition.

Memorandum: Highly Confidential

To: Researcher

From: Chairman, British Fashion Institute

It has long been the British Fashion Institute's belief that, due to market characteristics, (see attached tables), the British fashion retail sector is unlikely to encounter any significant threat from a prospective foreign market entrant.

Unfortunately, this assumption would appear unfounded. Indeed, two French fashion retailers, Morgan and Kookai, have made significant gains within the UK.

The British Fashion Institute Executive have called for an investigation into this matter. Further research questions will be passed to you later. In the meantime, we require that you:

(a) identify these market characteristics and explain why Morgan and Kookai were nevertheless able to make significant gains within the UK;
(b) explain their motivations for market entry, classifying the push and pull motivations;
(c) identify and explain their market entry strategy.

Table 2.1 UK fashion retailing: market structure

Consumer expenditure on clothing 1994	£24.7 billion

Average growth in consumer clothing expenditure:
    1985–9
    1990–4
	11%
	 3%

Number of retail clothing businesses 1994	24,923 (down 20% from 1990)
Number of retail clothing outlets 1994	51,319 (down 15% from 1990)
Number employed in retail clothing sector	264,000
Gross margin % of turnover 1994 1989	41% 46%
Own brand market share	60% – highest in Europe

Source: EIU Retail Trade Review 9/95 (35)

Table 2.2 Major UK clothing retailers (by market share 1994)

Marks and Spencer	16%
The Burton Group	12%
C&A	4%
Storehouse	4%
Sears	4%
Littlewoods	4%
Next	2%
Total	**46%**

Source: Keynote, 1995

   After considering the above memo and the tables you decide to undertake
market research along two lines of inquiry:

1   You arrange to receive press cuttings on recent activity.
2   You arrange interviews with key informants.

Table 2.3 UK fashion retailers (by turnover of business, 1994)

	under £1m	£1m–£9.9m	£10m–100m	£100m+
Number of businesses	24,161	659	86	17
Percentage of total	96.9	2.6	0.3	0.1
Number of outlets	31,500	4,749	6,654	8,413
Percentage of total	61.4	9.3	13.0	16.4
Average sales per outlet (£'000)	105.5	359.7	389.5	571.3
Retail sales as a percentage of total	19.7	6.7	14.9	58.7

Source: EIU Retail Trade Review 9/95 (35)

MORGAN AND KOOKAI: COMPANY BACKGROUND

French in origin, both Morgan and Kookai have undertaken significant market expansion within the UK over the past four years. Morgan operate eight stores and six department store concessions, which are owned by their UK master-franchise partner, Paris Mart. In addition, the company have 15 shops operated by sub-franchise holders, and supply to 200 wholesale stockists. Kookai operate 17 stores and seven department store concessions. All are owned and controlled by their UK master-franchise operator, Adjustbetter. In France, both Morgan and Kookai enjoy considerable market success. Kookai operate 175 stores, while Morgan operate 60 stores, with wholesale relationships with a further 100 independent retailers.

Morgan:

Target market: female, aged 15–28, fun, fashion leader types.

Merchandise strategy: highly innovative, fashion led. Morgan seek to replicate the latest high fashion trends quickly and cheaply.

Brand identity: strong French associations, heavy emphasis upon advertising and promotional investment.

International activity: operate franchise and wholesale arrangements with 19 countries.

Kookai:

Target market: female aged 25, but with a client base between 18–35. Fashion forward, but not a fashion victim. Strong sense of personal style.

Merchandise strategy: feminine, up-to-the-minute fashion ranges, with a mix of casual and fashionable workwear.

Brand identity: heavy Parisian overtones, with direct associations with French culture in advertising and promotional campaigns.

International activity: 50 per cent of company turnover from international trading, primarily from franchise arrangements in Europe, the Far East, United States and Australia.

Press Cuttings

From the BFI library, the following clippings have been made available for your information.

THE FASHION RETAILER, *October 1991*

'... But as to whether fashion retailers adopt a strategic approach to foreign market development is still under debate. Recent research has suggested that foreign market expansion is likely to occur "by accident" and that many French retailers fail to undertake pre-entry market research, "product-test" the market or even develop specific market objectives ...'

FASHION TODAY, *November 1991*

'... and market evidence suggests that those fashion retailers who have developed a clearly defined strategy for international development are more likely to be successful in the long term ...'

THE FASHION RETAILER, *November 1991*

'... Young womenswear fashion chain, Kookai of Paris, are set to offer their range of up-to-the-minute fashions within the UK next month. The company have set up a whole-sale agreement with the British fashion distributor, Adjustbetter. A company spokeswoman said "The lack of product differentiation, particularly within the young female fashion segment in the UK provides Kookai with a tremendous market opportunity. British fashion retailers are not prepared to take a risk and this provides a real market niche for innovative and focused companies like us. ..." '

DAILY TRIBUNE, *September 1990*

THE PUSH AND PULL OF RETAILER INTERNATIONALIZATION

'... the DTI report, published today, suggests that domestic markets characteristics, such as market saturation, act as a "push" which encourage British retailers to seek overseas markets. On the other hand, the DTI maintain that niche market opportunities have acted as a "pull" for retailers, such as Burberry, who recognize that foreign shoppers are attracted to their very British image ...'

FASHION WEEKLY NEWS, *March 1993*

'... French womenswear retailers, such as Morgan and Kookai, have identified a variety of reasons for setting-up in Britain. Despite what we might think, the British market is perceived to be highly prestigious and an important market to be involved in particularly if you want to develop an international brand reputation. A Morgan spokesman said "When you tell prospective franchise partners that the Morgan brand is doing well in the UK, they become much more interested. The British association definitely opens doors for us".

In a similar vein, Kookai suggest that the British fashion consumer has become much more cosmopolitan in their fashion outlook. In particular, the British female shopper likes the kudos of having an Italian or French brand. "This has obviously been to our advantage at Kookai ... and this, coupled with our innovative and differentiated product, has given us a significant opportunity" said an Adjustbetter director ...'

CLASSIFIEDS

PARIS MART,

EXCLUSIVE WHOLESALE PARTNER OF MORGAN, FRANCE,

INVITE APPLICATIONS FROM INDEPENDENT FASHION RETAILERS INTERESTED IN STOCKING THE PRESTIGIOUS MORGAN BRAND. ALL ENQUIRIES TO ANNIE JONES, AT PARIS MART, LONDON. 0171 335 4678

FASHION REVIEW, *November 1992*

KOOKAI TO FOCUS ON FORGOTTEN SEGMENT – young, female casual/businesswear.

FASHION HERALD, *January 1992*

'... Adjustbetter, the wholesale arm of Kookai, are to cease offering the Kookai brand on a wholesale basis. Instead, the company, who have just signed a master-franchise agreement with Kookai, will develop a chain of stand alone Kookai stores. As part of the master-franchise deal, Adjustbetter will gain exclusive distribution rights within the UK for the Kookai brand. In addition, Kookai will provide access to their award winning advertising and promotions campaign, as well as autonomy to develop the Kookai brand within the spirit of Kookai's image.

Kookai's Export Director explained that one of the major benefits of entering a foreign market via wholesaling was the opportunity to develop a prospective franchise partner, such as with Adjustbetter ...'

FASHION NEWS, *June 1992*

'... Adjustbetter, the master-franchise partner of Kookai in the UK have recently opened a new Kookai store in London. It is the second Kookai store in the UK ...'

FASHION NEWS, *May 1994*

'... Kookai, the French fashion retailer, have opened their latest store as part of their franchise partnership with Adjustbetter. The company now have 7 stores in the UK. In relation to the rate of store opening, a company spokeswoman said "The company plan to have around 20 stores open by the end of 1995, excluding concessions. Since Adjustbetter have kept a firm control over the expansion programme, the rate of growth has not been as dramatic compared to other companies. But considered growth has meant that we can wait for the most appropriate high street locations, and we can get our distribution and management structures in place to match our expansion needs ..." '

FASHION INTERNATIONAL, *April 1994*

'... Paris Mart, the UK franchise partner of Morgan, have announced a dramatic reduction in the number of Morgan wholesale stockists. Currently wholesaling to over 300 independent retailers, the company want the Morgan brand to "only be available in the right environment". The decision to reduce the number of stockists comes in response to speculation that wholesale stockists have been undermining the Morgan brand through non-standard pricing, merchandising and promotion activities ...'

FASHION WEAR, *September 1993*

'... French fashion chain Kookai have recently unveiled the new look for their Paris stores. The new design is based upon the shopfits developed in the UK by their British franchise partner, Adjustbetter. According to a company spokesman, "one of the benefits of operating in the UK which is a world leader in visual merchandising, store design, and operations is that the home market benefits from the UK experience ..." '

FASHION NEWS, *December 1992*

'... It's official. British women are the most experimental and daring in Europe. Not just that, they are prepared to pay higher price points for fashionable garments, compared to their European counterparts, suggests a survey conducted by ...'

FASHION NEWS, *March 1992*

'... Morgan the French fashion chain currently available by wholesale in the UK have signed a master-franchise agreement with Paris Mart, their wholesale partner. As part of the deal, Paris Mart will have control over the distribution and operation of Morgan retail within the UK. Paris Mart intend to open their own Morgan stores, while at the same time operating sub-franchises. It is anticipated that the wholesale arm of the business will remain unchanged. A Morgan press link maintained that the availability of a dependable franchise partner was an important incentive for developing within the UK ... "We really got to know Paris Mart through our wholesaling. We are confident that their expert knowledge and experience will make Morgan Retail a success in the UK ..." '

FASHION WEEKLY, *October 1994*

'... Morgan is to open a sub-franchise store in Belfast, as well as in Manchester, Newcastle, Windsor and Bath. A company owned London store in Oxford Street will open in early 1995 ...'

FASHION WEEKLY, *September 1994*

'MORGAN

IT HAS COME TO OUR ATTENTION THAT COPIES OF OUR DESIGNS HAVE BEEN MADE AND WE ARE PURSUING THE OFFENDING PERSONS THROUGH THE COURTS.

WITHOUT FURTHER NOTICE, WE WILL NOT HESITATE TO TAKE LEGAL ACTION AGAINST ANYONE FOUND TO BE IMITATING OUR PRODUCT.

EXCLUSIVE UK DISTRIBUTOR – PARIS MART'

FASHION WEEKLY, *September 1995*

'Morgan are to open new sub-franchise stores next year as part of a rigorous expansion campaign. Paris Mart, the UK partner, have been inundated with applications from potential franchise holders. These will all benefit from Morgan's commitment to promotion including posters, swing tags, and bags featuring the images from Morgan's world-wide advertising campaign starring Calvin Klein model Albert Delegue and Channel model, Tricia Helfer ...'

FASHION WEEKLY, *March 1995*

'... Morgan licences and wholesale stockists are to benefit from a London Underground advertising campaign, as well as a national poster site initiative. The company are also negotiating for a network TV advertising campaign for A/W 1995 ...'

DRAPER'S RECORD, *November 1994*

'MORGAN IN LEGAL BATTLE-WITH FASHION STOCKISTS

'... A Guildford independent fashion retailer alleged this week to have lost thousands of pounds after a deal to stock Morgan clothing collapsed. The claim comes as a result of Morgan's decision to back out of a deal to supply the retailer after it had been agreed. However, Morgan have withdrawn from the deal, "due to the fact that a Morgan store is opening in the Guildford area. The shop will now have exclusivity in the Guildford area" said a Paris Mart director ...'

FASHION NEWS, *December 1994*

'... the British retail fashion sector has now become an important new market for French fashion retailers. Companies, such as Chipie, Naf Naf, Morgan and Kookai, have made significant progress in their UK development plans over the past three years. Home market saturation, a declining youth population and economic recession have encouraged many French retailers to consider foreign market expansion. The UK is an obvious target on the grounds of physical proximity, improvements in logistical infrastructure, as well as similarities in terms of fashion preferences ...'

TRANSCRIPTS OF INTERVIEWS

You have undertaken interviews with key informants from both Morgan and Kookai and you now have the interview transcripts.

Transcript A. Interview with Kookai Representative, December 1995

You: denoted by **M**.
Kookai representative: denoted by **K**.

M. Can you explain the master-franchise relationship between Kookai and Adjustbetter?

K. A master-franchise is first and foremost a partnership. It brings together our experience in fashion retailing, the strength of our brand and joins that with the local knowledge and experience of the local partner. It is really about a sharing of risk, of resources and of opportunity. How does it work? Well, on the Kookai side, we control what the product is, and so master-franchise partners must stick to our product range and are not allowed to change that in any way. They also get the benefits of having our brand – one that has an international reputation, which we believe has universal fashion appeal. The final element is our Global Advertising Campaign. Local franchisees are not allowed to deviate from what we are saying, in terms of images and messages. We want to be consistent throughout the whole world in terms of our message. Now, other than product and promotion control, we leave the operational running of Kookai in the UK to the local franchisee. They are the experts, after all. So they manage site selection, they can develop a store environment according to their own designs, but we would step in if we felt that their image was not in keeping with the Kookai brand values, but that would be unlikely, since our partners understand what we are about so well. They decide on local pricing and how they are going to distribute the goods. We do not tell them how exactly we want them to expand, but as the copy of the franchise agreement shows (see appendix), we do have certain stipulations which state exactly what our expectations will be with regards to their expected rates of growth. We really have very little to do with what goes on with regards to the day-to-day running of the stores and the local businesses.

M. So what exactly would you say was being internationalized in this process?

K. The franchise agreement is really about the transference of three elements: Kookai brand, Kookai product and Kookai advertising/promotion. There is no financial sharing of investment, in terms of Kookai, France providing loans or help for expansion etc. within the UK. It is purely a transactional agreement, we give the Kookai package and the master-franchisee gives us the money! We do not share managers, but we will advise on issues or problems, as and when necessary. There is no international sourcing or involvement by the local partner in the buying process. I suppose that it is really about the transference of what I said at the beginning, the transference of a concept.

M. Can you identify the problems or obstacles that are likely to arise as part of this process of internationalization?

K. Whenever a franchise agreement occurs in any situation, disagreements are bound to arise. It may be what I call perceptual incompatibility – and that basically means that both sides do not see things in the same way. It may be that a franchiser thinks that its product is of a better quality than it is perceived by a franchisee. An example in the UK had to do with the fact that Adjustbetter raised Kookai's market positioning in the UK, mainly through higher prices and very elaborate store environments. Initially, the reaction in France was negative and we feared that Kookai would not work in the UK. But Adjustbetter knew that the market would take it and they were proved right. It is interesting to note that in the recent refurbishment of the French Kookai stores, the main design idea came from the UK experience and the French prices have now been brought in line with those in the UK. I suppose it is true to say that at Kookai we have tried to create a global brand, one that does not need to be modified to suit local markets. And it is true to say that most fashion retailers follow this route. But in the UK we found that the most vibrant colours, the daring styles were the most popular and that surprised us. It also gave us something of a problem. We did not have enough of the things which were in demand in our ranges and, therefore, the British felt that we were not capitalizing upon the market opportunity. An integral part of a globalization strategy is connected to your marketing communications strategy. We wanted to have a Kookai message that was uniform, consistent, telling the same story. It is true, however, that some of the messages, with their cultural references, were too French – and those in other countries did not get the meaning. Also, we used characters or personalities who did not have an international reputation. Therefore, these people were of little interest to our world-wide market.

M. So how were these problems resolved?

K. We revised our communications strategy, so that we no longer had specifically French personalities or French references. For example, the Fashion designer campaign, whereby we had designers like Yves Saint Laurent and Karl Lagerfeld commenting about Kookai, was based on our realization that these were people who were internationally recognized and respected. We were pleased that this was such a successful campaign. In terms of product, we had to think of ways of capitalizing upon the demand. The only way that we could do that was to listen – and therefore I would say successful international fashion companies are those that are prepared to be flexible, to develop a learning culture and so become responsive to local market needs. We achieved that in two ways. The first was to develop capsule collections which were specifically for the UK market. Obviously that meant a reduction in scale economies. But we looked on it in a different manner. We saw it as a way to test and develop new styles and so research customer reaction. The interesting thing that now happens is that the UK capsule collections now feed in to the main overall design collection. The second method that we used was to include British designers, and those from other important countries, in the earliest stages of design. We take on board what they think is key to their market and we then try to create a Mega-Range that hopefully will suit the world-wide Kookai consumer. We also present the range to each master-franchisee each season, to explain what we have tried to say in our collection in design terms. At this stage, we get very important feed-back as to their acceptance of the range, as well as clear ideas for how they think future seasons ought to further develop.

END OF INTERVIEW

Transcript B. Interview with Morgan Representative, December 1995

You: denoted by **M**.
Morgan representative: denoted by **G**.

M. Can you explain the master-franchise relationship between Morgan and Paris Mart?

G. Morgan are an international company. Our market is wider than just France. Why? Well demographically, in France our target age group, women aged between 15–25, is in decline. Added to this, France has suffered a long recession and our customer is spending less. But that is not our motivation for going outside France. We know that we have a brand and a product with international appeal. When you want to internationalize, but you are a relatively small company, you do not have the resources to expand and take the risks that are associated with new market entry. It is sound business sense to find a partner to share the glory but also the risks from this type of growth. Now, with Paris Mart, we have a retailer and wholesaler who have a solid grasp of the local market and they know where we ought to open, who we should sell to and the product ranges that will work. In return, we give them the Morgan formula – the brand name, the brand identity, the advertising, the shop fits, the product range, the carrier bags, the rules for merchandising, all the main guidelines as to how we want the Morgan brand to look. As for the administration, such as who they are going to sub-franchise to, or sell on to through wholesaling, then we leave that to them. We do have expectations for growth and turnover which we agree at the beginning of the franchise deal, then regularly review. But after that, it is totally up to them. We leave all of the operational activities, such as distribution and stock control, to them.

M. So what exactly would you say was being internationalized in this process?

G. The Morgan brand, our expertise in presenting a brand that is up-to-the minute and totally unique in all of fashion retailing. We are internationalizing an approach to product management that is based upon a clear understanding of the very latest trends, a tightly controlled product development system with a highly integrated manufacturing approach which allows us to get to the stores long before the competition. And through our design and advertising, we are internationalizing a look, an attitude and a feeling, and that is what fashion is all about. Ours is a globalization strategy. We take the same image and product and offer it to the world. Successful international fashion retailing can only be done through the development of a strong, identifiable brand image and identity. The offer has got to say something directly and have a universal appeal. You can never nationalize a fashion brand – chopping and changing things in order to fit the local market. Immediately, you loose control and then the brand identity. The fashion world is truly a global village. The media gives people access to what is happening everywhere – MTV is based upon shared views and ideas and that is what

fashion does too. If you tell a different fashion story, say in Italy, then immediately those in Germany are going to say, 'that's not Morgan, I am confused
about what this brand is saying about me'. So to answer your question,
Morgan are about internationalizing an attitude, a way of living, a lifestyle,
that people everywhere are happy to buy into and so be a part of. There are
other business and management dimensions, but these are just there to
support the underlying premise, which is that we are internationalizing our
message in fashion.

M. Can you identify the problems or obstacles that are likely to arise as part
of this process of internationalization?

G. Logistics! The French are notoriously bad on delivery! But seriously, I
think that there is often the problem of who is responsible for what ... we
take control of certain things, like product design and we jealously protect
that. But a new franchise partner may think that they can go ahead and get
products from a different source, or alter the range in some way. There may
be disagreement over who is responsible for operational decisions. An area
of contention is often related to investing in new facilities or communications methods. One side often thinks that the other will gain greater benefits
and therefore they ought to pay more for something. Issues relating to conflicts over responsibilities do lessen as you get to know each other better.
Relationships mature and partners get to know each other. A major problem
with this form of internationalization is that as a company you lose a certain
amount of your business control. For example, Paris Mart are totally
autonomous in terms of how they expand their UK operation. Now, both
sides wanted to ensure that Morgan had maximum exposure within Britain,
but that became a problem whenever Morgan was sold through wholesaling
to some people who did not, shall we say, fully appreciated or care for what
we were trying to do at Morgan. They were undermining the brand's
integrity. Consequently, we became very frustrated at what was happening
but there was a limit to what we could do. However, Paris Mart were very
professional and they also recognized the problem. To their credit, they
acted swiftly to reduce the number of wholesale partners and through legal
actions were very tough on those who were copying Morgan designs. Other
issues arise in international partnerships, such as those related to foreign currency fluctuations – the British pound has been very unstable over the past
few years and, as a consequence, that has put major pressures on our British
partner in terms of pricing and the like. It is an added pressure, another consideration. Then you also have issues over whether you are really taking all
the opportunities that are available in the local market. Local partners always

think that something else could be done in order to improve things. But they sometimes forget that we have the same opportunities in 20 other countries and we can only do the best that we can!

M. So how were these problems resolved?

G. There is rarely a quick solution to these issues. I do believe that as a relationship develops, both sides get to know each other and understand the variations in corporate culture. Then again, there are problems, shall we say, that are born of national cultural differences. It is important that both sides make an effort to learn about the other's national culture and to make allowances for that. But it is also vital that efforts are made in order to ensure that a flexible approach is taken, an ability to adapt to these other cultures. In the case of Morgan, I think that it is true to say that we have sought to develop a true corporate commitment to internationalization. This means that we have put international trading at the heart of our philosophy. It is not a second thought, or something which we happen on. We have a willingness to pursue foreign market opportunities, to develop a strategy for the development of these markets. I suppose this is really about having a marketing-led orientation, and being prepared to listen to the needs of local markets. This leads me to another facet: developing effective communications structures, not just for the flow of ordering information etc., but for the transference of management ideas and opportunities, talking, arguing and coming up with new solutions. I would say that we have a culture of learning from experience. We do not know all the answers, we do make mistakes, but at least we have a philosophy that is prepared to learn from these. Often, we will review what we have done, and try to pull out the lessons, the good and the bad and we take that forward and make this the basis of our future developments and decisions. We endeavour to develop a learning culture, where we share and exchange and are better able to make a more informed decision. Developing a learning culture means that we adopt an adaptive approach – nothing is written is stone. You can and must make changes in this game. I do not think that I have given you any really explicit actions, or explicit details here. But what I want to do is tell you about the wider issues or ideas and values that are vital if you are a retailer who wants to manage our business across a variety of national markets.

END OF INTERVIEW

————— QUESTIONS —————

Further instructions have arrived from The British Fashion Institute. They want to know the following:

(1) Identify the problems and obstacles encountered by Morgan and Kookai on their entry into the UK.

(2) Explain how these problems were resolved by the companies.

Appendix

KOOKAI, FRANCE

DETAILS OF FRANCHISE AGREEMENT WITH FOREIGN PARTNER

Kookai will grant the exclusivity of a territory to a foreign partner who is a local fashion retail professional, and who is bound by legal contract, as a master-franchisee. The master-franchisee will hold the rights to exclusively franchise, distribute and sell the Kookai brand and product within their country. The master-franchisee is the guarantor in respect of the Kookai concept and image within their country.

The master-franchisee must submit a business plan consisting of:

1   An agreement of a contract duration from 3–5 years maximum (can be extended after satisfactory review), allowing for exclusive control of the Kookai product.

2   The candidate must forecast precisely over a 3–5-year period, a shop opening prediction as such:

> year 1: opening of . . . shops
> year 2: opening of . . . shops
> year 3: opening of . . . shops.

3   Buying budgets are linked directly with the opening of new stores. These must be calculated on the basis of a basic budget of approximately 500,000–700,000FF per shop, per year.

4   Brand positioning – the master-franchisee must position the Kookai brand as a French ready-to-wear brand of international reputation, using the best means of promotion to include press, posters and TV. Kookai will provide all advertising materials to be used in all campaigns, including negatives for catalogues, publicity etc.

All other details, with regards to master-franchisee financial commitments and specifications of Kookai's percentage royalty are specific to each country and the aspirations of the proposed business plan of the master-franchisee.
(Translated from the original French document.)

Further reading

Alexander, N. 1990: Retailers and international markets: motives for expansion. *International Marketing Review,* 7(4), 75–85.

Brown, S. and Burt, S.L. 1991: Special issue on retail marketing: international perspectives. *European Journal of Marketing,* 26(8/9).

Dawson, J.A. 1994: Internationalization of retail operations. *Journal of Marketing Management,* 10, 267–82.

Economist Intelligence Unit 1995: *Retail Trade Review* No. 35.

Forward, J. and Fulop, C. 1993: Elements of a franchise. *Service Industries Journal,* 13(4), 159–78.

Hopkins, D.M. 1996: International franchising: standardisation versus adaptation to cultural differences. *Franchising Research: An International Journal,* 1(1), 15–24.

Keynote 1995: *UK Clothing and Footwear Report.* London.

Mendelsohn, M. 1992: *Franchising in Europe.* London: Cassell.

Salmon, W. and Tordjman, A. 1990: The internationalization of retailing. *International Journal of Retailing,* 4(2), 3–16.

Sanghavi, N. 1991: Retail franchising as a growth strategy for the 1990s. *International Journal of Retail and Distribution Management,* 19(2), 4–9.

Welch, L.S. 1992: Developments in international franchising. *Journal of Global Marketing,* 6(1/2), 81–96.

3

IKEA: International Development

NATHALIE PRIME

OVERVIEW

This case study considers the issue of the international development strategy of the Swedish world-wide leader in the furniture market, IKEA. The major issue is the need to adapt an essentially European concept to American market conditions. The standardization versus adaptation strategies are considered. The international development and marketing strategy are then defined at the global and American levels.

KEY WORDS

Global marketing and development strategy, Internationalization of retailing

◇

INTRODUCTION

In July 1992 the IKEA store in Plymouth Meeting, 20 miles from Philadelphia, celebrated its seventh anniversary. The commercial success of this store, the first to be opened by the Swedish furniture distributor in North America, had played an important part in IKEA's establishment on this territory. By the end of 1992, the IKEA network totalled ten sales outlets, seven of which had been operating for over two years. For Bjorn Boyle, president of the IKEA subsidiary in the United States, the time had come for a strategic look at results achieved and future prospects. His first step was to review what he knew of the culture and achievements of IKEA. Only then could he begin to plan a strategy for the next stages of development.

IKEA'S ROOTS

In its name and the colours it uses, IKEA carries the identity of its founder, Ingvar Kamprad from Elmtaryd farm in the village of Agunnaryd in Sweden. While remaining loyal to its origins, the business also represents a shop-window on Swedish lifestyle. It was in 1947 that Ingvar Kamprad, then 22 years old, started up in mail order sales of flower seeds and ball point pens. Encouraged by his success with this method of marketing, he was not slow to consider applying the same system to furniture produced by local craftsmen. A catalogue was subsequently drawn up offering products at unbeatable prices, an advantage obtained by leaving it to the purchaser to assemble his own furniture (Ready To Assemble or KIT concept).

Competitor reactions were lively. Local suppliers operated a boycott against Ingvar Kamprad, who then had to find new sources of supply without loosing competitive advantage on prices. IKEA's founder then proved his ingenuity and placed the foundation stone of a new concept of distribution whose originality is seen in the methods used to supply and market furniture in kit-form or loose parts. In this way, for example, the seat, frame and metal supports making up a single chair can come from three different suppliers. This supply strategy has led to the development of a network of some 2,487 suppliers spread over 71 countries. By doing this, IKEA could continue to offer 'quality at the lowest price for a consumer who buys, transports and assembles his own furniture'.

Ten years ago, Ingvar Kamprad gave the presidency of the board of directors to Anders Moberg. The founder of IKEA, at 70 years old, is the president of the surveillance council but keeps a large involvement in the group. He announced that none of his three sons would take his place as the leader of IKEA. His sons are the shareholders of Ikano, which owns Habitat.

IKEA's Expansion

The IKEA concept certainly made a fortune for Ingvar Kamprad, whose personal assets in 1990 were valued at 1.9 billion ECU, ranking him amongst the wealthiest people in Sweden. From the first store he opened in 1954 at Almhult in the forest of Smaland in Sweden with 15 co-workers, up until the 131 sales outlets in 27 countries employing 30,500 co-workers, this distributor of 'kit furniture' has experienced an incredible expansion. IKEA's turnover in 1995 amounts to 8,763 millions of NLG (1 NLG = US$ 0.58 = SEK 4.44).

IKEA's spatial expansion went through three stages which could be termed respectively as Scandinavian, European and world-wide. The first stage covered the 1950s and 1960s, years during which IKEA consolidated its position in Scandinavian countries. In 1963, following the success at home, the first IKEA store outside Sweden was opened by the distributor in Oslo, Norway. Scandinavian expansion was followed by the opening of other sales outlets in Norway and Denmark which provided optimal coverage of the territory.

As a second stage, IKEA planned to extend its European territory. A first trial was made in 1973 in Zurich, Switzerland. The performance of this new sales outlet, in a market which had the reputation of being conservative, provided the motivation for IKEA's continued development in Europe. After Switzerland, expansion continued with outlets opening in Germany, Austria, France and Belgium. At the start of the 1980s, IKEA stores could be seen in many countries of Western Europe. Parallel to this European expansion, IKEA experimented with some of the more distant markets during the 1970s, notably Canada and Australia. In both cases, IKEA's presence was established through franchising.

The results of these experiments allowed IKEA to enter the final expansion stage of the world-wide development. Markets situated outside Western Europe were tackled at this point, in particular North America and Eastern Europe. By 1996, IKEA owned six stores in Central Europe which shows signs of being a very promising market because consumer demand has greatly overtaken distribution forecasts. New projects are under way. The Swedish group opened four stores in Poland, one in Slovakia, one in Hungary and, after many disagreements with the Soviet authorities, one store in Moscow. It is working also on several projects in the Czech Republic.

In 1996, 85.3 per cent of IKEA's sales were in Europe, with 10.6 per cent in Sweden, 22.7 per cent in Belgium, Denmark, the UK, Norway, the Netherlands, 29.9 per cent in Germany, 20.3 per cent in Austria, France, Italy, Switzerland, and 1.8 per cent in Hungary, Poland, the Czech Republic and Slovakia. The USA and Canada account for 13.6 per cent of sales.

The UK, where IKEA has been present since 1987, constitutes the highest growth market in Europe. 'Our London store has produced sales increases of 20 per cent per annum in a recessive market' confirmed Birger Lund, who started up the development in this country. With its purchase in 1992 of Habitat's British and French subsidiaries for 700 million French francs, IKEA is becoming the leading furniture distributor in the UK. The sixth store opened in 1995 in Leeds but the potential network is about 15 stores.

France also represents an important market. IKEA France is managing nine stores in the suburbs of large cities (Paris, Lyon, Marseille, Lille, Bordeaux and Toulouse) producing a turnover of 2.6 billion francs in 1995. The latest store to be opened is in Villiers-sur-Marne and is claimed to generate the highest turnover of any IKEA store in France. The total area is 23,000 m² with 13,500 m² sales area, reducing the percentage of non-sales area from 50 per cent in earlier stores to 30 per cent. The potential network in France is estimated at between 20 and 25 stores, with smaller stores in medium-sized cities (10,000 to 12,000 m² contrary to the usual size 18,000 to 20,000 m²). For the first half year of 1995, the turnover increased by 2–3 per cent in France and 5 per cent in the rest of the world.

IKEA prospects new markets with the objective to penetrate a maximum of two new countries each year. In 1996, two stores opened in Spain (Barcelona and Madrid), one in Finland (near Helsinki), and one in Italy (Milan). They are interested in possibly expanding into Turkey and Greece.

Although IKEA's development efforts have been heavily concentrated on Europe and the United States, the distributor is already present in some Asian markets and is analysing the opportunities of the Chinese and the Japanese markets. IKEA know that the group must be circumspect on the Chinese market because the legal environment is permanently fluctuating. None the less, IKEA hopes to open five to ten stores in the next ten years. The beginning of a subsidiary company was created in Peking with an area manager. The IKEA network also comprises more modest-sized sales outlets in Kuwait, Australia, Hong Kong, Singapore, Canary Islands and Iceland.

IKEA's expansion on the international market was accompanied by the upstream development of a network of 2,487 subcontractors in 71 countries. In 1995–6, in terms of volume the Nordic countries now represent only 32 per cent of purchases, compared to 13 per cent for East Central European countries, 30 per cent for the rest of Europe, 5 per cent for North America, and 20 per cent for the Far East. The Polish business started in 1960, following the boycott by Swedish manufacturers. The main task of the purchasing offices in each country is to maintain contact with the many suppliers and so to do their utmost to find the ideal 'purchasing mix'.

IKEA's globalization strategy relies on the standardization of its offer. 'We treat Eastern European markets the same way as other markets', explains Aulin, 'although we are forced to make some specific concessions to local conditions'. In practice, the product range offered by IKEA in the different stores can be reduced and partly adapted due to local circumstances, such as local income levels, regulations and specific needs. Thus, producing furniture for the German market takes into account the statutory safety standards as, for example, when promoting a line of 'click-clack' convertible sofas which was particularly popular in France.

IKEA's GUIDING PRINCIPLES

Whatever the territory being served, IKEA's mission remains the same as expressed by its founder, Ingvar Kamprad: 'To offer a wide variety of functional furniture for the house, of a quality and at a price affordable by a majority of people.' To achieve this goal, quality and economy are the two core principles of the company.

The principle of quality is applied at three points in the life of products offered by IKEA, i.e. creation, range and use. In the first case, contrary to what is usually the case in this sector, IKEA does not restrict itself to the distribution of furniture produced by manufacturers: each of its articles is designed by and for IKEA, within its ten 'laboratories', among which five are concerned only with furniture design. Each product has a name rather than a code. This way a television unit can be called RALF, TIMMERMAN, KOMPASS, or SALEN while a plant pot holder can be SUSPEKT, METAFOR or RESON. The reason is that IKEA wants to project the feeling that the products are a part of the family. Lars Westman, president of IKEA France, explains 'we have 12 full-time designers and over 100 checkers'. Research and development is carried out in the IKEA 'laboratories' thus allowing continual creation of new products, sometimes up to 20 per cent of what the stores have on offer.

Quality is designed into the products at the level of product ranges on offer. Each item for sale in the stores, whether furniture or other product, is part of a coherent whole, designed in accordance with the expectations of a specific segment which can be: young or old, high or low income, modern or classic, etc. In this way, IKEA offers some 12,000 items to fit out a house, from flower pots to carpets, via dishes, lamps and wall paper.

Finally, beyond this continual creation and marketing of new products with great attention being paid to their integration, quality as understood at IKEA also affects the third stage of the product life cycle, that of its use. IKEA furniture is submitted to three types of trial which test strength and workability as well as surface and resistance. All IKEA furniture which is tested carries the quality label Möbelfakta. The 'Möbelfakta' label, adapted from the Swedish standards system, identifies materials, construction and durability characteristics on a scale of A, B and C.

'At IKEA, quality and low prices go hand in hand', and the principle of quality is associated with the principle of saving money. To propose such low prices several methods are used by IKEA to make savings with the help of customers: IKEA develops its own products, focuses on flat-packs and buys in quantity, whereas customers help themselves, take away their own purchases and assemble their own furniture. IKEA covers the entire chain of operations from design and product development through to the sales outlet.

IKEA strives to create more programmes to protect the environment. For four or five years, the catalogues have been printed on paper that has been bleached without using chlorine and they do not use wood from old growth forests. They also initiated a recycling programme for their catalogues and other company's catalogues. One chair is made of 30 per cent recycled wood and their shopping bags are made of 30 per cent post-consumer recycled plastic. The company is currently testing a system that uses reusable bags instead of cartons on deliveries of custom upholstery items.

$$\diamond$$

IKEA'S MARKETING MIX

IKEA's marketing mix is based on the twin principles of quality and economy, and targets the modern family. 'Our target consumer is the baby boomer, 25–49, but customers come to IKEA to shop for furniture based on changes in their life, getting married, getting divorced, having a child, having children, moving out, buying a new home' says spokesperson Pamela Diaconis. IKEA spreads its client base by making furniture for small industries with less than 20 people or for customers working at home.

The products are the same world-wide. The furniture design is modern and light, textiles are often in pastel colours. Products are not delivered, but IKEA co-operates with car rental companies that offer small trucks at low cost. A mail order service is offered in Europe and Canada. IKEA has built its own distribution network, with outlets located outside the city limits of major metropolitan areas. The prices are low and the firm tries to keep its price image consistent. IKEA's promotional efforts are mainly through catalogues, and its advertising is based on getting attention. Media choices vary from market to market.

IKEA's marketing mix has to a great extent altered the very act of buying furniture. In fact, to benefit from the price advantage of IKEA products, consumers have to carry out tasks themselves which are normally the responsibility of the manufacturers and distributors. But this is all worth the effort as prices can be 30 to 50 per cent lower than competitors.

In compensation, IKEA provides additional services. First, the catalogue has the same low prices for a full 12 months. Since 1947 when the business was founded the IKEA catalogue has represented the communication tool 'par excellence'. 'The catalogue is our main shop-window and guarantees availability and prices for one year' points out Claes Ehrnfelt, design director. The catalogue is printed in 32 languages and 60 million copies are distributed world-wide as from 1 August each year. It is presented in four main editions (Europe, North America, Australasia, the East); minor modifications in response to regional specifics are made to each of these editions. Half of the promotional budget is spent on creating and distributing the IKEA catalogue. Some 150 people are involved in its development, about 60 of whom work on preparing 600 ICAP (IKEA Catalogue and Advertising Production) studio settings.

Secondly, outlets services include the Swedish restaurant, a supervised children 'ball room' and free cartoon cinema, the IKEA payment card, stock information over the phone, a 24-hour information service, a kitchen service package, gift vouchers and special services for corporate clients. The Home Interior Service can provide customers with all the help and advice needed, free of charge, when customers plan to furnish a whole room or an entire house.

Thirdly, making the search for furniture an agreeable occupation is IKEA's pledge backed by its many outlets services. Usually located at the edge of urban areas, IKEA stores are easily recognized by their blue and yellow colours and their relatively large floorspace (20,000 m² on average). An IKEA store looks more like an amusement park rather than a furniture department store. IKEA supports an open, spacious selling space with a warehouse exhibiting single-piece furniture. The idea is to create an atmosphere different from the typical, oppressive furniture store. If they want, visitors can request the advice of a salesperson. They can even ask for specialist advice on kitchen-fitting for example, to help them draw up their installation plans. Moreover, if the customer feels confident enough to put things together but needs some guidance, he can get a do-it-yourself video.

Fourthly, IKEA offers an after-sales guarantee. In respect of policies on returned products, with only a few exceptions, an item which is unused and intact, in its original packaging and accompanied by its sales receipt, can be returned and refunded within the prescribed time-limit, usually 30 days. Any item showing a manufacturing defect can be returned, even outside of pre-scribed time-limits. Since 1995, new services are available: instant credit is available through the IKEA credit card, home-delivery and assembling of the furniture and wedding lists.

Customer service is extremely important because IKEA considers that it is not only competing with the furniture and home improvement suppliers, it is also competing with firms which sell television sets and holidays.

IKEA'S COMPETITIVE POSITIONING

Application of the IKEA concept has allowed this Swedish business to occupy a position 'apart' in the furniture distribution sector, differentiated by its supply and marketing policies. Its policy of supplying world-wide in kit form allows IKEA to achieve excellent quality/price ratios through supplier selection and economies of scale. For its STEN storage system, for example, IKEA goes so far as to emphasize that the selling price is lower than the purchase price of the raw wood used to make it. It is also pointed out that IKEA would need a fleet of lorries stretching from Paris to Madrid to load all the stock contained in the distributor's 12 warehouses. The largest of these terminals, 135,000 m^3 capacity, is situated at Almhult, IKEA's place of origin, and is capable of fitting out 20,000 three-room dwellings. As seen above, IKEA is also distinguished by its marketing policy for kit-form furniture. This policy requires much greater participation from purchasers but, on the other hand, offers them additional support services.

IKEA is an international organization whereas its main competitors are usually leaders in their own market, like MFI in UK, Concorde in Germany and Conforama in France. Indeed, Conforama owns 162 stores but it is only present in Sweden, Luxembourg and Portugal.

In France, new competitors, struggling to sell at the lowest price, have appeared. Many hypermarkets (like Carrefour, Leclerc, Lapeyre, Castorama) started to sell furniture and, furthermore, two new brands were created in 1994: Basika and Hilary. On the other hand, the furniture sector shows a decreasing turnover for the last five years. In 1994, the leaders in France, Conforama and But, using the hard discount concept, had growth in sales but IKEA France had a decrease in sales. Therefore, the retailers are merging like Darnal and Pier Import to form Pier Import Europe or IKEA with Habitat in 1992. The strategic goals are similar amongst competitors: to increase the number of stores, to extend the network outside of France and to extend the range of customer services.

IKEA AND NORTH AMERICA

The slow-down of growth prospects in Western Europe and in its original markets, associated with increased competition have persuaded IKEA to consider the large American market. The Swedish distributor has been involved in North America since 1974 when it opened in Canada. IKEA management was, at that time, able to benefit from experience acquired by several major European retailing businesses that had previously set up in Canada and the United States. Opinions of success factors from European retailers in the US emphasize the following aspects. Americans have already shown that they like a total-concept store, and it is not always easy to transplant a store as it existed in Europe without adaptations. Any European retailer is in danger during the first three years because there is the product risk, the location risk and the cross-cultural management risk. Using American management to run the US operation appears to be more successful than using expatriates. American consumers prefer large shopping areas and advertising is extensive. Low price outlets attract the biggest market.

IKEA's beginnings in North America did not go beyond Canada which was then considered a major market not only because of its own potential but also as a test market for the wider American market. Maybe there also appeared to be similarities between Sweden and Canada, as both countries were situated in the north and were forested. Presence was established by franchises. Results of this first trial were inconclusive and IKEA directors attributed this to franchise management opting for reduced lines of the IKEA ranges. Consequently, IKEA decided to buy back the franchises and to operate its own network. This proved to be more successful.

A market development plan was then drawn up for the United States forecasting the opening of three stores per year. The first American store opened in July 1985. It was backed by a vast communication operation: sending personal invitations to a sample of the target segment (active, town-living adults aged 25 to 35, with an annual family income above $50,000), distributing a million catalogues and running an advertising campaign using all the media – television, radio, newspapers, bus side-panels. Situated in Philadelphia, this first IKEA store to open in United States met all the distributor's criteria

– floorspace of 15,100 m², situated within a built-up area at the edge of the city, and with extensive car parking and motorway access.

A second store of 14,800 m² was opened in Washington in Autumn 1986, followed by a third of 19,400 m² in Baltimore at the end of Summer 1988 and a fourth in Pittsburgh a year later. Now, there is one store in New Jersey (Elizabeth), one in New York State (Long Island) and one in Houston. Stores in the East of the United States were supplied by two large distribution centres, one in Montreal, Canada, and the second in Philadelphia. On the West coast of the United States, the IKEA network includes five stores in Los Angeles and one in Seattle.

North American development took off well with IKEA's purchase of four sales outlets at a cost of $19.8 million from STOR, a competitor who had been unable to reach the critical mass which would allow it to be profitable. In 1996, the 13 stores located in the United States generated a turnover of $510 million. In accordance with IKEA's long-term plans, two or three new stores are to be opened each year over the next 20 years with higher concentration on the North East of the United States and Canada. In fact, five stores opened in 1992, none in 1993, one in 1994 and none in 1995.

IKEA has apparently broken several of the rules of international retailing:

1   enter a market only after exhaustive study;
2   cater for local tastes as much as possible; and
3   gain local expertise through acquisition, joint ventures or franchising.

IKEA does not spend much money or time on studies. The managers use their eyes and make qualitative judgements. Then, they may adapt, but quite often they stay with the original format. This iconoclasm was successful in Europe, but it generated problems in the United States. European products jarred with American tastes and sometimes physiques. Swedish beds were narrow and measured in centimetres. IKEA did not sell the matching suites that Americans like. Its kitchen cupboards were too narrow for the large dinner plates needed for pizza. Its glasses were too small for a nation that piles them high with ice. Therefore, the managers decided adaptation was necessary. The firm now sells king- and queen-sized beds, in inches, as part of complete suites. In all, IKEA has redesigned around one-fifth of its product range in America. Its kitchen units are next on the list.

The firm has changed its American operations in other ways too. At the beginning, it was shipping the furniture from Europe, adding to costs and problems of stock availability. Now 45 per cent of the furniture is produced in America. Because Americans hate queuing, the firm has installed new cash registers that speed throughput by 20 per cent, and has altered store layout. Moreover, it offers a more generous returns policy than in Europe and a next-day delivery service.

THE AMERICAN FURNITURE MARKET

The American furniture market is estimated at approximately $22 billion. It is generally considered to be a stagnant market. In any case, IKEA management compares this situation to Germany in 1974 and France in 1982. They also propose to make changes. A demographic analysis of the American market makes it possible to predict considerable population changes. Children born during the baby-boom between 1945 and 1965 are now between 30 and 49 years old, have high incomes, have an inclination to buy more expensive furniture and seem to place importance on the quality of life and family values. This is the 'cocooning' age now prevalent in the United States, an age when particular care is taken to create a pleasant house interior.

This tendency could become stronger by the year 2000, with the aging of a population where the age range 35–44 will be predominant. According to experts, the adult population will show the following preference when buying furniture: 47 per cent furniture shops, 29 per cent so-called specialty stores such as Pier Import, 16 per cent department stores, 8 per cent others.

COMPETITION IN THE UNITED STATES

Competition to IKEA in the United States is found naturally in the furniture distribution sector, but also comes from the household electric appliance sector and, in a wider and indirect sense, from the leisure activities sector. Two main types of direct competition can, however, be identified. Specialty furniture stores make up the first category. While Levitz, the market leader, was achieving a turnover of $879 million in 1987 with 105 outlets, IKEA was ranked 21st with sales of $77 million and two outlets.

The second category of direct competitors includes full and discount department stores. Sears was top amongst these in 1987 with sales of $780 million. With a higher sales–space productivity in furnishings than for several other consumer products, these big stores extended the marketing of such items and made substantial efforts to promote them.

Among the various categories of furniture offered by distributors, ready to assemble kit furniture was a segment that was growing in the United

States, with annual sales in 1988 of $2 billion. The top three retailers were K Mart ($110 million, discounter), Wal Mart ($95 million, discounter), and IKEA ($90 million, lifestyle positioning). Beside the large stores and furniture specialists, so-called specialty stores, home centres and wholesaler groups also sold ready to assemble furniture, often in association with domestic equipment products. In particular, home centres were positioned as the best sales point for this category of furnishings. For example, Heilig-Meyers, who offered a huge range of domestic equipment items, from household appliances to garden equipment, noticed the possibilities for expansion in the furniture market. In addition, the very nature of kit-form furnishings was advantageous for mail order. Thus J.C. Penny sells its range of ready to assemble furnishings by catalogue. However, in spite of the potential of ready to assemble furnishings, one of the biggest challenges to the furnishings distribution sector was how to change the negative attitudes of American consumers with regard to ready to assemble.

Despite a huge and dynamic competitive environment, IKEA believes it has two distinct advantages. The first is attached to its offer of a complete range of furnishings and not just a limited number, as is the case for a majority of retailers. The second resides in the strength of its marketing mix which goes beyond the task of selling ready to assemble furnishings. According to its directors, IKEA's major competitors in America are specialty stores such as Pier One or Conran's and department stores. In addition, IKEA is well placed to service a promising new segment, office furniture for the home.

$$\diamondsuit$$

Prospects for the Future

After some 40 years in operation, IKEA is today considered to be the world-leader in furniture distribution, a position it has reached thanks to the two principles of quality and economy. These guiding principles underpin all activity from product creation right through to after-sales service. What are the prospects for the future?

IKEA must in particular remodel its company culture in order to cope with its growth. The rural roots of its founder, Ingvar Kamprad, have had a significant effect on IKEA's way of functioning. Company employees, nick-named 'Smalanders' are thought of in Sweden as entrepreneurs, but also as thrifty people who understand the value of money. Company people take pleasure in saying that, while English is the dominant language, 'Smaland' is the cultural language. 'We share strong social values' emphasizes Anders Moberg, President of IKEA since 1986. 'We think we are doing something useful for people. That creates a family feeling at IKEA, a feeling of harmony and liberty which allows development but can also lead to mistakes.'

In any case, there is a risk that the egalitarian management style which encouraged staff loyalty and gave workers their sense of mission may be lost with the arrival at IKEA of directors moving over from other companies. The recruitment of Göran Carstedt from Volvo in 1991 to take over responsibility for North American operations, and of Jan-Erik Engvist from a Swedish pharmaceutical group, also contradict the tradition of internal promotion followed until then.

The paternalistic influence of Kamprad may be reduced if other high level executives join the business. 'The biggest restriction to expansion of our company is not money but finding experienced managers' confirms one IKEA executive. 'Our growth is so rapid that our internal managerial development policy is not sufficient to fulfil our top level management requirements.' Moberg explains: 'It is difficult to find executives capable of adapting to the IKEA philosophy. We take great care with our recruitment and we spend a lot of time on training beforehand.'

'Being bought by IKEA is like taking holy orders' says Sir Terence Conran, the founder of Habitat. He suggests that just as a monastery has its rules so in IKEA there is Almhult where rules are instilled into the novices. As all the vital functions are concentrated at Almhult, initial training consists of explaining 'the family feeling for its origins'. In this philosophy there is certainly no question of being better seen than the company. The overarching message which is handed over at Almhult is based on IKEA's slogan: 'Save money'.

The arrival of so many 'foreigners' in IKEA's management could well, if not destroy, at least profoundly alter the company spirit and its dynamic marketing, which constitute its two essential strengths. Moberg recognizes that this holds a long-term risk: 'It would be dangerous to integrate too many foreigners at once. We must maintain a balance between our wish to acquire outside experience and the preservation of our values.'

The risks of explosion and loss of identity which are linked to giantism are serious. Already, over the last two years, IKEA has had to reorganize into three 'regions' with intermediary managers (Europe, North-America, Asia-Pacific). After ten years with the company, Bernard Furrer remembers nostalgically: 'Before, when in doubt, we telephoned straight to Ingvar Kamprad ...'. This growing bureaucracy at IKEA even scares the 'barons' trained on the job. The time of the eternally faithful self-made managers seems over. New managers are more qualified and professionally trained, for example Per Kaufman studied for his MBA at INSEAD, and they are no longer systematically Swedish. Germany, Switzerland and Denmark are managed by nationals and Italy has had a French director since the autumn of 1992.

The organizational and human questions linked to company development are not the only ones being asked and requiring answers. New strategic and marketing decisions need to be taken now because sales turnover abroad will have to compensate for stagnation in the original market. In fact, IKEA's traditional customer-base in Western Europe has reached maturity today and the distributor hopes to hold on to this market by evolving towards higher range products, in the post-modern style. In addition, contextual constraints have led to distortion of the original IKEA concept. First of all, the Swedish distributor had to acquire some of its sub-contractors when they were threatened with bankruptcy by the break-up of the Eastern Bloc countries. In this way, IKEA found itself the owner of three factories in Poland, with all the problems of raw material supplies and production inherent to a manufacturer.

The second distortion to the IKEA concept concerns the distributor's principle of product homogeneity. Some products of necessity have to be modified in response to the standards of countries where they are sold. Changes made may appear to be only minor anodyne details, such as adjusting the size of quilts to American requirements or the development of exclusive products to take into account the low purchasing power in Warsaw. They do, however, reveal new market trends which require localization of the offer. Pessimistic prediction from a competitor: 'If they start to build different ranges in different countries, they will lose their soul and, above all, the advantage of heavy standardized volume which allows them to practice such competitive pricing.'

Buying Habitat could be IKEA's reply to this problem. Its very first acquisition will enlarge the group's scope. 'Excellent idea' admits Terence Conran, 'Habitat will become their top of range'. Demonstrating the strategic importance given to this operation, management responsibility was put into the safest hands, those of Jan Aulin, Kamprad's deputy since 1968. 'I'm just the man he has known the longest', concedes Jan Aulin, who is the companion who has taken part in all the key decisions on IKEA's existence. Jan Aulin now finds himself in charge of a difficult project, getting IKEA out of the 'ghetto' of 'top furniture supplier for young couples'.

This weighing down of the Swedish distributor's structure also risks hampering its capacity to act, leaving openings for local competitors who are more quick to react. In this way, in France, Marc Bisch, general manager of Fly furniture (0.8$ billion turnover achieved by 122 stores with only two sales outlets outside of France (New Caledonia and Tahiti) as opposed to

$2.5 billion for IKEA with nine sales outlets in France) puts his money on flexibility. While he considers the Swedish distributor to be 'a national standard', he congratulates himself on being able to 'change a collection in two months'. A second advantage for the Fly network is its number of stores. Although certainly smaller than IKEA, they are present in urban concentrations which facilitates better access by consumers. An IKEA customer, on the other hand, must drive to get to the store and, if 'the chair of his dreams' happens to be out of stock, he could well change his mind about the distributor.

To try and maintain growth, IKEA is considering diversification outside of the furniture market. Development of a hotel chain, Swedish Inns, is being seriously considered. This could become reality by joint participation in a project between Inter Ikea Holding and the Canadian businessman, Jonathan Myette, who controls the Allegiance Hotel group. Swedish Inns would be economical hotels, entirely fitted out by IKEA; they would be promoted through the IKEA catalogue and the first ones would be situated close to the distributor's outlets. This type of diversification is not innovative in itself since, some thirty years ago, Kamprad had a hotel built at Almhult to welcome IKEA visitors. In any case, any steps taken towards developing Swedish Inns will be cautious and only a $5 million investment has been agreed for the first one to be built at Montreal. This trial will serve to assess concept feasibility which, according to Per Ludvigsson, President of Inter Ikea Holding, should create synergy between IKEA's original trade and the hotel sector.

Acknowledgement

Copyright © ESCP – CEDEP 1996.

——— QUESTIONS ———

Using the information supplied in the case and drawing on your studies on the course expand on the following topics:

(1) Analyse the company's position in its global environment and on the American market. What are the opportunities and threats on international markets, company strengths and weaknesses?

(2) Assess IKEA's international development strategy. Identify the company's key success factors. Has IKEA pursued a classic standardization strategy?

> (3) How might IKEA develop in the future? Consider carefully:
>   (a) American expansion.
>   (b) Global development of the company from the point of view of strate-
>   gic responses to major trends distinguishing the principal markets.
>   (c) How the company could benefit from the Asian growth.
>   (d) Critical factors, particularly internal ones, which the company
>   should monitor in order to face up to new challenges in its world-
>   wide expansion.

Further reading

Czintoka, M.R. and Ronkainen, I.A. 1990: Ikea in the USA. In: *International Marketing*, second edition, Dryden Press, 203–7.

Miller, N.M. 1986: The new immigrants. *Chain Store Age Executive*, February, 16–18.

Terptra, V. and Sarathy, R. 1990: Ikea. In: *International Marketing*, Dryden Press, 291–6.

—— 1993: La petite révolution culturelle d'IKEA. *Points de Vente*, No 536, 15 décembre 1993, 18.

—— 1994: IKEA furnishing the world. *Discount Merchandiser.* 34(10), 46–8.

—— 1994: Completing the span of 'bridge to boomers'. *Advertising Age*, 7 November, S–8.

—— 1994: Management brief: furnishing the world. *The Economist*, 19 November, 83–4.

—— 1995: IKEA. *Marketing Magazine*, 3, April, 16.

—— 1995: Global retailers get ready for new shopping empires. *Advertising Age*, 66(37), 18 September, I–35, I–42.

—— 1995: IKEA dans la course aux ouvertures. *Libre Service Actualite*, No 1458, 18–19.

—— 1995: Temps de travail: l'avancée d'IKEA. *Libre Service Actualite*, No 1469, 135.

—— 1996: L'Asie, le troisième pied d'IKEA. *Libre Service Actualite*, No 1485, 24–5.

—— 1996: IKEA: la croissance soft. *Le Figaro économie*, lundi 13 mai 1996, 1–8.

—— 1996:Villiers sur Marne: tout le savoir-vendre d'IKEA. *Libre Service Actualite*, 1491, 74–5.

—— 1996: Higher quality furniture, better displays boost fast growing category. *Discount Store News*, 35(15), 5 August 82.

IKEA catalogue 1997.

IKEAFAX 1995/96.

Press articles published in *American Demographics, Fortune, The Weekly Home Furnishings Newspaper, The Wall Street Journal, Business Week, Retail and Distribution Management, Le Figaro économique, Eurostat.*

4

Aer Rianta International (ARI)

MARY WILCOX AND EDMUND O'CALLAGHAN

OVERVIEW

Aer Rianta International is a subsidiary company of Aer Rianta, a fully commercial semi-state company responsible for the management of Dublin, Cork and Shannon Airports in the Republic of Ireland. Since 1992, Michael Patton has been the driving force behind Aer Rianta International's global strategy of controlled diversification and expansion, mainly in the area of duty-free retailing. Joint venture companies played a significant role in this expansion. The company developed on the basis of its core competencies and the matching of these competencies to market opportunities. This required a flexible strategic approach. It invested heavily in building competitive advantage. Formats and procedures were standardized; areas such as sourcing, distribution, and human resources received particular attention. ARI faced many challenges in adapting to diverse business cultures and is confident that it is well positioned to face the future.

KEY WORDS

Retailing, International, Duty-free, Cultural diversity, Joint venture companies, Managing interdependencies, Risk-exposure, Airports, Strategy, Competitive advantage, Human Resources.

INTRODUCTION

Since 1992, Michael Patton has been the driving force behind Aer Rianta International's global strategy of controlled diversification and expansion. Under his leadership the company located duty-free retailing outlets in the Middle-East, the Far-East, Eastern Europe, Western Europe and the UK. His vision is clear: Aer Rianta International (ARI) will work to develop ownership and management of airports internationally. The company's skills traditionally lay in managing the interdependencies between retailing activities and airport operations, and he would continue to capitalize on this. The impending removal of intra-EU duty-free sales in 1999 meant that Aer Rianta had three years remaining in which to build up its overseas businesses to offset the expected loss of its highly profitable duty and tax-free sales in Ireland. It looked to its subsidiary, ARI, to close the revenue gap. Patton did not discount the challenges facing the company, but as 1996 began, he was confident that ARI was well positioned to face the future.

Aer Rianta is a fully commercial semi-state company and is the Irish Airports Authority responsible for the management of Dublin, Cork and Shannon Airports in the Republic of Ireland. The total annual passenger throughput of these three airports exceeds 10 million. Aer Rianta has had a long history of involvement in the duty-free business and can claim to have invented the concept by opening the world's first airport duty-free shop at Shannon in 1947. Aer Rianta also operates seven hotels in Ireland, and its subsidiary company, Aer Rianta International, operates overseas in multiple locations. (Appendix 1, 'Milestones for ARI' details in chronological order ARI activities.)

In 1986, Michael Patton joined the accounts department of Aer Rianta as an accounts supervisor; on 1 April 1992 he became Director General of Aer Rianta International. Although Michael thinks he was 'lucky' to be in the right place at the right time, his meteoric rise through the company ranks is indicative of Aer Rianta's willingness to recognize and reward people's ability, dedication and hard work. He now controls his own division with overall responsibility for ARI, the subsidiary responsible for global expansion.

Shortly after his joining the company, Aer Rianta successfully bid for duty-free trading in Moscow Airport and Patton was part of the first team that went to Russia to establish the operation. In 1988 Aer Rianta International was formed and between then and 1992 the company expanded rapidly and profitably within the Commonwealth of Independent States (CIS).

THE GENESIS OF ARI

Since the mid-1980s, Aer Rianta's corporate strategy had been to grow, both in core and ancillary business. Because the size of the Irish economy constrained domestic growth and access to developed markets was limited and difficult, emerging markets in under-developed countries suited Aer Rianta's particular blend of skills.

Liam Skelly, a senior executive in Aer Rianta, pursued the initial opportunistic expansion into the CIS. Liam, a man with great charisma, a motivator, and a 'legend in the duty-free industry', capitalized on the already excellent relationship which Aer Rianta had with the Russian airline, Aeroflot, which had used Shannon Airport as a transit stop since the 1970s.

During the 1970s' oil crisis, Aeroflot had difficulty finding the vastly increased sums in foreign currency to pay fuel costs outside the former USSR. With the help of Aer Rianta, Soviet fuel was brought by sea to Shannon, and storage tanks were built for the Soviet fuel. Aeroflot and Aer Rianta entered into a barter agreement which allowed Aeroflot to pay all charges at the airport in fuel, which Aer Rianta then sold on to other operators at a competitive price thus enhancing Shannon as a transit stop. This arrangement helped cement the relationship between the two companies.

In the mid-1980s, the restructuring process which was taking place in the Soviet Union under Mikhail Gorbachev presented Aer Rianta with an opportunity to further develop this relationship with Aeroflot. Arising from a decree of the Praesidium of the Supreme Soviet on 13 January 1987, many undertakings in the then Soviet Union began to look for joint venture opportunities with Western partners. It was against this background that ARI was established and involvement in joint ventures in the CIS developed.

The Russians were interested in ventures which would generate an income in foreign currency and which would attract advanced technology and know-how. Recognizing a good opportunity, Aer Rianta decided to change from consultancy into direct operation and to propose to Aeroflot that they set up a joint venture company to manage duty-free shops in Moscow's international airport. They won this contract against stiff competition from other multi-national duty-free organizations.

Aer Rianta constructed the shops, provided experienced management and sales staff, sourced the goods and introduced state-of-the-art computerized retailing and stock control systems. The Russian partners provided the retailing sites and some of the staff.

A group of Aer Rianta core staff, supported by specially recruited contract people, were charged with establishing the Moscow shop. The challenge of this experience helped bond ARI staff into a cohesive team. Local staff were trained and gradually integrated into the business, while retaining a core group of Irish staff. The duty-free shop opened on schedule on 1 May 1988 and was a tremendous success. At the end of 1988 the shop won the internationally acclaimed 'Retailer of the Year' award for the world's best duty-free shop. Within a short time, joint ventures to operate duty-free shops were signed with the four largest airports in the then Soviet Union, Moscow, Leningrad, Kiev and Tashkent. The successful Russian venture helped establish Aer Rianta as a 'brand' in the duty-free industry.

MODES OF ENTRY TO THE DUTY-FREE INDUSTRY

Duty-free shops operate at airports, cross-border points, ferries, and most recently the Channel Tunnel. Competition for high-prestige, profitable locations is intense. The duty-free industry has major players (see appendix 2) but considerable secrecy still surrounds many of the companies that operate duty-free shops. A dozen or so companies are truly multi-national with operations in several countries. Mode of entry is at the discretion of the airport owner. Entering a new market is not easy and some markets have a tendency to favour domestic companies as concession holders.

Entry to the industry can take several forms:

Owners and management of an airport run the duty-free shops

This is Aer Rianta's position in Ireland where it owns and manages Dublin, Shannon and Cork Airports. Owning both the airport and the duty-free shops allows the interdependencies to be managed to maximum advantage.

Concessions

The most usual form of entry is that of concessionaire. Contracts to operate and manage duty-free shops are awarded on the basis of bids received. The successful bidder pays a guaranteed fee and a percentage of sales revenue to the airport owner. The bid also includes level of service to be provided by the concessionaire, product range to be stocked, etc. This mode of entry can be risky if the duty-free operator overbids in order to secure the concessionaire contract. The potential for overbidding increases as competition for contracts intensifies with concessionaire margins being squeezed. There is always the danger that duty-free prices may increase as a result of increasingly competitive tenders, thus eroding the perceived discount vis-à-vis high street prices.

Joint venture companies (JVCs)

These are set up between the duty-free operator and a local company in the foreign market. Sometimes the partnership can be with the airport owner, as was the case in many of ARI's Russian operations. JVCs are often the best method of entry into a market where the duty-free operator has limited knowledge of the environment; occasionally their formation is a legal requirement. Within the CIS, ARI had, by law, to establish a JVC with a local partner in order to bid for duty-free contracts. JVCs are appropriate for developing countries, e.g. CIS and Pakistan, because local companies may have neither the capital nor the expertise to set up duty-free shopping operations. The format offers substantial economic and political advantages. Investment and risks are shared. Some investment requirements can be eliminated through the use of the partner's existing infrastructure. Dealing with an existing agency, particularly one with well-established lines of communication and authority with government, helps to facilitate the venture.

Management contract

The final mode of entry is by management contract. The duty-free company is paid a management fee and receives a percentage of the turnover. Duty-free is a cash-rich business and, as such, can be an attractive business proposition. Management contracts rarely require the duty-free company to finance the working capital. Reward can be substantial in relation to risk exposure.

$\Diamond$

PUTTING A STRATEGY IN PLACE

On Liam Skelly's retirement in 1992, Michael Patton became Director General. By now ARI had joint venture companies operating duty-free shops in several CIS airports and central city duty-paid shops in hotel lobbies in Moscow and St Petersburg. They also had the beginnings of a business in Bahrain. Despite the initial phenomenal success, Patton was not entirely happy with his inheritance.

The pace of expansion had fuelled its own problems. When ARI was originally set up in 1988, all of its staff were drawn from within the Aer Rianta organization. As it expanded rapidly, it was found that in-house resources were finite. Between 1989 and 1991 a large number of people were recruited from the private sector, some of whom found it difficult to become imbued with the Aer Rianta culture.

When putting his management team together, Patton's strategy would have been to employ mostly Irish people and, where possible, to source them internally. If this was not possible, it was vital for them very quickly to acquire the Aer Rianta philosophy. He wanted top-quality people in finance, personnel and retailing to form part of his management team. Some of new recruits came from the private sector, but approximately half came from within the Aer Rianta organization.

Patton's style was different from Skelly's. The heady early days of expansion and success became myth. Many of the existing businesses had no coordinating mechanisms. Each was 'a little fiefdom in its own right, it was like running eight or nine entirely different businesses; no standardization existed'. For some employees the necessary stream-lining and structures were a poor replacement. Within two years seven middle-managers had decided to leave or were replaced. All of these were people who had been recruited externally and either did not or could not subscribe to Aer Rianta's ethos and culture.

The new Director General felt that the company needed a more clearly defined strategy: 'What businesses should we be in? Which countries should we operate in? What investments should we be making and at what levels? What exposures could we carry, what exposures could we not carry?' As a state company, all its operations were subject to scrutiny by the Auditor General and it was finally answerable to the Irish taxpayer. The company had invested IR£15m in rapid expansion in a variety of different ventures in high-risk areas; no exit mechanisms existed. It was time to ask questions and develop an overall strategy.

An in-house design team developed a retail format which could be modified and adapted to suit all locations. Structures were established which enabled people to work to 'reasonably the same procedures, while respecting the need for some autonomy'. Financial goals were set to reduce exposure to acceptable limits; companies were given cash-flow projections with targets set for monies to be repatriated within a time-limit.

Deciding on locations

ARI executives knew that duty-free retailing in Russia was a finite market. While the expertise and distinct competencies which they had built up by operating in Russia could be applied to other similar underdeveloped parts of the world, Patton's preference was for 'First World' locations. At this stage, lack of critical mass and bidding power made it difficult to enter developed markets.

Intensive market research was undertaken to ensure that bids for new locations would result in profitable ventures for ARI. Almost 95 per cent of the world's duty-free shops are run by third parties, largely via concessions. Liam Flood, Company Secretary says that 'ARI is involved in on-going research on duty-free outlets: when are they coming up for renewal? what way are they being offered? what are the logistics of moving goods? what are the political risks?'. This research involves sending members of the management team to talk to airport owners, 'to monitor the number of passengers passing through an airport, to see what kinds of goods were bought and what was not bought, and how much money was spent. What is it going to cost you to set-up out there? What is it going to cost you to pay people? What general overheads will you have to bear? You must try to work out your margin. There is no point in bidding more than it's worth. You may get the concession, but you lose'. The company needed to know what level of service the airport owner expected and what mode of entry was acceptable. If a local partner was essential for entry, then ARI would seek a suitable partner, establish a JVC and enter a bid for the duty-free contract.

Organizational structure

Although ARI had found JVCs invaluable as expansion mechanisms, Patton was becoming disillusioned with multi-partner JVCs: 'one partner is difficult, two is impossible and three is suicidal'. Even in Russia, where the experience had been generally very good, problems with a partner had made the company decide to sell the majority of their shares in Arbat House and the Valdai Centre, a prestigious central city shopping mall which they had been instrumental in building and running.

The company began to concentrate on bidding for duty-free management contracts. Such contracts may not be as lucrative as concessions, but profitability can be more satisfactory in terms of a risk/return ratio, because working capital does not have to be financed. As Liam Flood explains: 'Moscow is doing $5m dollars per week, and we must hold 5–6 weeks' stock. This is dead money sitting on the shelves'. Management contracts have other advantages in that they require fewer staff to be located overseas, and decision-taking is clear-cut.

ARI was successful in winning the management contracts for central city duty-free shops in Bangkok, the duty-free shops at both ends of the Channel

Tunnel, and, most recently, the duty-free outlets for Beijing International Airport.

Patton's ultimate vision was ambitious. He wanted ARI to own airports throughout the world. The combination of being able to manage and develop duty-free activities and offer expertise in full-line management services was seen as an important competitive advantage. This vision got its first tentative expression when ARI won the contract for managing all operational and commercial activities at Warsaw Airport.

The British government's policy of privatizing state-owned airports provided another opportunity for ARI in pursuance of its airport ownership objective. In February 1995, an unsuccessful Stg£36m bid was made for Cardiff Airport. Later that year, having formed a strategic alliance with NatWest Capital Ventures, ARI became the 'preferred bidder' for Birmingham Airport; an already profitable airport with growth potential. When the deal goes through, ARI will own 30 per cent of the Airport with the option to buy out NatWest. 'We will soon own a piece of British airport infrastructure.' ARI is interested in securing the management contracts for most of the privatized airports, including East Midlands, Southampton, Liverpool, Manchester and Glasgow.

In November 1995, ARI was invited to bid for the provision of airport management services in India. It may also bid for the management of duty and tax-free facilities. The Indian government's programme includes the development of 84 international and domestic airports throughout the state and the plan provides for the involvement of private companies in these developments. There are also possibilities for airport ownership in Turkey, South East Asia and Australia.

Because all locations reported on an individual basis, handling the multitude of problems which followed the company's rapid expansion put the management team, and Patton in particular, under severe time pressure. In 1995, the company was restructured on an overseas regional basis and regional managers now report to *Head of Operations* and *Head of Administration*, who in turn report to Patton. Now only major problems are referred to the Director General and time is available to deal with issues of strategy and with the often intense negotiations between preferred bidders and airport owners.

Handling Cultural Diversity

The cultural context

On a global basis, ARI executives identify three broad business cultures. The bureaucratic culture characteristic of Eastern-European countries, the less procedural, 'fix it' culture of some Far-Eastern countries and the capitalist culture of Western economies. There is an element of all cultures in all countries, but generally speaking, one culture tends to dominate. Each environment had to be accommodated, understood and mastered by ARI, in order to ensure a successful outcome.

Partnership agreements were endemic to ARI's initial foreign expansion, because JVC's were the principal mode of entry to such markets at that time. Partnership agreements are often potentially problematic and this tendency is exacerbated when diverse national cultures are involved. The mix of Western and Russian cultures or the mix of Western and Asian cultures could potentially provide a lethal business cocktail if not understood and managed properly.

In addition to its technical skills, ARI felt that being Irish was an advantage. Coming from an ex-colonial background, it demonstrated a greater sensitivity and respect for other cultures, a quality sometimes found wanting with other duty-free operators. Some duty-free companies tend to impose their *modus operandi* on each local culture they encounter. ARI's stated strategy was to 'seek long-term agreements, to give the partners a say in the running of the business and to maintain transparency and fairness in our business dealings'. The dividend of this strategy was seen most recently when ARI won the contract to operate duty-free shops at Beijing in the face of intense competition from the world's leading duty-free companies.

Staffing issues

Because airports tend to be state owned, often the giving of concessions is at the discretion of politicians who are sensitive to public opinion. A willingness to employ local people may be a prerequisite for winning a contract. In Russia, the employment of local people was seen as evidence of ARI's commitment to its JVCs. To do this made economic sense for the company in that an expatriate employee's wage would cost significantly more than a local person's wage (£20,000 pa versus £4,000 pa in the CIS). However, when local staff have no concept of either customer service or profit, and have few natural retail skills, intensive training is needed so that sales targets will be reached. ARI achieved productivity levels which were comparable to Western standards. Selective recruitment techniques, committing resources to staff development and providing appropriate incentives to employees were the methods used to achieve this end. In sharp contrast, staff in Bangkok are natural traders who require little formal training. Whatever its starting point, ARI puts effort into ensuring that local staff absorb the company culture and become integrated.

ARI considers that choosing the right manager is critical to the success of its duty-free outlet. Local employees, who must have a good command of spoken English, are invariably better educated than their counterparts in the English-speaking world. In some countries, professional people find that they can earn more with ARI than they can by pursuing their careers. The company has found that an autocratic management style rarely works to motivate employees. In any case, such a style is alien to the company culture. Appendix 3 shows current and past employment patterns.

Cultural variety

Each business culture differs. Each poses its own unique problems. For example, Western business systems consist of sourcing, production, marketing, distribution and customer service. By contrast, in most East European countries, decades of central planning over-emphasized production, at the expense of customer-related issues. The Far East provides another perspective. The Thais are an astute people with a developed trading tradition, who accept additional competition as a natural phenomenon. ARI can teach the Thais very little about the art of buying and selling, but has the purchasing power to interest the Thais.

Legal problems differ by country. Varying business ethoses and management philosophies present challenges with rapidly evolving legal and administrative structures. In Russia, rarely a month goes by without some new legislation being implemented. Asian business environments can lack regulation and control. In all business environments, ARI constantly monitors changes in legislation and administrative detail which affects its business. In this way, ARI avoids falling foul of local authorities and also avoids the heavy fines which can go with non-compliance.

History helps shape trading cultures. For example, Russia's business culture never had the opportunity to develop. They went straight from a feudal system to a communist system. On the other hand, the Poles never really accepted Communism, they were always good traders and keen business people. Yet many people from Western capitalist economies would stereotype all Slavs as having common characteristics. As one ARI manager put it: 'the Poles are as different from the Russians as the French are from the Germans, and the Germans are from the Italians. You must tune in to individual cultures'. This, he believes, is the secret of ARI's success.

◇

BUILDING COMPETITIVE ADVANTAGE

Product sourcing

For the duty-free industry, product sourcing is a critical element in maintaining a competitive edge. In any partnership arrangement, ARI maintains control over product sourcing. Sourcing is a key component of all partnership agreements and management contracts. ARI reasons that the relationship is more likely to be long term if it controls sourcing because partners would have neither the expertise nor the buying power to acquire goods at competitive prices. ARI's buying power allows for more competitive prices to be offered to customers, increasing the competitiveness of the duty-free shops.

The company installed a central purchasing department to bulk buy on the world market and are now strong enough to obtain the best possible prices. They established a network of buying specialists across Europe, Russia, the Middle East and Asia to meet international demands. They also restructured their buying mechanisms. Products stocked in their duty-free shops have become somewhat generic. In line with a world-wide trend, most items stocked are major international brands. At one time they had 700 suppliers and 10,000 stock items, now they have 200 suppliers and approximately 2,000 stock items. Greater purchasing power and more sophisticated sourcing and distribution techniques have improved all retail margins. The company has also concluded a number of agency agreements in the Middle Eastern region and are supplying merchandise to a number of outlets in this area. ARI's buying power increases with each additional new contract won.

Warehousing and distribution

The company also invested in a computerized world-wide distribution network which ships over 12,000 tonnes of merchandise to Russia every year and large amounts to other centres. Distribution and consolidation hubs have been strategically located in Europe, the Middle East and South East Asia to ensure that merchandise can be moved efficiently and cost effectively through a variety of global transport channels. Extensive warehousing resources, a state-of-the-art stock control system and local distribution networks allow merchandise to move safely and smoothly from bonded stores to shop floor. The scale of the company's international operations and purchasing and distribution channels allows ARI to pass on significant cost savings to each of its partners and principals.

Other benefits for Aer Rianta's foreign partners include the acquisition of management expertise, profit sharing, technology acquisition, training and an assured supply of quality merchandise.

Human resources and customer service

Fran Murphy, Head of Operations, is the company's human resource man. Fran started his career as a member of the airport police and is another example of Aer Rianta's ability to launch people on different careers. 'He's very, very good with people. He has a "feel" for who should be where, how people will work together, who should be put in charge.' Initially, the company recruited a lot of people who were transient, now they look for motivated people who are committed to ARI. Staff in the core business are given the opportunity to work in the overseas ventures for specific periods; ARI now has a pool of management talent with knowledge of the different businesses and their interdependencies, and this can be accessed as ventures are being researched or set up.

To provide a professional service, ARI developed an in-house retail management training programme which covers all theoretical aspects of retailing. Entry to this course is open to all ARI and Aer Rianta staff and there is a large demand for admittance. ARI use this course to identify 'the right people', people with retail flair and good interpersonal skills. 'We have good people at the top, but we also need good people on the ground to work with the locals.' The Retail Management Course is effectively a two-year induction course into how ARI manages its overseas ventures – 'the way we do things'. Two six-month placements overseas provide staff with work experience in different cultural settings. Irish staff, equipped with retailing and management skills, are then placed in supervisory and management positions in overseas duty-free shops. Trainee managers from Russia have also attended the retail course and ARI intends to encourage other indigenous staff to avail of the opportunity to become professional retailers.

Not All Plain Sailing

Major challenges had to be faced as ARI positioned itself as an international retailer. For example, changes in both business and political climates, problems with partnership arrangements and prolonged legal battles occasionally made life difficult.

Pakistan

Karachi experienced problems from its earliest days. As the highest bidder, ARI went into Karachi on a concession basis in a joint venture with a Bahrain-based businessman. Each partner owned 50 per cent of the company. In an agreement with the Civil Aviation Authority, the JVC was committed to paying the airport authorities a percentage of sales, which could not fall below a guaranteed minimum sum. The aviation authority in turn guaranteed a certain minimum passenger throughput level, but 'didn't deliver on it due to all sorts of regulations which they apparently imposed themselves. Customs were obstructive, and all kinds of stumbling blocks were put in the way'. At one stage, the government threatened to introduce new regulations drastically reducing the sale of duty-free goods in Pakistan. AerRianta Pakistan sought redress through the courts.

The major shortfall in expected passenger numbers, changes in policy and other restrictions on trading activities made it impossible to achieve the level of sales required to ensure the viability of the business. But AerRianta Pakistan was tied into a ten-year contract and faced heavy penalties if it attempted to pull out. In late 1993 it was apparent that the business was in serious financial trouble and executives drew up a cost-savings plan to take effect immediately. Cuts were sought in payroll and advertising, and efforts were made to renegotiate the shop's rental contract and concession fees with the Civil Aviation Authority. It seemed that the only way of operating successfully in Karachi was with a local partner. When a Pakistani Company expressed interest AerRianta Pakistan sold 89 per cent of its shares and reduced its exposure. The company still exists and is trading. ARI now has a management contract for Karachi and is paid a management fee.

Russia

In 1995, the last Irish staff departed ARI's joint venture shopping centre and bar business in central Moscow. The operating company, Sitco, which runs two pubs and the Valdai shopping centre, was set up in 1991. Originally, Aer Rianta held a 45 per cent stake, 5 per cent was held by a Shannon based company and the other 50 per cent was owned by Mostroi, a subsidiary of the city government and a Russian supermarket. ARI has reduced its holding in Sitco to 19 per cent and no longer has a management role in the business. The company say that the project has not cost it money, and that it was 'extremely satisfied' with the price it received for reducing its stake. Industry sources estimate that it received $7m for the sale of its stake.

Since Sitco started trading, the business climate in Moscow has suffered because of an increase in crime. The growth of competition from the number of Western companies operating there has made it too expensive for many joint ventures to pay Western wages to foreign managers and workers. Improved shopping facilities made shopping in hotel lobbies less attractive and ARI withdrew from these locations.

During 1991 the Russian government introduced tougher value added taxes and from 1994 the Russian Central Bank required businesses to trade in roubles. ARI found that 'the business environment in Russia in ordinary commercial sales had become more difficult' and many foreign partners in similar joint ventures have experienced problems. The Sitco partnership arrangement was creating its own problem; an extremely volatile Russian partner made commercial decisions impossible. The combination of these circumstances convinced ARI to reduce its holding.

ARI has deferred its plans to build a warehouse which would consolidate its distribution network in Russia, but they are going ahead with building a warehouse for Moscow duty-free.

Poland

The three-year contact between ARI and the Polish State Airport Authority has run its course and is up for tender. A dispute between the Polish Airport Authority and a previous duty-free operator went for arbitration to a third country. The decision went against the Poles, who were heavily fined and who do not have the means of paying. The Poles want any company willing to manage Warsaw airport to pay this fine and recoup this sum over several years' trading. ARI was not interested in this arrangement and have not tendered for the contract.

Channel Tunnel

While Eurotunnel duty-free is now operating exceptionally well, initially it was late opening and passenger numbers were lower than expected.

ARI had just formed a JVC with a catering company, Bewley Ltd and, in addition to bidding for the duty-free management contract, the JVC entered a bid for the catering contract for the two restaurants on either side of the Channel Tunnel. Aer Rianta Bewley saw the opportunity to get the Eurotunnel catering contract as a prestige development, rather than one which would earn it large profits. The catering concession was awarded and then withdrawn. This decision was challenged in the French court to no avail. Aer Rianta Bewley are appealing the decision on the grounds that Eurotunnel did not comply with the 1994 European tendering procedures when putting the concession out to tender. The action is expected to take about a year to come to court.

ARI are philosophical about the problems encountered in foreign markets. For example, the Eurotunnel duty-free concession sales have now grown to a degree that they are the largest single outlet which ARI manages and, despite the catering controversy, ARI's relationship with Eurotunnel plc is excellent. In the final analysis, ARI rarely fail to achieve a satisfactory return on investment, which is critical in terms of shareholder interest.

$$\Diamond$$

THE BOTTOM LINE

The Aer Rianta brand was launched internationally with the opening of the Moscow duty-free shop in 1988. By 1990, sales revenue had reached IR£33m from Soviet operations and ARI's profits amounted to IR£4m on an initial investment of approximately IR£10m. During its initial two years, business in the Soviet Union had grown to be almost equivalent, in employment and turnover, to its domestic retail business.

However, 1992 was a bad year for ARI. They recorded a loss of IR£602,000 due to the introduction of back value added tax in the CIS. Its overseas operations returned to profitability in 1993 with a IR£654,000 pre-tax profit on overall IR£102m sales. In 1994, the subsidiary made a £3m contribution to the group's profitability on a turnover of IR£112m. Its pre-tax profits rose by 39 per cent to a record IR£31.6m. Appendix 4 shows turnover figures for the JVCs.

Because of the nature of international duty-free shopping, most of its trade is either in hard currency, or in strong currencies. Occasionally the company may suffer a loss when a currency changes value, but sometimes it gains, especially when the US dollar is strong against the Irish Punt. The company is conservative in the accounting treatment of overseas operations and makes heavy provisions to cover the uncertainty of doing business in foreign countries. Profit figures tend to underestimate its trading strength and management appear to be satisfied with their 'bottom line'.

──────── QUESTIONS ────────

(1)   What are the key success factors for SRI's international expansion? How dependent are these on external environmental factors?

(2)   What are the human resource policies which ARI have used to underpin their expansion?

(3)   How has ARI addressed the cultural issue in international retail expansion? Is this cultural issue likely to become more or less important in the future?

(4)   Analyse the marketing environment for ARI using SWOT analysis.

(5)   Analyse the structure of the duty-free industry using Porter's five force model as a framework.

(6)   In terms of Ansoff's Matrix, identify the strategic options pursued by ARI.

(7)   What was the fundamental strategic issue facing ARI post-1992?

(8)   Analyse the organizational implications of expansion for ARI.

(9)   Identify the industry critical success factors for duty-free companies, and specifically those relevant to ARI within the former Soviet Union.

(10) How appropriate was ARI's choice of JVCs as a diversification strategy?

(11) Evaluate ARI's unique positioning strategy.

Appendix 1   Milestones for ARI

1988

In February an agreement was signed with Aeroflot to form a joint venture company called 'Aerofirst' to establish two duty-free shops in the departure area of Moscow's international airport, Seremetyevo II.

Duty-free sales commenced on-board international flights operated by Aeroflot out of Moscow.

In November ARI signed its second joint venture agreement, this time with Aeroflot–St Petersburg. The purpose of this joint venture was to establish duty-free shop facilities at Pulkova Airport in St Petersburg.

1989

In March, two arrivals duty-free shops were opened at Moscow Airport.

In April, ARI signed a third joint venture agreement with the Vyborg Regional Consumer Society for the establishment of a duty-free shop on the USSR/Finnish border at Torfionovka.

In June, the first duty-free shops at St Petersburg Airport were opened. ARI also opened bars at that airport and commenced in-flight duty-free sales from St Petersburg.

In August, ARI signed further joint venture agreements with Intour services and the Pribaltiskaya Hotel in St Petersburg to establish duty-free shops there and in other hotels in St Petersburg.

In October, ARI signed a contract to construct a maintenance hangar for Aeroflot at Moscow Airport. This project was completed at the end of 1990.

In December, the shop in the Pribaltiskaya Hotel opened.

1990

In February, ARI was awarded a contract for the management of a duty-free shopping complex in Bahrain Airport. Aer Rianta was responsible for the design of the complex, overseeing the fitting out, etc., as well as the on-going management of the duty-free shops. Aer Rianta's contract is with a private company, Bahrain Duty Free Shops Ltd which had obtained a concession for the provision of shopping and catering facilities from the Bahrain Directorate of Civil Aviation.

In April, a new joint venture with Aeroflot and other business partners in Moscow was registered to cover various other commercial undertakings in the Moscow region. In May, a second downtown shop was opened in St Petersburg and the shop on the Finnish border at Torfionovka also commenced trading.

In September, the Moscow departure shops were greatly extended. In December, a third shop was opened in downtown St Petersburg in the prestigious Astoria Hotel.

1991

In July, the Arbat Irish House/Shamrock Bar opened for business in downtown Moscow, operated by joint venture company SITCO (The Soviet Irish Trading Company). A new Irish Bar was opened at Moscow Airport.

1992

In early 1992 Aer Rianta International was awarded a major management contract by the Polish State Airport Authority (PPL) to manage all operational and commercial activities at Warsaw Airport. The three-year contract involved the assignment of a number of senior key personnel to Warsaw. This contract has now terminated.

In May, a new duty-free shop at Kiev airport opened for business and, in August, ARI secured a contract to run a new duty-free shop in the new Jinnah Terminal at Karachi.

1993

In October, ARI concluded a consultancy agreement to assist with the management of the duty-free shops at Kuwait's International Airport and a second border shop at Brusnichnoye on the Russian/Finnish border opened for trading.

1994

In January, ARI won the contract to provide duty-free shops at both ends of the Channel Tunnel. Aer Rianta designed and fitted out the duty-free shops at both tunnel terminals.

In March 1994, the first shopping mall in Russia, the Valdai Centre, was opened in downtown Moscow in the Nova Arbatsky. The mall extends to a total of 3,171 m^2 and houses nine retail outlets, a cafe, a restaurant and a bank.

In late 1994, in line with ARI's strategy of concentrating on its core business of Airport Duty-Free Shopping and Airport Management, the company reduced its direct involvement in a number of downtown ventures in both St Petersburg and Moscow, but have retained a minority shareholding in SITCO.

1995

In January, ARI was awarded a major duty-free contract in Bangkok by the Tourism Authority of Thailand. The contract covers the operation of a new 4,000 m^2 duty-free shop in the downtown World Trade Centre in Bangkok. This contract was won in the face of competition from over 12 of the world's main duty-free operators. In the latter half of the year, ARI was chosen as the preferred bidder for ownership of Birmingham Airport.

1996

In January, ARI won the contract for managing duty-free in Bejing International Airport.

Appendix 2   The World's Major Duty Free and Travel Retail Shop Operators

Rank	Company/operator	Travel retail sales (in US$ millions)
1	DFS Group, USA	2,100
2	Gebr. Heinemann, Germany	752
3	Allders International, UK/Int'l.	607
4	Weitnauer Trading, Switzerland	570
5	Duty Free International, USA	376
6	SAS Trading, Scandinavia	304
7	Stena Line Group, Sweden/Int'l	300
8	Greyhound Leisure, USA	300
9	Duty Free Philippines, Philippines	258
10	Alpha Retail Trading, UK	256
11	**Aer Rianta International, Ireland**	**223**
12	Japan Airport Terminal Co., Japan	217
13	Silja EffJohn, Finland	210
14	Saresco, France	203
15	Viking-SF Line, Finland	200

Source: Adapted from *General Publications*, 1995

Appendix 3   Number of employees

Staff	1988	1989	1990	1991	1992	1993	1994	1995
Ex-pats. (total)	36	30	115	142	139	122	107	67
Local Staff								
CIS	200	250	430	722	992	994	1032	709
Karachi						22	31	64
Bahrain						166	166	166
Eurotunnel								129
Bangkok								400
Kuwait								120

Source: ARI

Appendix 4   Aer Rianta International sales in joint ventures

JV turnover	1988 $000	1989 $000	1990 $000	1991 $000	1992 $000	1993 $000	1994 $000	1995 $000
Aerofirst	10,671	26,875	41,018	36,692	40,683	47,104	58,669	74,997
Sitco	0	0	0	10,276	35,222	41,032	37,750	0
Lenrianta	0	1,804	6,034	5,609	7,334	8,500	9,391	9,771
Intourianta	0	0	10,144	8,572	7,758	6,387	4,475	–
Sitop	0	0	1,591	6,205	6,344	6,497	16,080	36,430
Kievrianta	0	0	0	0	1,030	2,282	3,869	7,230
Karachi	0	0	0	0	880	7,517	7,003	4,631
Kuwait	0	0	0	0	0	0	9,938	14,640
Bahrain	0	0	0	3,337	24,548	25,937	33,391	39,000
Eurotunnel	0	0	0	0	0	0	3,336	58,232
Bangkok	0	0	0	0	0	0	0	2,151
TOTAL	10,671	28,679	58,787	70.691	123,799	145,256	183,902	247,082

Source: ARI

5

Free Record Shop: The Sky is the Limit?

EVERT HELFFERICH AND MARJOLEIN HINFELAAR

OVERVIEW

Free Record Shop Holding NV originated in 1971. The company exported its retail format Free Record Shop to Belgium in 1989 and is now market leader in the Netherlands and Belgium. In 1994, the company set up operations in Norway. This case study gives a detailed account of the internationalization process, paying attention to strategic marketing and management issues.

KEY WORDS

Internationalization strategy, Leadership, Adaptation, Organizational structure

---

THE COMPANY

Free Record Shop was founded by the entrepreneur Hans Breukhoven in 1971. The first shop in Schiedam (near Rotterdam) was the smallest record store in the Netherlands, being only 16 m². At the time, record shops had to be a member of the Dutch association of music retailers in order to be able to buy records in Holland. Avoiding these restrictive practices, Breukhoven imported records from England, Germany and France and sold them at a standard price of ƒ14.95, 25 per cent below the cartel price. In the course of the 1970s the company opened another 16 outlets and in 1979 Free Record Shop took over the record chain Disco Dancer (17 outlets). This caused several problems with the computerized stock control system, which could only handle 25 outlets. In the next few years, therefore, Free Record Shop sold the less profitable outlets and bought new ones in better locations, whilst modernizing the distribution system and store layout. The first step across the border was the takeover of the Belgian record chain Dilewijns Discount in 1986, subsequently restyling and renaming the stores. In 1989, the company entered the Amsterdam stock market in order to have more financial scope for expansion at home and abroad. The company took advantage of the booming market for CDs as almost the entire population was replacing its record collection, and it was one of the first music stores to stop stocking LPs. Steadily expanding, by 1994 the company had 101 outlets in Holland and 26 in Belgium (including a 1500 m² mega-store in the centre of Brussels). Free Record Shop Holding NV had a turnover of ƒ250 million for the financial year 1993/94 (see appendix 1).

The name Free Record Shop was chosen in 1971 to symbolize free selling prices and free trade. This informal mission statement, translated into the Free Record Shop retailing strategy targeting the average consumer in the age group 12 to 40, brought the company great domestic success in the 1970s and 1980s. Until recently, the product range was deep and wide with an emphasis on CDs. Free Record Shop is currently changing into a home entertainment centre also offering videotapes and CD-i software. With the help of the computerized cash register system, all Dutch and Belgian outlets can be supplied within 24 hours by the distribution centre at the company headquarters in Capelle a/d IJssel, near Rotterdam. The product range in each outlet can be closely matched with customer demand, taking into account regional or national differences in music taste, such as a larger range of French chansons for Brussels or Dutch sentimental ballads for Amsterdam. In order to get discounts, Free Record Shop purchases centrally from companies in various countries. Even so, Free Record Shop is not the cheapest music store anymore; prices are set nationally depending on the market situation. In an attempt to move up-market, the emphasis is put more and more on service and layout of the store. In the larger stores it is possible to look for CDs and videotapes with the help of a database. Levels of training are high and staff commitment is valued. The interior of these stores is spacious and well-lit, allowing a clear presentation of the goods and an open atmosphere. Many of the smaller outlets in Dutch towns and cities such as

Leeuwarden and Apeldoorn, however, do not yet meet these higher specifications. The characteristic bright yellow and blue store colours and the logo with the upturned fist and thumb make Free Record Shop a distinctive fascia on most Dutch and Belgian high streets.

The company uses various external communication tools to reach its target groups and generate more customer traffic. The key activity is publishing the magazine *Free*, available for free in every outlet, providing the consumer with information on developments in the picture and sound carrier market and the home entertainment business, and offering prize competitions. Furthermore, joint promotional activities are undertaken with a diverse group of companies: the Dutch national newspaper *Algemeen Dagblad*, Milka chocolate bar manufacturers, C&A clothing stores and Fleuril washing powders. The company avoids radio and TV commercials because it considers them too expensive and comparatively ineffective.

In Holland and Belgium, Free Record Shop is the market leader with a market share of approximately 20 per cent in 1994. Apart from the Free Record Shop format, two other formats are exploited for different target groups in the Netherlands. Van Leest is a professional and high quality store for the upper middle-class selling a wide range of titles with a particular emphasis on classical music. Fame Music in Amsterdam is the first music department store of the Netherlands with a sales area of 1850 m^2 and six departments specializing in pop, jazz, classical music, dance music, videos and games. The number of titles stocked is more than 100,000.

Free Record Shop is a subsidiary of Free Record Shop Holding NV. The basic organizational structure was not changed when Free Record Shop became an international company. Decisions about pricing, assortment and purchasing are made on a national management level, in close consultation with the company headquarters. Operations are headquarter-controlled by means of a fully automated stock control system providing up-to-date sales figures for each shop. In an attempt to motivate employees and to maintain a strong corporate identity throughout its outlets in three countries, Free Record Shop uses a two-way communication system: if an employee has an idea or a question to senior management at HQ, this should be answered within 24 hours. All senior managers have to spend at least a couple of days per year working alongside the sales assistants in one of the outlets. According to a senior executive, power distance (defined as the degree to which influence and control are unevenly distributed in the company) is low, because all employees have the opportunity to influence day-to-day decisions at store level and at HQ level. It is not known how regularly employees actually make use of this opportunity. The company has a strong belief in team spirit, which is badly needed in its current drive to improve efficiency and to continue to expand. The staff is never allowed to forget, however, that communication with the customer has priority: in its organizational chart consisting of five concentric circles, Free Record Shop places the customer in the centre and senior management in the outer ring.

The company's policy of openness as regards internal communication is also reflected in its willingness to co-operate with researchers and educational institutions. In 1995, Free Record Shop supplied two Dutch educational publishers with lesson material, and Hans Breukhoven is a regular guest lecturer at the Faculty of Economics, Erasmus University (Rotterdam).

THE ENTREPRENEUR

Hans Breukhoven was brought up in a working-class district of the sprawling city of Rotterdam in the 1950s. His father left the family when Hans was two years old, and his mother ran a successful school for beauty specialists. After leaving school, he spent a few years as a sailor with Holland-America Line before becoming a market trader in wigs and underwear. He found standing behind a market stall all day in winter rather cold and unpleasant, so he tried his luck opening a record shop. On his travels with Holland-America Line he had noticed that LPs were much cheaper abroad, so he regularly drove his van to London and Paris to buy his stock. Taking his company through slow, steady growth in the seventies and then accelerated growth in the 1980s and early 1990s, he started putting in more and more gruelling working days of up to 18 hours. He readily admits to being a workaholic, but emphasizes that the quality of life is all-important: the customers should find the CDs and videos that they want, the employees should find satisfaction in their work and he himself should provide the right leadership to his company and yet find enough time for his family.

A few years ago he married the glamorous Dutch media star, ex-singer and model Vanessa, in a fairy-tale wedding to which 1,000 guests were invited. The couple have four adopted children. He occasionally accompanies her to high society events, quite content to stay in the background while all the photographers gather around her. Having said that, Hans Breukhoven is by no means media-shy: he relishes giving interviews to newspapers, magazines and TV channels, in which he leaves a strong impression of being an ambitious, self-made businessman, always looking for creative and innovative schemes to open up new markets or beat the competition, whilst maintaining a rational outlook. His recent statement 'my heart is the check-out' could be indicative of the company's ambitions for the future. Another telling quotation was Vanessa's words in a recent interview: 'I'd rather die in a Rolls Royce than in a *bakfiets*' (a Dutch bicycle and cart used for deliveries).

Hans Breukhoven likes to keep in touch with Free Record Shop staff at all levels, so he pays regular visits to outlets irrespective of travelling distances, and talks to sales assistants to give them extra motivation. To this end he has a private helicopter, painted blue and yellow. He acquired it a couple of years ago with the intention of beating the daily traffic queues between his home in Wassenaar (near The Hague) and HQ at Capelly a/d IJssel, but the Dutch aviation authorities would not give him permission.

If the need arises, he does not hesitate to take firm control of operational details. After the financial year 1992, for example, the company accounts revealed a serious drop in profits (f8 million) in spite of rising turnover, and he concluded that those in management positions must have lost their customary prudence in financial matters because they had been blinded by the company's success. For three months, all expenses claims of managers were authorized by Hans Breukhoven personally. It earned him the nickname of 'the bookkeeper', but the strategy worked because overheads dropped significantly. In an interview with the commercial TV channel RTL4 in November 1995, he stated that his company should never forget its roots as a specialist store using price as its competitive weapon, and should not have its head in the clouds with too much talk of high service levels and attractive store atmosphere.

$$\Diamond$$

GOING TO SCANDINAVIA

The main motive for Free Record Shop to enter the Flemish-speaking part of Belgium in the 1980s had been that it was geographically close, there was no language barrier and the country had great market potential. In the 1990s, the motive for going international further afield was different: the market in Holland and Belgium was becoming saturated. In 1994, the Belgian market stagnated, but turnover in the sound and picture carrier sector in Holland actually decreased (1993 index 100, 1994 index 97), showing a much sharper decline than the overall downward trend of 0.5 per cent in the non-food sector. Average per capita spending now stood at f87. With non-store retailers such as book clubs slicing away ever more market share (8 per cent of videos and 18 per cent of CDs in 1994), market leader Free Record Shop had to keep on its toes. Along with some other prominent Dutch retailers the company joined 'Telekado', a scheme for sending presents through the postal service. The company wasted no time in approaching the biggest chain of petrol stations, Shell, and negotiating the right to sell its products through 70 petrol station shops around the country. Impulse buys in these shops currently account for 15 per cent of petrol companies' turnover, and these are expected to increase as the companies are investing more in developing convenience store formats, taking advantage of new legislation allowing longer opening hours. Once again, Free Record Shop responded. In order to catch those travelling by public transport as well, the company entered into a co-operation with the Dutch railways and opened kiosks in railway stations in major towns. By the middle of 1995, the total number of stores in the Netherlands including these small outlets had grown to 141. In its regular stores, Free Record Shop allocated more floor space to CD-i and CD-ROM software, targeting the growing market for multimedia products. All these strenuous albeit successful moves to consolidate the company's market position, however, could not satisfy Hans Breukhoven's thirst for more spectacular growth: he sought new adventures by going abroad again.

The company's search for further international opportunities had begun in the early 1990s. In spite of Hans Breukhoven's dynamic image, rigorous research was carried out before plunging into new markets. According to a senior executive, criteria guiding the decision whether to enter a new market are consumer buying behaviour, competitors in the market, projected market growth and political trade barriers. He states that the company will minimize risks and the objective is to transfer Free Record Shop's undiluted retail format through wholly owned stores. In 1992 the company acquired a store in Germany which was to serve as a pilot, operating it under its old name. In the event of disappointing results, it could easily be disposed of at minimal exit costs or damage to Free Record Shop's reputation. In fact, this is exactly what happened because Germany was found to have a saturated market and powerful competitors in the hi-fi equipment sector. After surveying the Spanish market extensively, it was deemed too small for expansion and very different from Holland and Belgium, which would have necessitated far-reaching adaptations of the format. In France, the hypermarkets dominated the market. The UK market was far too competitive. Eventually, Norway was chosen in 1994 because of its market potential and the perceived similarities between the Dutch and Norwegian music cultures. The entry decision in favour of Norway was unequivocal, because all the selection criteria were met. At the moment, Norwegians are the number one music buyers in the world with per capita sales of $f100$ per year. The market was expected to grow by 10 per cent in 1995. The perfect location for a pilot store was found in Karl Johansgate in Oslo, Norway's best-known shopping street. The store in Oslo, opened in December 1994, is seen as a foothold on the Scandinavian market, opening up great possibilities for future expansion.

The preparatory phase before operations in Norway could be set up absorbed a great deal of Hans Breukhoven's time and energy. Having discovered the Norwegian market potential, future competitors had to be studied. It was found that there would be three direct competitors (i.e. specialist chains) with a total market share of 30 per cent. Department stores also still had a considerable market share in music products. They used strong competitive weapons such as price, but did not offer the wide range and service level of the Free Record Shop home entertainment centre. A significant factor was that none of them were established on the prestigious main shopping street, Karl Johansgate. With the help of a business friend, a Dutch expatriate estate agent in Oslo, a successful offer was made to the owner of an ailing supermarket to buy the premises. The estate agent also acted as an interpreter in talks with local government officials, when legal technicalities became too complex for English to be used as a common language. The outlet in Karl Johansgate was to be run by an experienced Dutch Free Record Shop store manager, who played an active part in recruiting local sales staff. Two important requirements were that applicants should have sales experience in the music sector, so that Free Record Shop could get inside information about its future competitors, and that they should be fluent in the English language, to facilitate communication with the store manager and with HQ.

Several adaptations had to be made for the Norwegian market. In the Netherlands and Belgium the market will tolerate higher prices for CDs than in Norway, so in order to win market share the company had to adopt a penetration pricing policy; profit margins were squeezed by up to 20 per cent. Norwegian customers expect to see the prices of popular CDs displayed on large noticeboards, and will go to another store if the prices are marginally lower there. This has meant that the Oslo outlet has to be allowed much more freedom to respond to market conditions than all other Free Record Shop outlets. As for the assortment, a great deal of shelf space has to be allocated to classical music and to native Norwegian folk music as it was found that over 35 per cent of customers, even in the younger age groups, prefer this to English-language pop music. Norwegians are proud of their own traditional music culture, in a marked contrast with the average Dutch consumer. So the markets were not as similar as the company had originally thought. Even from the outside, the store looks different. The bright blue and yellow shopfront would have conjured up undesirable associations with the Swedish flag, because many Norwegians have still not forgiven the Swedes for annexing their country in 1814 and ruling it until 1905. Imitating IKEA, Free Record Shop chose bright yellow and red instead.

Political and legal factors have proved challenging for Free Record Shop when setting up in Norway. Partly due to the fact that Norway is not a member of the European Union, the company has had to contend with import restrictions. Management has had to adjust their buying policies accordingly, sourcing in Norway and forgoing the discounts they have negotiated with their usual suppliers. Films on videotape have to be approved by a government censorship agency, which involves extensive filling in of forms. Strict regulations on advertising have also proved an obstacle: joint promotion is illegal in Norway, so the company has resorted to short commercials on a local radio station and to putting up mini-billboards in pubs and restaurants and handing out leaflets at pop concerts. To improve name recognition, Free Record Shop also advertises on city buses in Oslo.

$$\diamondsuit$$

THE FIRST YEAR IN OSLO

The performance of Free Record Shop Oslo exceeded all expectations in its first month, with a turnover seven times higher than targeted. Customers were evidently taking to the open, well-lit atmosphere in this new music store with 350 m² of selling space, which compared very favorably with the cramped, dark and dingy music stores elsewhere in Oslo. In May and June of 1995, Free Record Shop was already monitoring customer perception with the help of retail management students at Asker School of Trade and Retail Management near Oslo. A survey carried out in the centre of Oslo proved that out of 200 respondents, 57 per cent had heard of Free Record Shop. A questionnaire to 169 customers of the outlet indicated that 86 per cent were in the 12 to 29 age group, and the vast majority were more than satisfied with the assortment, the prices, the service, and the location (see appendix 2). These results are highly encouraging, although the complete target market (age group 12–40) has not yet been reached.

On three different days and at three different times, mystery shoppers visited the store. They had been instructed to act like normal customers, observe the outside and the inside of the shop, approach a sales assistant with a couple of questions and buy a CD. Positive points they noted were the lay-out, the lighting, the helpful attitude of the employees and the database for CDs. Negative comments concerned the untidy racks outside, several junkies hanging around the pavement in the afternoon and the evening, and the fact that it was difficult to recognize the sales assistants because they did not wear name badges. None the less, when completing the questionnaire each mystery shopper expressed the intention to visit the store again. The final part of the survey consisted of a store count, whereby the relation between the number of visitors and the number of buyers was investigated during three days. It turned out that the percentage of buyers was the lowest in the busy slot between 14.00 and 17.00 hrs, and the highest during the extended opening hours on Friday (18.00–21.00). The store was open for at least one hour longer than the other retailers in Oslo every day, but so far had not advertised this fact.

Several recommendations were made to Free Record Shop on the basis of the survey results. First, senior management were advised to choose an alternative location in Karl Johansgate, at some distance from the railway station and the junkies. Secondly, the company should capitalize on the favourable visitor–buyer ratio in the early evening and promote the store's longer opening hours. Thirdly, sales staff should be more recognizable to the customers. Fourthly, in spite of the fact that 44 per cent of respondents in the centre of Oslo ranked price level as the most important factor when choosing a music store, as opposed to only 7 per cent selecting service level, the store should continue to emphasize its high standards of service because the customers did appreciate it. Fifthly, in view of the Norwegian market potential, it would be worthwhile for Free Record Shop to also try and reach the wealthier consumer in the age group 30 to 40. The store manager, however, could not give her full attention to implementing these recommendations. By the summer of 1995, she was too busy making preparations to open the second Norwegian Free Record Shop outlet in Kristiansand, approximately 100 kilometres down the coast.

◇

WHERE TO GO NEXT?

Free Record Shop now faces a multitude of questions. If the company wants to accomplish its goal of operating 20 Norwegian outlets by the year 2000, is it going the right way about it? With only 4.5 million inhabitants, expansion opportunities in Norway are limited, no matter how high the per capita spending on music products is. Should Free Record Shop try to conquer the rest of Scandinavia as well? Denmark, for example, has an even higher per capita income than Norway. And what about the range of other European countries that the company rejected in the early 1990s? Could there be a way of avoiding the risks Free Record Shop did not want to take then, and still expand into new markets? According to a senior executive, the five major success factors in international retailing are the added value of the retail format, the product range, the stamina of all those involved, an effective pricing policy and promotional activities. To the outsider, it would seem that the company possesses these qualities. Alternatively, there might be ways of further differentiating in the countries where the company has a secure and well-established position. Or has it exhausted the possibilities in that direction? And what to make of Hans Breukhoven's views on the company's positioning strategy, an apparent contradiction of official policy? Even so, could Free Record Shop ever survive without Hans Breukhoven, the lifeblood of the company? And finally, does the company's actual profile really match the ambitious and adventurous picture painted in some of the media? These challenging questions, and more, are now food for thought for top management.

Acknowledgement

The authors are indebted to Free Record Shop Holding NV.

————— QUESTIONS —————

(1) Analyse the growth strategies adopted by Free Record Shop to date.

(2) Using the results of the customer survey shown in appendix 2 identify what promotion policies should be considered by the company.

(3) Discuss advantages and disadvantages of alternative options the company might pursue in future international expansion.

Appendix 1   Key figures in Dutch guilders (consolidated)
Financial year as of 30 September

	1993/94	1992/93	1991/92	1990/91	1989/90
Results (×1,000)					
Net turnover	249,627	221,796	185,714	167,740	134,106
Gross margin	82,035	73,875	61,094	59,580	46,268
Operating result	13,163	12,950	6,778	15,107	12,537
Result before taxes	12,419	9,646	1,401	14,136	11,514
Net profit	8,379	6,548	1,090	9,283	7,439
Depreciation	7,873	7,051	6,908	5,131	4,021
Cash flow	16,252	13,599	7,998	14,414	11,460
Retail outlets	148	137	122	107	97
Employees	1,047	931	751	708	504
Full-time equivalents	731	632	557		
Equity (×1,000)					
Shareholders' equity	46,777	40,647	37,404	37,267	29,004
Balance sheet total	99,261	96,570	80,288	60,370	62,647
Number of ƒ1 shares	3,495,103	3,495,103	3,495,103	3,400,500	3,400,500
Data per share (in Dfl)					
Net profit	2.40	1.87	0.31	2.73	2.19
Cash flow	4.65	3.89	2.29	4.24	3.37
Shareholders' equity	13.38	11.63	10.70	10.96	8.53
Dividend	0.75	0.50	0.30	0.30	0.20

Source: Free Record Shop (1995) *Annual Report 1993/1994*, Capelle aan den IJssel.

Appendix 2   Results of customer survey in Norway

Age of the respondents

Age	Percentage	Cumulative percentage
<20 years old	48.5	48.5
20–30 years old	38.0	86.5
30–40 years old	7.0	93.5
40–50 years old	4.1	97.6
50–67 years old	1.8	99.4
67 and older	0.6	100.0

Sex of the respondents

Sex	Percentage	Cumulative percentage
Male	69.8	69.8
Female	30.2	100.0

Occupation of the respondents

Occupation	Percentage	Cumulative percentage
Student	61.4	61.4
Full/part-time employment	34.5	95.9
Looking for work	1.8	97.7
Working from home	1.1	98.8
Retired	1.2	100.0

Frequency of visits to Free Record Shop

Frequency	Percentage	Cumulative percentage
First time	16.4	16.4
Once a month or less	17.5	33.9
Twice a month	25.2	59.1
Three times a month or more	40.9	100.0

Opinion about price level of products in Free Record Shop

Opinion	Percentage	Cumulative percentage
High	6.0	6.0
Above average	13.2	19.2
Average	46.1	65.3
Below average	25.1	90.4
Low	9.6	100.0

Opinion about the assortment in Free Record Shop

Opinion	Percentage	Cumulative percentage
Incomplete	5.4	5.4
Below average	9.6	15.0
Average	13.9	28.9
Above average	46.4	75.3
Complete	24.7	100.0

Opinion about the employees in Free Record Shop

Opinion	Percentage	Cumulative percentage
Unfriendly	3.6	3.6
Below average	3.6	7.2
Average	9.5	16.7
Above average	30.3	47.0
Very friendly	53.0	100.0

Opinion about the location of Free Record Shop

Opinion	Percentage	Cumulative percentage
Unattractive	2.4	2.4
Below average	5.5	7.9
Average	12.1	20.0
Above average	26.1	46.1
Attractive	53.9	100.0

The number of visitors and buyers on Friday the 5th of May

Time	Visitors	Buyers	Buyers in %
10.00–11.00 hrs	77	20	26.0
11.00–12.00 hrs	100	20	20.0
12.00–13.00 hrs	113	24	21.2
13.00–14.00 hrs	209	48	23.0
14.00–15.00 hrs	213	40	18.8
15.00–16.00 hrs	257	54	21.0
16.00–17.00 hrs	221	58	26.2
17.00–18.00 hrs	147	36	24.5
18.00–19.00 hrs	127	40	31.5
19.00–20.00 hrs	133	52	39.1
20.00–21.00 hrs	112	35	31.3
Total	**1709**	**427**	**25.0**

Source: Brunsveld, H., Kimmel, J. and Smulders, T. 1995: *Free Record Shop Goes Scandinavia*, Retail Management School Leeuwarden/Asker School of Trade and Retail Management

Further reading

Alexander, N. 1996: *International Retailing*. Oxford: Blackwell Publishers.
Bartlett, C.A. and Ghoshal, S. 1989: *Managing Across Borders, the Transnational Solution*. Massachusetts: Harvard Business School Press.
Hellriegel, D. and Slocum, J. 1992: *Management*. New York: Addison Wesley.
Johnson, G. and Scholes, K. 1993: *Exploring Corporate Strategy*. New York: Prentice Hall.
Joned, G.R. 1995: *Organizational Theory: Text and Cases*. New York: Addison-Wesley.
Levy, M. and Weitz, B.A. 1995: *Retailing Management*. Chicago: Irwin.
Lewison, D.M. 1994: *Retailing*. New York: Macmillan.
McGoldrick, P.J. and Davies, G. 1995: *International Retailing, Trends and Strategies*. London: Pitman Publishing.
Knee, D. and Walters, D. 1985: *Strategy in Retailing, Theory and Application*. Oxford: Philip Allan Publishers Ltd.
Pellegrini, L. 1994: Alternatives for growth and internationalization in retailing. *International Review of Retail, Distribution and Consumer Research*, 4(2), 121–48.
Usunier, J.C. 1993: *International Marketing, a Cultural Approach*. New York: Prentice Hall.
Warnaby, G. and Woodruffe, H. 1995: Cost effective differentiation. *International Review of Retail, Distribution and Consumer Research*, 5(3), 253–70.

The Body Shop International: Options for Expansion

PAUL FREATHY

———— OVERVIEW ————

The objective of this case study is to examine the options available for a retailer wishing to undertake a strategy of corporate expansion. The case examines the Body Shop from the perspective of a small retailer who has successfully grown into a medium-sized organization. The study indicates that the company is now at a critical juncture in its growth phase and must look at methods of growing from a medium-sized enterprise into a large international player. While the Body Shop has traditionally used the franchise method of expansion, this study questions whether this approach represents the only option for the company or does it have altern-ative methods of securing its future in the cosmetics industry.

———— KEY WORDS ————

Retail strategy, Franchising, Chain store development

BACKGROUND

For many the Body Shop International (BSI) embodies the very concept of niche retailing. It sells a limited range of toiletry and cosmetic products to a number of targeted consumer groups. Founded by Anita Roddick (chief executive) and her husband Gordon Roddick (chairman), the Body Shop has become synonymous not only with retailing but also with environmental and animal protection, fair trade and human rights activities. Operating from its headquarters in Littlehampton, West Sussex the company has expanded rapidly over its 20-year existence by franchising its brand name and product range.

This case study examines how an organization is able to expand its operations while at the same time maintaining its market position. The Body Shop is used as an illustration as it is a company that has demonstrated significant market growth over the past two decades but has now reached a critical point in its development. It will be argued that the Body Shop now faces a series of difficult strategic choices over the future direction the company should take. The main issue arises as Body Shop attempts to redefine its market position from a small/medium-sized niche retailer, into a much larger more strategically capable player in the international retail market.

Prior to an examination of the Body Shop's current strategy and operations, it is useful to provide a brief overview of the company's development. The first Body Shop was opened in 1976 in Brighton with a second following later that year in Chichester. The product range consisted of toiletries and cosmetics developed from natural ingredients. At this stage, all manufacturing was through third-party suppliers. One of the chief sources of differentiation for the company during this time was the recycling of its containers as a method of reducing costs. In 1978 the first UK franchise was awarded and the company began its overseas expansion with outlets opening first in Brussels and then in Stockholm. At this stage, franchising consisted of licensing the Body Shop name and products in return for the franchisee putting forward the capital to open a shop. It was not until 1982 that the first charges for licensing a franchise were made with a fee of £3,000. The company was now averaging two new store openings a month and in October of that year opened a new warehouse and offices. During 1983 the company began in-house manufacture and opened its first store in Australia.

Over this period the company continued to differentiate itself through its product offer. Because its merchandise was sold in standard-sized containers and no monies were devoted to product launches, the risk associated with failure was relatively low. The Body Shop was therefore able to experiment with a wide variety of products and ranges. For example, in 1986 the company became one of the first multiples to offer a toiletry range for men. In 1988 the first American branch was opened in Manhattan, this was possible only after the company had bought the exclusive rights to the Body Shop name in the US and Japan for $3.5m from the Sanders and Short families. In 1989 the Body Shop was voted retailer of the year and distribution began from its current site at Watersmead. As a method of increasing its penetration in the US market and establishing it as a trade mark, the Body Shop catalogue was also launched in 1989 with a 25,000 print run. In 1991 the Body Shop opened its 600th store and later that year its 700th store. The Body Shop acquired Cos-Tec Ltd a manufacturer of colour cosmetics, skin care and toiletry products. By the end of that year retail sales in the United States had reached $22.8m and mail order of $3.2m. By the end of 1994 the company was operating 1,210 stores in 45 countries. The personal stake of Anita and Gordon Roddick in the company was 25.4 per cent.

BODY SHOP POSITION, STRUCTURE AND OPERATIONS

Reflecting the trend of many organizations to explicitly provide a statement of their guiding principles and organizational philosophy, the Body Shop's Annual Report 1995 states:

> We aim to make the best, most authoritative skin, hair and body care products which simultaneously embody our values and satisfy our customer needs.

The company, however, positions itself as having interests other than the accumulation of profit and market share. These principally revolve around environmental and animal welfare concerns, fair trade and human rights campaigning. This commitment is displayed in a number of ways. For example, recent projects have included investing £500,000 in a wind farm, establishing a trading charter which details the company's method of conducting business, collecting 3 million signatures for the CITES campaign and backing a campaign against the Nigerian government on its human rights abuses.

The company's philosophy is further illustrated by its declaration of non-material values. The objectives are:

1 to sell toiletries and cosmetics with the minimum of hyperbole and packaging;
2 to promote health rather than glamour. The company's stated aim is to promote reality rather than any 'dubious promises of instant rejuvenation'. As is stated in the Annual Report 1995, 'the very concept of beauty is not one with which the Body Shop empathizes (our concept of beauty is Mother Theresa not some bimbo)';
3 to use naturally based, close-to-source ingredients wherever possible;
4 not to test ingredients or final products on animals;
5 to respect the environment.

This market positioning is reinforced through a vertically integrated structure. The Body Shop owns three manufacturing subsidiaries, and a wholesale arm which supplies all outlets and acts as the chief franchisee in the UK and the United States. In addition to the main trading arms, the group itself consists of a number of subsidiaries (table 6.1). In the 43 other countries where the Body Shop trades, wholesale and retail activities are carried out by independent franchisees. The exception remains Singapore, where the stores are directly operated by the group. The size of store varies from 300 ft^2 to 1600+ ft^2 but the preferred size for new store openings is between 1000 ft^2 and 1200 ft^2. Its product range comprises approximately 450 core lines which are regularly updated through the organization's research and development facilities. The company's objective is to increase its internal manufacturing capacity to 70 per cent by the end of 1995.

In 1995 the Body Shop made a profit before tax of £33.5 million on a turnover of £219.7m. The UK still accounts for the largest proportion of sales and profit. The United States, whilst being the second largest region in terms of turnover, remains behind Europe in terms of its profit contribution to the group.

Body Shop International, the holding company, is responsible for the siting, design and layout of the stores. The centre also provides promotional material and decides upon the programme of store refurbishment. In addition, the Body Shop acts as guarantor on franchise leases. Rents are limited by the company to 10 per cent of estimated sales. Franchisees who take out a Body Shop franchise must buy 90 per cent of the product from the Body Shop; the remaining 10 per cent they have some discretion over but must seek prior approval from the company before stocking the product.

Table 6.1 Body Shop principal subsidiaries 1995

Name	Activity
The Body Shop Worldwide Limited	Control of activities of overseas head franchisees
The Body Shop UK Retail Company Limited	Responsible for the group's retail activities in the UK
The Body Shop Supply Company Limited	Materials management and product manufacturing and procurement of the group's products
Colourings Limited	Marketing of colour cosmetic products
Jacaranda Productions Limited	Video production
Soapworks Limited	Manufacture of soaps and related products
Skin and Hair Care Preparations Inc	Holds some of the group's trademarks in the United States and Japan
The Body Shop Inc	US trader of the group's products
The Body Shop Film Company Limited	Film and television series production
Cos-Tec Limited	Creation and manufacture of colour cosmetics, skin care and toiletry products
Normaland Limited	Operates two of the group's UK outlets
The Body Shop (Singapore) Limited	Operates group's Singapore retail outlets

Source: Extel 1995

Since the first offer was made in the late 1970s, the Body Shop has experienced few problems with their franchises. One main advantage of the franchise option has been a quick and relatively inexpensive roll out of stores. Franchisees are required to contribute £10,000 towards legal fees and up to £50,000 for stock. In the overseas division, the company appoints a head franchisee who will be responsible for a designated area. Typically, the head franchisees sub-contract stores to third parties, as well as running some stores themselves. In return for being granted a head franchise, the franchisee will typically invest in a warehouse and take responsibility for the management of inventory.

Royalties are not standard everywhere and it is possible for a franchisee to have a period of grace. The exception is Japan, where no free period is allowed. A typical free period in the United States would be 3–5 years with no royalties, then 5 per cent of retail sales. The initial franchise fee is $40,000 plus $300,000 to cover all initial expenses. The royalties themselves are considered an insignificant part of the earnings mix. The Body Shop aims for a 50 per cent gross margin on the delivered product while the franchisees themselves achieve a gross margin of between 35 per cent and 50 per cent.

◇

STRATEGIC ANALYSIS

In undertaking an analysis of the Body Shop, it is possible to identify a range of strategic and operational criteria that have contributed towards its success. It is also possible to identify a number of factors that continue to make the organization vulnerable in the international market. The objective of this section will be to consider these issues.

One of the main strengths of the Body Shop is its strategic positioning. Using Porter's (1985) generic strategies model, it can be argued that the Body Shop has followed a strategy of differentiation focus. The processes that lead a company to internationalize are extensive and outwith the remit of this case (see, for example, Alexander 1995a; 1995b; Burt 1995; Treadgold 1988; Salmon and Tordjman 1989). However, the aim for the Body Shop has been to target a relatively narrow group of consumers across a wide number of countries with a standard product concept. The Body Shop formula internationalizes well and the company has utilized local knowledge in order to overcome cultural difference, institutional prejudices and legal complications.

While there remains some debate as to the importance of personalities in retailing, Anita Roddick remains a central strength to the company. The guiding principles identified earlier stem primarily from the values she sets. This remains accurate not only in the context of day-to-day operations but in the transmission of the broader, strategic values of the organization. Her input remains a central strength in the company's fortunes.

The Body Shop has become an established part of the large and growing toiletry industry. It has successfully developed itself as a brand name. This will provide it with the benefits traditionally associated with branding (increased identity, created loyalty, security and reduced risk) and help to offset the danger of the Body Shop concept becoming a fad. It already successfully competes against the large multiple retailers such as Boots and Superdrug in the UK and has outlived other niche retailers such as the Body and Face Place.

As a method of rapid international expansion, franchising has become a recognized growth strategy. Burt (1995) notes that in the 1980s, franchising accounted for 24 per cent of all British retail investment overseas (as compared to 3 per cent in the 1960s). The benefits of franchising are well documented (Manaresi and Uncles 1995) and include rapid expansion, transfer of risk, improved buying power and access to capital. The Body Shop has illustrated its ability to utilize the franchise route while at the same time maintaining close strategic and operational control over its operation. As noted above, relatively few difficulties have been experienced with the franchise method, however where there have been problems, the Body Shop has illustrated its ability to control its franchisees.

Although there remain some notable exceptions, retailing has traditionally been a national rather than international activity. The Body Shop has developed significant overseas experience. In the early 1990s it restructured its European franchise operation and increased the accountability of individual franchisees. Management control has remained at the head office and the company's vertically integrated structure has meant that product quality been centrally maintained.

Despite having successfully competed at the national and international level, the Body Shop is not immune from difficulties and an examination of its environment, structure and operations reveal a number of weaknesses. First, one may consider the company to be underpositioned. Again, drawing upon the work of Porter (1985) it is feasible to suggest that the company's position as a focused differentiator means that it has a relatively small market share. In the UK for example, the chemist and drugstore sector is becoming increasingly concentrated. While it still remains possible to identify a number of smaller chains, the sector has been characterized by intense acquisition activity. Boots remains the dominant player with over 1,300 outlets and 60 per cent of market share. However, companies such as Lloyds, AAH and Unichem have grown by absorbing small chains and pharmacies. Lloyds itself is now the subject of a takeover bid by Unichem. Currently, the Body Shop has a 3 per cent market share and is the fifth largest operator in the UK (Corporate Intelligence, 1995).

Even within the UK market, therefore, the Body Shop is a relatively small player. To reposition itself as a serious contender in the international market, the company has to consider an effective growth strategy that extends its currently limited consumer base. Undergoing such a major structural and operational transition will effectively develop the Body Shop from an entre- preneurial organization to a more formal and bureaucratically controlled company (Mintzberg and Quinn, 1991).

A second issue of concern for the company is its size. Although it has an international presence the Body Shop still remains a comparatively small retailer. Sales for 1995 totalled £219.7m with an operating profit of £34.5m. This has led to concerns over the future of the Body Shop. The Roddicks' combined equity amounts to approximately 24.5 per cent of the total share- holder value and the lack of a majority shareholding interest has led some to comment on the vulnerability of the Body Shop to take over. Moreover, the nature of the Body Shop products means that it is very sensitive to discre- tionary spending. Despite the company being an established and well-known brand, the danger still remains of substitute products or fascias continuing to erode market share. Boots and the supermarket chains have all brought out rival ranges of natural cosmetic products.

While it is undeniable that Anita Roddick has been the central character in the development of the Body Shop concept, there always remains some concern about an organization that revolves around one person. In particular, one has to question what the contingency strategy would be if Anita Roddick was to leave the Body Shop. It is possible to draw parallels with Laura Ashley the women's fashion and home furnishings retailer. When in 1985 the founder Laura Ashley died in an accident, the future of the company remained unclear and the strategic direction of the organization was arguably lost.

One of the most remarked upon aspects of the Body Shop is its relation- ship with institutional investors and the City. One of the features of the company's history has been the scant regard it has paid to the financial institutions. A love–hate relationship has existed between Anita Roddick and the City and the media has made much of the animosity that has existed between company and investor. Traditionally, the Body Shop has been crit- ical of the short-term views of the Stock Exchange and its focus upon profit maximization and quick financial returns. Anita Roddick once described the City as, 'those pin-striped dinosaurs in Throgmorton Street' (Roddick, 1992).

For its part, the City has tended to tolerate the Body Shop, the level of its borrowing has remained low and it has provided higher than average returns since it was floated in 1985. However, there are indications that the tolerance afforded the Body Shop may be changing as two quotations from the Stock Exchange illustrate:

The city's love affair with the Body Shop appears to be on the wain, it is jittery about the existing management and its ability to expand the eco-friendly beauty brand.

Given her current record it is doubtful whether the self-styled Miss Mega Mouth would make the top ten in any popularity stakes. (Panmure, 1993).

The City's volte face may stem from the transitory pressures that the Body Shop is now facing and an apprehension in the way in which the company will react to them. The company is operating in a highly competitive, mature market and a concern has been expressed that the Body Shop is reaching a level of saturation in the UK high streets. This has resulted in a cannibalization of the existing sales base. When a new store opens, it has been estimated that between 5 and 10 per cent of sales may be taken from an existing Body Shop. The third store opening on Oxford Street led to a 20 per cent reduction in sales for the nearest other unit (Panmure, 1993).

ISSUES IN STORE FOR THE BODY SHOP

It may be argued that the Body Shop is at a crucial stage in its strategic development. As an article in the *Sunday Times* (May, 1995) indicated: 'The Body Shop is on the brink of transforming itself from an unconventional modest-sized outfit into a thrusting global corporation. It is a difficult transition to make and many companies have failed it before.' Such considerations were not new as the NatWest Securities Strategic Assessment (1994) exercise noted: 'All companies go through this difficult transitional period where original skills and drive have to be supplemented by an organizational structure.' The developments that the Body Shop faces parallel those described by Mintzberg and Quinn (1991) where an organization's entrepreneurial spirit and method of operation no longer remains an adequate means for operating the company. In its place it must develop a more mechanistic organization with a formal hierarchy, bureaucracy and reporting structure.

The Body Shop can therefore be seen to be at a juncture in its organizational development. An imperative remains to reposition itself away from being a medium-sized international organization into an internationally active large corporation. If it fails to undertake this transition then it will suffer the risk of stagnating in a highly competitive market environment. Worrying signals have already begun to appear. For the 1995/96 financial year, interim profits for the 26 weeks to August dropped from £12.3m to £9.1m. Control of operating costs remains an issue, with the United States in particular providing the organization with difficulties. Despite improving their network of stores, sales in the United States have proved to be slow, hindered in part by the intense competition. While the 65 new store openings in the 1994/95 financial year helped to improve year-on-year sales by 7 per cent, they disguised a 3 per cent decline in like-for-like sales. Interim results for the current year have reported a £2.4m loss in the United States.

To undertake effectively the transition into a large international player will require both capital and management expertise. The company has already embarked upon a strategy to assist in this transition. It has restructured the organization into strategic business units as a method of improving communication. However, the costs of restructuring the group are set to outstrip estimates by more than £3m. The obvious fear remains that if the Body Shop is to undertake further restructuring, its independence as a medium-sized organization may be compromised. The share capital held by its founders would be further diluted in favour of City institutions and the basic guiding principles which have been a factor in its success may be lost.

The company has sought to develop its international management structure. In so doing it has had to look outside of the firm and not rely upon internal promotion. Senior individuals have been recruited from industry including executives from Coca-Cola and American Express. In the United States, the company has appointed Terry Hartin, a main board director who will take over as the chief operating officer for the subsidiary.

The Body Shop has traditionally relied upon its campaign activities to generate necessary publicity. Given the difficulties experienced in the United States the company has had to rethink this approach and set about developing a more coordinated advertising campaign.

One of the most radical strategies proposed to date has been the recent announcement that the Roddicks are considering buying the company's shares back and returning the company to private ownership. At this stage such a strategy has only been speculated upon, but it is known that there have been preliminary discussions with the investment bank Morgan Stanley.

Overall, the Body Shop demonstrates a high degree of centralized control, good staff relations and an international profile. Despite being small relative to other international players in the retail market, its experience and good communications structure have allowed it to compete successfully. The company has innovative product designs and through its process of vertical integration it has control over the product quality and the merchandise mix and, with more than 1,000 stores operating, a critical mass has been achieved.

QUESTIONS

(1) Using the Body Shop as an example, discuss the benefits and problems of using franchising as a method of international expansion.

(2) What alternative methods of corporate expansion could be suggested for the Body Shop?

Evaluate the strategic issues that stem from each alternative method? For each strategy you decide to recommended, you should consider the following issues: Whether any of the strategic growth options suggested will undermine the relative independence that the company currently enjoys. Whether its market position as an environmentally friendly, ethical retailer will be compromised by its need to raise financial capital. If the Body Shop succeeds in buying back its equity from the City, will this affect the plans you recommend for future expansion.

(3) What are the main threats to the organization if the current strategy continues in its present form?

Appendix   Consolidated profit and loss account for Body Shop International Ltd (£m)

YEAR	1991	1992	1993	1994	1995
SALES TURNOVER	115.6	147.4	168.3	195.4	219.7
Cost of sales	(50.4)	(68.2)	(78.0)	(89.5)	(89.6)
GROSS PROFIT	65.2	79.2	90.3	105.9	130.1
Distribution costs	(27.5)	(32.0)	(37.5)	(43.0)	(50.7)
Administration expenses	(15.7)	(19.3)	(28.5)	(32.8)	(44.9)
TRADING PROFIT	22.0	27.9	24.3	30.1	34.5
Interest income	0.5	0.5	1.3	1.0	1.4
Interest payable	(2.5)	(3.2)	(4.1)	(2.5)	(2.4)
Exceptional profits	–	–	–	1.1	–
PROFIT BEFORE TAX	20.0	25.2	21.5	29.7	33.5
Tax	(7.3)	(8.7)	(7.6)	(10.1)	(11.7)
PROFIT AFTER TAX	12.7	16.5	13.9	19.6	21.8
Minority interests	(0.6)	(0.1)	(0.1)	(0.2)	–
NET INCOME	12.1	16.4	13.8	19.4	21.8
Ordinary dividends	(2.3)	(3.0)	(3.2)	(3.8)	(4.5)
RETAINED PROFIT	9.8	13.4	10.6	15.6	17.3

Source: Extel 1995

References

Alexander, N. 1995a: Internationalization: Interpreting the motives. In P. McGoldrick and G. Davies (eds), *International Retailing; Trends and Strategies*. London: Pitman.

Alexander, N. 1995b: Expansion within the Single European Market: A motivational structure. *International Review of Retail Distribution and Consumer Research*, 5(4), 472–87.

Burt, S. 1995: Retail internationalization: evolution of theory and practice. In P. McGoldrick and G. Davies (eds), *International Retailing; Trends and Strategies*. London: Pitman.

Corporate Intelligence 1995: *The Retail Rankings: 1995*. London: Corporate Intelligence Group.

Manaresi, A. and Uncles, M. 1995: Retail franchising in Britain and Italy. In P. McGoldrick and G. Davies (eds), *International Retailing; Trends and Strategies*. London: Pitman.

Mintzberg, H. and Quinn, B. 1991: *The Strategy Process; Concepts, Contexts and Cases*. New Jersey: Prentice Hall International.

NatWest 1994: The Body Shop: International exposure. *NatWest Securities Strategic Assessment*. London.

Panmure 1993: The Body Shop – company report. *Investment Report*. London: Panmure Gordon and Co. Limited.

Porter, M. 1985: *Competitive Advantage*. New York: Free Press.

Roddick, A. 1992: *Body and Soul*. London: Vermillon.

Salmon, W. and Tordjman, A. 1989: The internationalization of retailing. *International Journal of Retailing*, 4(2), 3–16.

Treadgold, A. 1988: Retailing without frontiers. *Retail and Distribution Management*, 16(6), 8–12.

7

The Impact of Foreign Involvement on the Greek Department Store Sector: The Bhs–Klaoudatos Experience

CHRISTINA BOUTSOUKI AND DAVID BENNISON

OVERVIEW

The recent involvement of foreign companies in Greek retailing has contributed markedly to the creation of a much more competitive environment for the country's indigenous retailers. This case study details how one of the largest department store firms, Klaoudatos SA, responded to the new circumstances by entering into a franchising agreement with British Home Stores. It describes the wide range of operational and strategic issues which needed to be resolved by the management of both companies as they came to terms with major differences in outlook, culture and practices.

KEY WORDS

Greek retailing, Foreign involvement, Impact, Franchising, Department stores, Management practices

CONTEXT

In response to major changes in its economic, social and political environments, Greek retailing has started to undergo dramatic structural and organizational developments, which many commentators have described as a retailing revolution. The changes began in the food sector, where large new supermarket and hypermarket formats have appeared, but the non-food sector, and in particular the department stores, have proved susceptible to the new pressures. In the process, Greek firms have adopted a more professional and sophisticated approach to management in place of the intuitive, casual and unstructured style that typically has been prevalent. Since this could not be easily achieved alone, Greek department stores have looked to foreign retailers to provide them with the knowledge and experience necessary to compete effectively. This case study examines the issues involved in one such partnership, between the Greek firm of Klaoudatos SA and the UK retailer, British Home Stores, and shows the variety of management problems that both companies have had to deal with as they come to terms with major differences in outlook, culture and practices.

Retailing in Greece traditionally has been dominated by small family owned and operated enterprises. A high number of shops per head of population, a low number of employees per outlet and a high proportion of self-employed have all been symptomatic of a distribution system characteristic of a less developed economy (table 7.1). The demand for more retail floorspace produced by the growth in incomes and consumer expenditure in the post-war period was mainly accommodated by a continuous expansion of store numbers up until the mid-1980s, rather than by any overall increase in the average size of outlets (Bennison and Boutsouki, 1995). Increasing social and economic pressures for more modern retail provision began to emerge in the 1980s but were largely constrained by legislation which, among other things, controlled prices, limited opening hours and made it impossible to employ people on a part-time basis. It was the sudden removal of these constraints in 1991/92 as part of the government's efforts to liberalize the economy in preparation for the Single European Market, and the simultaneous rise in interest in the Greek market by foreign retailers, that triggered fundamental changes in the structure and organization of retailing.

The most visible and most rapid changes have occurred in the food sector where the last few years have seen fierce price competition, the construction of hypermarkets and large supermarkets, and vigorous merger and acquisition activity as retailers have sought to gain economies of scale. In the

Table 7.1 Retail densities and employment in Greece and selected European countries

	Outlets per 10,000 population	Average Employment per Enterprise	Percentage self-employed
Greece	170	1.8	71.1
Denmark	87	4.2	16.0
France	83	4.5	23.8
Germany	59	5.6	15.4
Spain	129	3.2	53.4
UK	61	8.7	15.8

Source: Corporate Intelligence Group. *European Retail Statistics*, 1993

non-food sector, the major development has been the rapid growth in franchising by foreign retailers, especially in the clothing/fashion sector, building on the bridgehead established by Benetton in the previous decade (table 7.2).

Against this overall background, the department store sector has found itself under increasing pressure. Consisting of a small number of, mainly family owned, companies, they have traditionally occupied sites in the centres of Athens, Piraeus and Thessaloniki, with a few stores in some of the larger provincial towns such as Larissa and Patras. The growth of the specialist franchised stores and the challenge from the new hypermarkets selling a wide range of non-food items has added to the problems posed by already intensive intra-sectoral competition and the effects of a prolonged recession. Moreover, their difficulties have been further exacerbated by the impact of rising car ownership, which has led, on the one hand, to restrictions on private cars in city centres, especially Athens, and, on the other, to the growing popularity of accessible suburban centres.

To become more competitive and retain or even expand their market share, many department stores have undertaken collaboration in some form with foreign retailers. The first to come into the Greek market in this sector was Marks & Spencer, who entered a franchising agreement with Marinopoulos SA in 1990. There is little doubt that this provided a sharp stimulus to the other Greek operators, and Klaoudatos entered its agreement with British Home Stores in the following year. Since then, the other two large department store companies, Minion and Lambropoulos, have also developed links with foreign retailers. Minion made an arrangement in 1993 with Galleries Lafayette that gave them exclusive rights to selling the French

Table 7.2 Foreign retailers operating in the clothing and footwear sector in Greece in 1995

Company	Country of origin	Mode of entry*	Year	Number of outlets
Benetton	Italy	F	1979	140
Laura Ashley	UK	F	1980s	2
Yves Rocher	France	F	1980s	2
Natalys	France	F	1980s	3
Prenatal	France	F	1980s	4
Escada	Germany	F	1980s	4
Alain	France	F	1980s	12
Naf Naf	France	DI	1980s	7
Versace	Italy	F	1980s	I
Jaeger	UK	DI	1980s	1
Max Mara	Italy	F	1985	6
Palmers	Austria	F	1985	2
Stefanel	Italy	F	1987	3
Mothercare	UK	F	1987	6
Mulberry	UK	F	1990s	2
Ted Lapidus	France	F	1990s	1
Essential	France	DI	1990s	1
Emporio	Italy	F	1990	3
Jacadi	France	F	1990	7
Paparazzi	France	DI	1990	2
Mondi	Germany	F	1991	3
Kid Cool	Belgium	F	1992	1
Chipie	France	DI	1992	1
DAKS	Japan	C	1992	1
Zannier	France	F	1993	1
Zara	Spain	F	1993	2

*C – Collaborative agreement; DI – Direct Investment; F – Franchising

company's merchandise in Greece, and provided them with guidance on improving their management. This was followed by a similar agreement between Lambropoulos and J.C. Penney.

KLAOUDATOS: A TRADITIONAL GREEK RETAILER

In 1957 members of the Klaoudatos family founded a company under the name 'G.A. Klaoudatos & Bros.' The company was created in order to import and export products, and to represent foreign companies in Greece. Although quite diversified in its activities, the company became known to the wider public through the Klaoudatos department stores. Located in prime locations in the city centres of the larger Greek cities, the department stores represented 75 per cent of the company's total sales. The company attempted to achieve a wider coverage of the Greek market than its competitors by operating more stores but of smaller size. Klaoudatos was the first ranked company in the Greek department store sector in terms of number of operating stores but only third in terms of retail sales, after Minion and Lambropoulos.

From its earliest days, Klaoudatos identified the importance and attraction of foreign products for Greek consumers. Out of the personal interest of a few of the family members, it started specializing in ski-wear and formed agreements with a number of foreign manufacturers that allowed it to act as the main supplier and distributor of specific ski-wear brand name products in Greece. This led to the development of the 'Klaoudatos Sport Centres' located in shopping centres in Athens suburbs as well as to two ski-wear outlets in winter resort centres.

The acquisition of stakes in other Greek companies was another form of expansion for Klaoudatos. In 1977 it acquired 50 per cent of two companies which operated department stores in Rhodes and Patras. Both outlets were located in the town centres and each had about 3,000 m² of selling space. In addition, Klaoudatos acquired 30 per cent of Sirinian SA, a company that operated a department store in Larissa (5,000 m²) as well as a discount store (1,500 m²) located on the outskirts of the town. Klaoudatos also operated another discount store under a different trading name located in the Greater Athens area which had 3,000 m² of operating space and parking facilities (Company Report, 1993).

Service was never an important element in Klaoudatos' policy. The company put an emphasis on price at the expense of product quality, variety and service. This created the company's down-market image that tended to be underlined by the existence of street vendors operating around some of the stores. Despite attempts to upgrade the company's image the name 'Klaoudatos' was linked in the mind of the Greek consumer with low-quality products usually displayed in big baskets at low prices.

There was no clear management structure or strategy in the Klaoudatos company. Family members were 'employed' in top management positions. The company's management was divided into two sectors: the Athens area and the rest of the country. A board of directors formed by a general manager, two managers and a 'consultant' were responsible for the company's overall control (see figure 7.1). The board of directors was

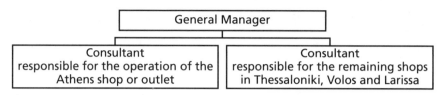

Figure 7.1 The Klaoudatos management structure, pre-1992

elected by the shareholders, mainly other family members, for a period of two years. As a family company, Klaoudatos lacked the flexibility and efficiency of a well-established modern retailer. As a result, a strategy of cautious expansion was adopted in order to minimize any financial risks.

However, the recession and the increased competition by a number of foreign and local retailers, forced the company to review its operations and attempt to become more competitive. Being a down-market department store, Klaoudatos needed to upgrade its image and become a more efficient retailer in order to move in line with the wider developments in the Greek retailing sector. A franchising agreement with British Home Stores was seen as an opportunity that could provide Klaoudatos with the managerial expertise and the foreign concept that could give the Greek retailer the necessary competitive advantage to overcome the financial difficulties it was increasingly facing (table 7.3).

◇

BRITISH HOME STORES: THE FOREIGN INFLUENCE

British Home Stores (Bhs), was founded in 1928 with two stores operating in the London area. The company's marketing strategy was based initially on price. Later the emphasis on price alone was enhanced with a policy of quality and value for money. A change of image was considered to be vital for the survival of the company and an effort was made to link the Bhs brand name with 'consistently superior products offering the best value for money'. However, Bhs appeared to lack the flair and style that seemed necessary to succeed effectively in the retail environment of the 1980s, although the company was perceived as being friendly, honest, solid and conservative, giving sound value (Warnaby, 1993).

Over the last few years there has been an increasing harmonization of the product offer across department stores. Therefore, in fashion, price and quality, Bhs appealed to the same target customer. Listening to the customer and getting the product right were constant factors of concern and a large part of the marketing budget was spent on market research.

Table 7.3 Klaoudatos' performance 1988–1992

	1988	1989	1990	1991	1992
Sales (000 drachmas)	4,179,286	4,871,217	5,227,486	5,498,599	5,754,925
Net Profit (000 drachmas)	172,027	109,360	287	(43,493)	(359,167)
Return on Assets	6.36%	3.36%	0.0085%	(1.08%)	(8.41%)
Stock Turnover (days)	99.8	108.4	100.1	109.6	101.5

Expansion in new markets was made an attractive option due to the highly competitive UK market, as well as the existence of niche markets where Bhs could be a prosperous operation. An overseas market expansion strategy was developed as part of the company's objectives and emphasis was put on franchising as the means to achieve this. The opening of only one new outlet in the UK as opposed to the operation of a total of 35 outlets abroad in 1994 highlights the current importance of overseas expansion to the company. It was expected that the number of Bhs outlets operating abroad would reach 50 by the end of 1995. Expansion in the overseas markets was a key element of the Bhs operation; according to Paul Gould, divisional merchandiser in the Bhs franchising department, 'Effort will be put in the overseas market where expansion through the franchising format has very little financial risk for Bhs and it is very profitable.'

BHS–KLAOUDATOS: THE MERGING OF TWO FORMATS

Development

The Bhs–Klaoudatos co-operation started in April 1991 and quickly proved to be very profitable for both parties. The franchise operation initially covered 27 per cent of the total sales of the Klaoudatos company. In the first two years of their joint effort, against a recessionary background, sales kept at the same level, even in the centre of Athens where government restrictions on private car access had caused a general decline in retail sales of up to 50 per cent. In 1993, sales were 5.85 billion drachmas and in 1994 reached 6.6 billion drachmas (*Self Service Review*, 1994). Profits were expected to rise even more in 1995 with the operation of sub-franchise outlets.

The Bhs concept became successfully established in Athens and Thessaloniki. However, the small size of the market in the rest of the country was considered to be an impediment to expansion since it was difficult to find the appropriate retail space for the operation and generate adequate profit. Nevertheless, operations in the existing Klaoudatos' outlets in Larissa and Volos have proved to be very profitable, and further expansion in Agrinion, Crete and Patras was planned in 1995 in company-owned stores that would operate as individual Bhs outlets. Expansion was also sought through the satellite store format and a network of 15 outlets was believed to be close to realization.

Appropriate financial backing and the ability to operate the stores to the standards of Bhs were the basic requirements Klaoudatos had to fulfil. The Greek retailer was asked to produce a five-year business plan, stating the number of shops it planned to operate and justifying the selection of the possible locations. The burden of risk stemming from the need to provide capital for expansion was passed almost entirely to Klaoudatos, while in return Bhs provided the concept and the managerial expertise. Initial plans were for Bhs to operate in all Klaoudatos' stores and eventually expand further through the creation of sub-franchise stores with Klaoudatos acting as a master-franchiser. This form of co-operation enabled better control of the operation since everything was monitored by Klaoudatos, who worked closely with Bhs. At the same time, it provided rapid growth and expansion of the Bhs concept throughout the country with the least possible financial risk. The success of the operation was considered vital for Bhs's further expansion as well as the establishment of the Bhs brand name in the European market.

Establishing a brand

'Bhs–Klaoudatos' was kept on the shop fronts so as not to alienate Klaoudatos' old customers. Bhs was entering a foreign market, and it was therefore thought easier and safer for the company to start providing for the existing group of customers as well as trying to attract new ones. With both retailers operating from the same building in the Athens and Thessaloniki department stores, it was considered necessary for both names to be displayed on the shop fronts. It was expected that this situation would eventually lead to the upgrading of Klaoudatos' shops to Bhs standards.

According to Bhs, the idea of the concept was that the franchise outlets in Greece would look the same as the stores in the UK in terms of product range, product quality, store layout and service provision. The ideal target

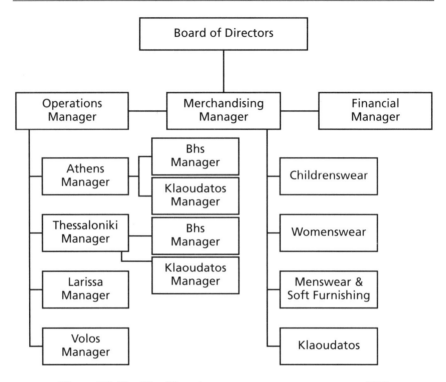

Figure 7.2 The Bhs–Klaoudatos management structure, post 1992

group was identified as the young working woman and her family. At the same time it was considered vital to retain as many of the existing core of loyal Klaoudatos' customers as possible.

The new management structure

The franchising arrangement with Bhs forced Klaoudatos to adopt the Bhs management structure. Three areas of responsibility were established: operations, merchandising and finance and administration (see figure 7.2). The operations manager, assisted by a group of store managers was responsible for the overall operation of the outlets. In each store the operations manager was then supported by the Bhs and Klaoudatos managers. The merchandising team consisted of the manager and a group of merchandisers responsible for the various ranges of products. They were responsible for marketing the products and arranging the shop layout. The finance manager was responsible for the company's budget and any financial issues deriving from the master-franchising operation. Sub-franchisees were expected to work closely with the operations manager and the merchandisers in order to get maximum assistance in the establishment of their operations.

Establishing the Bhs–Klaoudatos outlets

Bhs's initial plan was to operate in all existing Klaoudatos outlets where the operation could be facilitated by existing staff and equipment. Although these provided a reasonable coverage of the Greek market, further expansion through sub-franchise stores was planned. The location of these outlets was a major concern in the establishment of the sub-franchise operation. The aim was to operate in prime locations in city centres. The Athens and Thessaloniki areas were originally preferred because of their size, population density and higher per capita expenditure on clothing and footwear. The selection of store sites was accomplished through accumulated experience and judgement as opposed to being based on market research made by Bhs in its home operation. One of the criteria for the selection of a location was the existence of a Marks & Spencer or a Zara outlet in close proximity. The store network is listed in table 7.4.

Satellite shops that would complement the department stores were also planned. These shops would be located in shopping centres around hyper-markets in out-of-town locations, and were planned to operate with a limited range of Bhs-only products.

The space in each of the Athens and Thessaloniki stores was divided between the Bhs and the Klaoudatos sections, with the Bhs section operating from 2,500 and 1,700 m^2 respectively (31 and 37 per cent of the total floor-space). Bhs was located on the ground and lower floors where it could be easily accessible. Initially, the differences between the two stores were very striking, but constant efforts were made to upgrade the Klaoudatos section. The crammed floorspace characteristic of the Klaoudatos departments was gradually reformed following the Bhs pattern. The changes included a reduction in the number of items on display and the distinct presentation of different ranges of products. A store refurbishment programme was introduced aimed at the gradual improvement of the shop's environment. Windows are arranged with a combination of Bhs and Klaoudatos products in order to attract both new and old customers.

The gradual upgrading of the store layout, the livelier and friendlier environment and the new range of products, were the most immediate changes identified by the consumers, particularly in the Athens and Thessaloniki outlets where the two sections were operating from the same building.

Table 7.4 Stores operated by Klaoudatos in 1995

Type of operation	Location	Year of operation
Wholesale store	Athens	1983[a]
Department stores	Thessaloniki	1968
	Volos	1981
	Athens	1984
	Agrinio	1991
Specialist ski-wear outlets	Parnassos Winter Resort Centre (2 outlets)	1981
Klaoudatos sport centre outlets	Ethrion Shopping Centre in Athens	1989
	City Plaza Shopping Centre in Athens	1991
Bhs franchise outlets	Thessaloniki[b]	1992
	Athens	1993
	Larissa	1994
	Volos	1994
	Athens Glyfada	1994
	Thessaloniki[c]	1994
	Crete	1995
	Patra	1995
	Turkey (Istanbul) (2 outlets)	1995
	Rhodes	1996
Bhs sub-franchise outlets	Athens	1994
	Larissa[c]	1994
	Athens	1995
	Piraeus	1995
	Thessaloniki[c]	1996

[a] This store replaced the original wholesale store set up in 1963.
[b] The Bhs franchise outlets in Thessaloniki, Athens, Larissa and Volos were created in existing department stores operated by Klaoudatos.
[c] Satellite store operating with a limited range of Bhs products.

The results of a survey conducted in these stores in 1994 in an attempt to identify consumers' attitudes towards the franchise arrangement showed that 96 per cent of respondents liked the Bhs layout and 76 per cent were pleased with the modified Klaoudatos' layout. Furthermore, 81.5 per cent of the consumers liked the Bhs range of products compared to 51 per cent who approved of the Klaoudatos ones.

The new product

The existence of a company-owned warehouse (1,400 m^2) in an Athens suburb, as well as an established distribution system using a separate logistics company, was at first considered something that would facilitate the combined operation. However, the system proved to be inefficient for the storage and distribution of Bhs products. Although Klaoudatos has so far managed to distribute its own products satisfactorily to its outlets, the nature of the Bhs merchandise required greater efficiency and punctuality in order to meet the levels of customer demand. Fast and regular stock replenishment became important. Klaoudatos' inability to meet such targets resulted in Bhs products being imported and distributed directly to the stores. Local sourcing, although difficult to control by Bhs headquarters, was initially considered as an option. However, such plans were quickly abandoned after an unsuccessful first attempt when it was found that products had made their way to street vendors selling outside the store at a much lower price within a day of their introduction.

A friendly environment

Improved levels of service and the creation of a friendly shopping atmosphere became priority targets for Klaoudatos. There was no staff training policy at a company level. A pleasant personality as well as efficiency were the most important criteria in the selection of employees. Staff in each store were closely monitored in order to achieve the required standards of service. Respondents to the survey reacted positively to changes in the service offered – 'at last there is somebody available to help me' – with a few exceptions who were annoyed by what they considered over-attentiveness – 'they don't let you browse'. Although there was a slight distinction between the level of service in Bhs and Klaoudatos, the majority of the consumers (92.8 and 88.9 per cent) found employees in both Bhs and Klaoudatos friendly and helpful.

Operating the new company

'It is a massive learning curve that we all have to go through together.' When the manager of Bhs in Athens made that statement he indicated the difficulties involved in such a co-operation. He was appointed by Bhs in order to monitor the development of the franchise operation and to provide managerial expertise to the Klaoudatos family members. Klaoudatos had to learn to operate as a modern and efficient retailer, and this was expected to be achieved by the new generation of Klaoudatos' managers, coupled with the organizational skills of Bhs managers appointed to the stores for the first few years of their operation.

However, there was no EPoS (electronic point-of-sale) system or any other form of information technology connecting the franchise operation with the Bhs headquarters in London. As a result, stock replenishment became a lengthy process for Klaoudatos that also affected the company's pricing policy. Price was determined according to the exchange rates. The fluctuation of the drachma against the pound created financial constraints in the company's operation. In order to be able to overcome such difficulties and cover any possible losses Klaoudatos decided to trade with a higher profit margin. As a result, Bhs products became more expensive in Greece than the UK, creating some inconsistency in the image Bhs was trying to establish. Despite such problems, Bhs products were successfully imple-mented in the Greek market: in the 1994 survey 65 per cent of respondents stated that Bhs products were good value for money compared to 16 per cent who found them expensive (19 per cent of them were uncertain).

The new customer

Greek consumers' receptiveness to foreign concepts enabled the quick and successful implementation of the Bhs brand in the market. Respondents to the 1994 survey appeared to welcome the Bhs–Klaoudatos operation: 58.1 per cent of the old Klaoudatos customers said that they visited the shop more often, and 77.6 per cent of them who had not been regular customers had started visiting the stores since the co-operation.

The target customer group became the young consumer. This seems to have been largely achieved since 57 per cent of survey respondents were less than 35 years old and only 20 per cent of them were more than 55. Most were attracted to the Bhs concept: 62 per cent of the people visiting the outlets preferred to shop at Bhs. Moreover, average expenditure in Bhs was approximately £13 whereas in Klaoudatos the average amount spent was £5. High levels of satisfaction were expressed with the range and quality of products: overall, 82.5 per cent of respondents were pleased with the quality of Bhs products, 65 per cent felt that Bhs products were good value for money, and only 16 per cent thought that they were expensive. Even higher levels of satisfaction were expressed by those respondents aged under

35: 86 per cent of them liked the quality of the Bhs products and 70.2 per cent were satisfied by their price.

──── QUESTIONS ────

(1) In what ways has Klaoudatos benefited from its alliance with Bhs?

(2) What are the inter-firm tensions which are likely to arise in the type of relationship existing between Klaoudatos and Bhs?

(3) From the account of the experience of Klaoudatos and Bhs identify the controls which a franchisor can exert over a franchisee's retail operations.

(4) What measures of success might Klaoudatos and Bhs apply to evaluate the joint activity?

References

Bennison, D. and Boutsouki, C. 1995: Greek retailing in transition. *International Journal of Retail & Distribution Management*, 23(1), 24–31.

G.A. Klaoudatos Company Report, 1985.

G.A. Klaoudatos Company Report, 1993.

Storehouse Annual Report and Accounts, 1993.

Storehouse Interim Report, 1993–94.

Warnaby, G. 1993: Storehouse. *International Journal of Retail & Distribution Management*, 21(3), 27–34.

8

Czech Retailers Face a Heavy Attack of International Chains

TOMÁS DRTINA AND TOMÁS KRÁSNY

OVERVIEW

As a result of the economic transition and privatization, accomplished in the early 1990s, the structure of Czech retailing became very fragmented. At the same time, foreign retailers started substantial expansion into the country. Czech retailers are seeking ways to survive in this strong competitive environment. The case of a local chain Interkontakt group is presented. Interkontakt has succeeded in introducing radical changes, after which it has turned 30 loss-making ex-state enterprises into profitable operations. Currently, Interkontakt group is the largest retailer in the country.

KEY WORDS

Retailing, Czech Republic, Transition, Internationalization

RETAIL DEVELOPMENTS IN THE CZECH REPUBLIC

History

Shortly after the Second World War, private retail distribution was virtually removed from the economy. Co-operatives were allowed to operate but their role was very limited. State retailing was dominant. Distribution could be carried out by only a limited number of trade companies, usually mono-polistic within one branch of a trade and one region (INCOMA Praha, 1991). The amount of selling space per inhabitant was three times lower than in developed West European countries (Krásny and Drtina, 1989).

The events of 1989 changed the situation in the country dramatically. Following all necessary enabling laws, the setting of guidelines for private entrepreneurial activities, price liberalization and, in particular, privatization itself, massive changes have occurred in the distribution system. In 1991, and especially in 1992, the Czech retail network became enormously fragmented. Within a framework of public auctions (small privatization) more than 11,000 outlets have been privatized and, through restitutions, a further 7,000 former state outlets have come into private hands. The number of co-operative stores has fallen from 18,000 to 7,000, mostly due to restitution and through selling of these shops to private entrepreneurs. Furthermore, tens of thousands of new outlets, mostly small ones, have opened. Most of the wholesale enterprises were privatized as part of the large-scale privatization scheme in 1993 and 1994. Whilst these steps were very desirable from the general political point of view, they nevertheless saw the atomization of retail distribution (Drtina, 1995).

This upheaval resulted in a completely different outlook for the whole Czech retail and wholesale trade. The increase in the number of active retail and wholesale companies was enormous. Czech entrepreneurs discovered a market niche after the breakdown of the old distribution channels. During four years the number of trading companies had increased 100 times, with retail companies of fewer than 25 employees responsible for two-thirds of all sales in the Czech Republic (Czech Statistical Office information).

In contrast to the radical organizational and ownership changes, there has not been a radical change in the physical structure of distribution outlets. Larger stores were mostly formed by reconstruction of former warehouses or revitalization of old shops which had been closed. The average size of outlets remains low, being about 90 m^2 of sales space. In spite of the enthusi-asm of Czech entrepreneurs, their financial backing is mostly not substantial enough to support the development of large-scale retail facilities.

Current developments

Under pressure from market forces, the situation in Czech distribution has altered considerably since 1994. Competition is under way – only the strong can survive. The number of companies operating in the market is declining and there is re-concentration of the retail sector. Numerous small companies have gone bankrupt and some former state enterprises have been liquidated. The importance of integrated distributors, for example multiple retailers, especially international ones, and regional chains, is increasing. Voluntary chains and buying groups operate in the market in both overt and hidden ways. Franchising has been introduced.

From the ownership point of view, state-owned companies are declining and the private sector with a 90 per cent market share dominates the market (Krásny, 1995). Co-operative enterprises, after significant decline in 1991–3, succeeded in stabilizing their position, due to the introduction of a system of centralized purchasing for some products and the improvement of the structure of their outlets with new discount shops and supermarkets.

Generally, discount stores and cash & carry operations are of growing importance with cash & carry wholesalers often serving the final consumer and in effect operating discount stores. New distribution channels have appeared, including petrol stations and home delivery of foods, although their market share is still very low. Likewise, the first out-of-town facilities and the first specialized large-scale non-food outlets have been established to provide, do-it-yourself merchandise, furniture or carpets. There are no accurate data on the total numbers of outlets. A survey by INCOMA Praha has generated the estimates presented in table 8.1. The number of food distribution points had reached 85,000 by the end of 1995. The importance of particular food retail formulas is shown in table 8.2.

◇

Retail Companies

In spite of re-concentration starting in 1994, the market share of large companies is still extremely low by West European standards. In 1994, only the whole Interkontakt group reached a market share exceeding 1 per cent. The combined shares of the largest five distributors was only 4 per cent of the Czech market. The largest 50 Czech distributors account for only 15 per cent of the market. In the case of food, the largest five distributors have an approximate 6 per cent share. Total sales of the major companies are shown in table 8.3.

Table 8.1 Retail outlets selling food in the Czech Republic

Type of outlet	Number of outlets
Supermarkets (with more than 400 m^2 selling space)	450
Food shops 201–400 m^2	930
Food shops 101–200 m^2	3,830
Food shops with 100 m^2 and less	32,800
Department stores	200
Discount shops	300
Cash & Carry	200
Non-food stores	40,000
Kiosks	3,000
Petrol stations	850

Source: INCOMA Praha estimate, December 1995

Table 8.2 Structure of food retailing in the Czech Republic

Type of outlet	Per cent share of sales
Supermarkets (with more than 400 m^2 selling space)	10
Wide assortment food shops	49
Specialized food shops	16
Mixed stores	13
Department stores	1
Co-operative shopping centres	6
Discount shops	3
Other outlets	2

Source: INCOMA Praha estimate, 1995

The major organizations in the market can be divided into five main groups.

1 Retail chains:
   – the most dynamic part of the Czech retailing,
   – typically operating from 20 to 100 supermarkets and some smaller outlets,
   – the main representatives are: Euronova, Pronto Plus, Julius Meinl, Tesco, Delvita, Plus Discount and Billa.
2 Integrated distribution systems:
   – groupings of small and medium-sized local companies financially connected and centrally coordinated, for example for joint purchasing,

Table 8.3 Top ten retail (and wholesale) companies in the Czech Republic in 1995

Rank	Company	Retail/Wholesale/ Cash & Carry	Main assortment	Regional activity	Total sales in CZK billion
1	Interkontakt group	R, W, C&C	food retail companies, department stores household products	region	10.5
2	M-Holding[a]	R, W, C&C	food + pharmaceuticals	region	5.9
3	KMart[a]	R	department stores	six cities in region	4.3
4	Euronova[a]	R, W, C&C	food	region	4.0
5	Pronto Plus	R, W, C&C	food	region	3.5
6	Spar[a]	R, W, C&C	food	region	3.5
7	Julius Meinl[a]	R	food	region	2.7
8	Delvita[a]	R	food	region	2.4
9	Plus Discount[a]	R	food	Bohemia	2.3
10	Quelle[a]	mail order	non-food	region	2.1

[a] Foreign capital participation.
Source: INCOMA Praha, March 1996

    – market share is growing, especially due to the activities of Interkontakt group, M-Holding and Food Union.
3 Retailer co-operatives:
    – co-operation in a franchise-type relationship or within a framework of unofficial buying groups,
    – these activities are represented by Spar, Lido or Vega.
4 Consumer co-operatives:
    – 75 independent regional co-operatives cover the whole country, called 'Jednota' or 'Konzum',
    – particularly strong in rural areas,
    – although in total they have a food market share of 10 per cent, only a very small part of joint purchasing is undertaken through the umbrella organizations, for example COOP Centrum, COOP Morava.
5 Small and medium-sized independent companies:
    – although they still make up more than 50 per cent of total food sales, their importance is declining, with many of them fighting for survival.

◇

INTERNATIONAL RETAILERS IN THE CZECH MARKET

The role of foreign retailers has become very important. During the early 1990s, hesitation and fear was generated by an ambiguous system of legislation, an unfriendly bureaucratic system and low prevailing purchasing power (Drtina, 1992). However, since 1993 the market share of foreign chains has increased rapidly. The biggest increase is expected to come in the second half of the 1990s, with the development of large shopping centres, along with further concentration and integration. International know-how, links to foreign suppliers and sufficient capital resources for large investments are the main benefits.

While in 1992 Kmart was the only foreigner within the largest ten Czech retailers, in 1993 Spar joined this group and, in 1994, Ahold's subsidiary company Euronova and Delvita of Delhaize le Lion also joined this group. In 1995, Plus Discount (Tengelmann), Julius Meinl and Quelle were added to the top ten companies.

The first big foreign investment came to Czechoslovakia from overseas. In the early 1990s, Kmart succeeded, within a privatization process, to win a majority stake in 13 large department stores of which six were in the Czech Republic and seven in Slovakia. With annual sales exceeding CZK 4 billion,

Kmart became the second largest retailer in the country. In April 1996, Kmart had to withdraw (due to its situation in the United States) and the European operation was sold to Tesco from the UK.

Until now the second biggest foreign investment has been managed by the Dutch group Ahold. Their subsidiary company Euronova launched its first supermarket in 1991. Initially, they were not very successful. Nevertheless, during the period 1994–6, they increased their market power, partly through taking-over the GF company. Euronova operates 90 supermarkets, called Mana or Euronova, ten Sesam discount shops and three cash & carry stores, many in the Moravian region, and have their headquarters in Brno. Their Mana shops are very popular with customers. Euronova is one of the five largest Czech distributors and the senior managers of Euronova plan to enlarge their network of supermarkets to 200 by the end of 1996 with some being operated as franchises.

Several other foreign food retailers have entered the market. Spar, from Germany and Austria, planned to cover all regions in both republics with approximately 1,000 licenses and to reach a 20 per cent market share by the end of 1994. The reality did not materialize with about 200 stores in operation at that date. Faster growth was partly limited by a dependence on supplies and control structures from abroad, although they developed three local wholesale bases. Another example of the 'western model' of retailing is provided by Delvita, a subsidiary of the Belgian supermarket chain Delhaize le Lion. Delvita operates 20 supermarkets in Prague and is now expanding to other regions. Currently, two Austrian retail chains are gaining a strong market position. Billa opened its first supermarket in Brno in 1993 and operates 14 outlets. Julius Meinl shops already existed in Czechoslovakia before the Second World War. In 1994, Meinl purchased 10 supermarkets, most of them in Prague, and in 1995 the South Moravian company Pramen Brno was taken over and rapid expansion continues. By the beginning of 1996, they had 55 stores. Discounters are proving to be successful, particularly the German chains of Tengelmann (with its discount line Plus with 26 stores in operation by 1996), Norma and Edeka.

However, not all foreign retailers have been successful. For example the Spanish grocery group SYP Supermercado had the two largest hypermarkets in the Czech Republic; both were located in densely populated block-housing-areas in Prague. Problems over legal issues, a wrongly balanced product mix, a sometimes too arrogant attitude towards suppliers and, last but not least, the lack of experience with large-scale outlets were the main reasons for a low level of consumer attraction and sales lower than expected. In early 1994, all SYP outlets were sold to Billa.

Developments in the non-food sector have been less rapid but none the less significant. The department store 'Krone' in a prime Prague location is operated by the German group Kathreiner AG. Nico, from Italy, has its large-scale outlet selling shoes and fashion on the edge of Prague. In addition, hundreds of brand names have appeared in textile and clothing, positioned both in exclusive shops and discount shops. In the shoe sector, Bata, the Canadian shoe producer and distributor with Czech origins, owns 43 outlets across the country. Brand shops, for example Salamander, Humanic, Leiser, Herto and Bama can also be seen on Czech shopping streets. The voluntary groups of Garant and Nord-West-Ring have been formed. The Reno brand have left the market because its concept did not fit Czech consumers.

In furniture there are IKEA, Europa-Möbel, ASKO and Möbel Walther. In do-it-yourself, a completely new type of specialized large-scale outlet, Bauhaus, Baumax-X, Götzen and Obi have entered the market strongly. German retailers DM and Rossmann have launched their drug discounters. Herlitz started its McPaper line of stationery shops. A more detailed description of foreign involvement in the retail trade has been given in Drtina (1995).

The influence of foreign distributors has two aspects: their increasing share in the total market is clear, but they also serve as an example for the ambitious and dynamic local distributors, who observe their competitors and try to copy those strategies and operations which could potentially contribute to a successful development of their own businesses. The local companies with the most dynamic growth are Pronto Plus, M-Holding and, especially, Interkontakt group.

Interkontakt Looks for the Right Strategies

Interkontakt group, with a turnover of CZK 10.5 billion and 7,000 employees, is the strongest distribution system in the Czech Republic. It is a joint-stock company without foreign capital. Interkontakt group is a good example of a local company which is successfully facing strong competition from the international chains.

History of the company

After the changes of 1989, a group of managers created a company specializing in import/export businesses and barter trade. These activities brought both an accumulation of capital to be used for later purchases of retail and wholesale outlets, and a knowledge of the supply structures in the market. This knowledge was used to define Interkontakt business policy. After 1992, the management of Interkontakt were able to take advantage of the opportunities of the Czech privatization system by buying up food supermarkets and department stores which were too big to be included in auctions of small privatization and at the same time too small, or non-profit making, or with too complicated structures to be of interest to foreign investors. The two main sources for the growth of Interkontakt and its rapid expansion into all regions of the Czech Republic were the accumulation of apparently non-attractive properties and the purchase of the complete network of loss-making regional ex-state enterprises for very low prices, for example about 100 ex state-owned food shops (Pramen) and 11 state department stores (Prior). The advantage of this procedure was a quick accumulation of assets which enabled Interkontakt to gain a dominant position in the market and deal with suppliers from a position of strength, thus obtaining good business terms. The greatest disadvantage was problems associated with the physical and economic state of companies, which looked and behaved like typical socialist enterprises. Prompt and effective change of this legacy into a dynamic market-oriented company was the most difficult mission of Interkontakt management.

The transformation of a former state-owned enterprise

In all the former state-owned companies Interkontakt had to introduce the following steps (Tlàbaba, 1996):

Careful examination of the state of the enterprise

Thorough analysis of the situation of the enterprise was a necessary condition prior to any action. All papers had to be carefully checked starting from real estate and land register through to stock levels.

Restructuring of assets and liabilities

The enforced sale of useless properties was one of the first necessary steps of the restructuring process. Both fixed and current assets which did not comply with a new strategy of the company were immediately offered for sale. Improvement of the stock was an especially difficult matter. The former socialist enterprises often bought goods just for storage with the space of storage rooms often being bigger than the selling space. A strict reduction of goods in stock was realized under the motto: 'to sell anything is just a matter of price'. In spite of inevitable short-term losses, the benefit of stores freed from old stock overhangs was worth that effort.

Collection of outstanding amounts

Ex-state enterprises were burdened with numerous problematic claims and debts from retailers, for example from winners of auctions in small privatizations who paid an enormous amount for a shop but had no money left for buying goods, or from a particular kind of business adventurer who appeared in the early 1990s and behaved more like a gold-digger than a business partner. In these matters radical action was required. Interkontakt initiated bankruptcies or prosecutions of debtors, tax deduction of claims, etc. The main goal was to clear the accounts of these old claims so that they did not affect the balance sheets any more.

Changes in management structures

New definition of statutory bodies was necessary, as well as changes in boards of managers in all companies which became part of Interkontakt. Interkontakt Holding as a majority stock holder in all companies concentrated its main managerial functions in the hands of a board of directors of the holding company.

New structure of the labour force

For former state enterprises, a very high over-employment, consistent with very low output, was typical. A 20 to 30 per cent reduction, on average, of the number of employees in all enterprises was inevitable. Savings from labour costs were used for refurbishment of shops and other investments. It was necessary to introduce all the changes rapidly, in order to achieve rapid results. A department store, called Laso, in Ostrava illustrates the situation. Within one year the number of employees of Laso decreased from 500 to 320 and over the same period sales increased by 20 per cent. A trading loss of 12 million CZK turned into a profit of 12 million CZK after one year.

Marketing

Interkontakt undertook a detailed analysis of the market situation and formulated its marketing strategy. Important shifts were made in defining a new profile for the shops and an assortment policy corresponding to the purchasing power of inhabitants in individual areas. Strong points of trade activities were supported, weak points were corrected or reduced. For instance, carrying a full assortment in department stores turned out to be too complicated and sometimes even a loss-making business. Therefore, about 10 to 15 per cent of selling space in most department stores were offered for lease. In this way Interkontakt reduced its internal problems and at the same time retained the range of services required by customers. Changing the appearance of shops was not considered to be of first importance. More attention was given to better management of shops. Any necessary recon-struction resulted primarily in an increase of selling space against storage space. Historically, shops had individual designs and kept their old local or regional names. This began to change in 1996 alongside the construction of new supermarkets.

Integration

The whole process is finalized through integration of individual enterprises into a single system. The most important change concerns centralization of decision taking and concentration of management policy in one centre. Senior management and decisions on business policy, financing, control systems and expansion plans are concentrated in the headquarters of the Holding Company in Prague. Integration effects prove its importance, espe-cially in the sphere of purchasing with negotiation of lower prices and better business terms from suppliers.

Logistics and information technologies

Optimization of logistic links helped to reduce costs. Introduction of information technologies enabled higher profitability of all component com-panies.

The above process was applied in the 30 enterprises which were integ-rated into Interkontakt Holding. All these originally loss-making ex-state enterprises have become profit-making ones.

PERSPECTIVES AND EXPECTATIONS

Due to the rise in new activities, the Czech retail scene has increased its variety and improved its quality. In the past, the producer dictated the market and the retailer (or wholesaler) could only slightly affect the quality of distribution. Currently, the role of both actors on the market has funda-mentally changed. While producers have to face the heavy rise in competi-tion, both local and foreign, retailers are much more powerful than before.

Economic transformation has brought retailers the power to choose the best strategy. They finally have an opportunity to conduct 'real trading'; they can look for, and decide, the most relevant concepts targeted to a specific market segment, the most efficient sources of supply and purchases, the most reliable suppliers and business partners, the most fitting product mix and price level, the most profitable locations, the best ways of how to meet consumers' requirements and how to keep the customer satisfied. Those who can manage their way through this labyrinth without major mistakes will be the survivors. Those who are able to recognize the main priorities are the winners.

The possible growth of the capacity of distribution patterns emerges from the comparison with West European states. To get closer to a Western level of retail supply, massive development of the distribution patterns must come in the next 10–15 years (Krásny, 1995). Already in the second half of the 1990s, independent food retailers are having to find their role in a strongly competitive market; their chances to persist are either in strict specialization, for example orientation to the tourist business, or co-operation within buying groups, voluntary chains and the franchise system.

Retail multiples will have major opportunities as chains of discount shops, supermarkets and hypermarkets. A strong position will be taken by international chains. Other integrated distributors also will gain more power over suppliers. Large-scale retail outlets will increase in number both with new constructions on greenfield sites and with reconstructions of warehousing and redundant factories. The number of cash & carry stores and discounters will grow. Smaller wide assortment shops, under 400 m^2 selling area, will decrease in number and market power, although their part in the next years will be still very important. Some will be rebuilt into discount shops and more specialist shops. Many small mixed shops will fail because they are not able to compete on price, range or quality. In three to five years it is likely that their number will decrease by between 5,000 and 6,000. The future prospects of kiosks are similar.

Internationalization will become the key factor of the future retail development. It is quite clear, that within three to five years the present low levels of concentration will be replaced by more concentrated structures dominated by integrated distributors and big international companies.

—————— QUESTIONS ——————

(1) What advantages does Interkontakt have, compared with foreign retailers, in developing a successful retail operation in the Czech Republic? Do foreign retailers have any advantages over local retailers in economies in transition from socialist structures?

(2) What are the environmental threats and opportunities faced by Interkontakt?

References

Drtina, T. 1992: SFR: Handel öffnet sich Europa. *Dynamik im Handel*. 92(12), 38–40.

Drtina, T 1995: The internationalization of retailing in the Czech and Slovak Republics. In: G. Akehurst and N. Alexander (eds), *The Internationalization of Retailing*. London: Frank Cass, 191–203.

Krásny, T. 1995: Retailing in the Czech and Slovak Republics. *The European Retail Digest*, Summer 1995, 12–17.

Krásny, T. and Drtina, T. 1989: *Mezinárodní srovnání vyvojovych tendencí maloobchodní sít*, VÚO Praha, 40.

INCOMA Praha 1991: *Le Commerce Intérieur Tchécoslovaque*, 110.

INCOMA Praha 1995: Vysledky TOP 50 roku 1994. *Moderní obchod* 6/96, 23–6.

Tlàbaba, J. 1996: Transformace byvalych státních podnik na trn orientované spolenosti. Paper at the second Conference on Czech Retailing, Prague, February 1996.

—Part II—
The Retailing Mix

◇

Introduction to Part II

The retailing mix contains more interacting components than the traditional marketing mix. The concept of the retailing mix is similar to that of the marketing mix but it differs in several important ways. The retailing mix represents the totality of the offer made by the retailer to the potential customer. In addition to the usual managerial dimensions of product, price, promotion and location, it also includes aspects of store design and in-store merchandising, customer service broadly defined and beyond simple employee interaction with customers and employment practices. The retailing mix defines the positioning of the shop and the firm; it also defines the store format. The retailing mix governs the cost structure of the store and of the firm. Defining these psychological positions, physical attributes and operational costs of retailing is the core concept of retail management. The retailing mix is what determines whether customers are enthusiastic or not and so whether the retailer is successful or not.

The 11 case studies in Part II consider both the totality of the mix and specific components. Marc Benoun provides an initial review of the overall position of a firm with a case study on Nature et Découvertes. In this company, a strongly defined position is established, supported by all aspects of the retailing mix. The case study of Shoe Express by Lynn Stainsby shows an attempt to create a new store format within the constraints of a currently operating firm going through a difficult trading period.

Product issues in the retailing mix represent a strong component of the overall positioning of the store. The link between product and positioning is explored in the case of Benetton by Frédéric Fréry. Product issues are here seen as extending beyond the issues of design, range and display, and into the arena of sourcing. Price issues are considered in the case study on Häagen-Dazs by Marc Dupuis and Élisabeth Tissier-Desbordes. The issues of having a premium product distributed through multiple formats, in effect different distribution channels, is the key issue addressed. The topic of low price positions is also considered by Enrico Colla in the case of Coop Italia. As with the earlier case study by Lynn Stainsby the topic of how to create a new format is considered, but, in the case of Coop Italia, it is within a strategic rather than operational context. The price issue is again addressed by Gilles Paché in the case of Intermarché. The low cost logistics system has the potential to provide the foundation for one aspect of the marketing mix, namely low price, but if a wider consideration of costs is taken then the underpinning of the discount format becomes unstable.

The 'right' location is assumed to be critical in the retailing mix. Paul Whysall considers what is meant by 'right' with a case study on J Sainsbury. There are many different beneficiaries of the retailing mix which eventually emerge for a store and the competing rights of these beneficiaries are explored in this case study. A key stakeholder group in the mix are the employees. Jacqui Gush considers one group of employees and explores their views of the company in which they work and its operations.

The final three case studies each consider a different aspect of the design and merchandizing aspect of the retailing mix. Malcolm Lochhead and Christopher Moore consider the overall design issues of Princes' Square Shopping Centre resulting from a Christmas promotional campaign. The involvement of non-retail organizations in the management of the retailing mix poses important issues of inter-organizational communication. The case of La Caisse d'Épargne by Frédéric Jallat and Élisabeth Tissier-Desbordes illustrates the difficulties of introducing new work and store designs within a very conservative savings bank. The attempts by The Olympic Museum Shop to create a store design which reflects the Olympic Spirit are the focus of the case study by Lluís Martínez-Ribes and María Dolores De Juan Vigaray. As with the first case study in Part II, the issue is the creation of a total retailing mix which generates a store which reflects the mission of the firm and which is also a profitable operation. Ultimately, the shop is the product for the retailer.

Key questions raised in the case studies in Part II of this book are:

1 What are the dimensions of the retailing mix?
2 How are the various aspects of the retailing mix balanced to create the total offer?
3 How do the strategic aspects of the retailing mix interact with the operational aspects?
4 What are the dynamics of the retailing mix and how easy is it to change the various dimensions?
5 What is the role of the entrepreneur manager in the creation of the retailing mix?

The retailing mix is the key aspect of the firm which requires management. The case studies in Part II show the complexity of this management process and again show why management in retailing is a very different activity from management in a manufacturing firm.

9

Nature et Découvertes Company

MARC BENOUN

─────── OVERVIEW ───────

In 1989, during a trip to San Francisco, Mr François Lemarchand found a store concept based on nature-related quality products. Mr Lemarchand decided to import and adapt this formula in France, further enhancing the original concept through a new dimension of discovery of nature and science. Founded in France in 1990, Nature et Découvertes enjoyed immediate success and, at the end of 1994, the company had 24 stores with an additional five stores projected for 1995. In the spring of 1995, Mr Lemarchand was interested in reviewing the future development strategy of his company. He had initially forecast locating approximately 40 stores in larger towns, with a population of over 500,000. But Mr Lemarchand raised the question as to whether he should not look into expanding his company by locating stores in smaller trading areas than originally forecast.

─────── KEY WORDS ───────

International store concept, Store adaptation, Development strategy

BUSINESS START-UP AND CONCEPT

The Nature et Découvertes company is based on an American formula that the stores' founder Mr François Lemarchand saw during a trip to San Francisco. In 1990, when Nature et Découvertes stores were established in France, Mr Lemarchand was no newcomer to the marketplace, since he had previously taken over Pier Import stores, which he first adapted to the French market and then developed successfully. In the 1960s, a warehouse called 'Pier 1', located in the San Francisco wharf area, offered merchandise from the mysterious, exotic world of the Orient and the Far East. This bric-à-brac concept was developed by two entrepreneurs from Texas, Charles Tandy (founder of Tandy computer stores) and Luther Henderson, who subsequently opened over 400 Pier 1 Imports stores throughout North American in the 1960s and 1970s. In 1972, the Pier 1 Imports chain expanded to Europe, growing at a rapid pace with close to 50 stores located in the UK, Belgium, Germany, the Netherlands and France. In 1976, the American entrepreneurs reached the conclusion that the original concept as developed in the United States did not adequately correspond to Europe, and particularly France. Hence, they decided to sell the 11 Pier 1 Imports stores in France. Having just completed his studies at Harvard Business School, the Frenchman François Lemarchand, seized the opportunity of buying the Pier 1 Imports stores in France through a LBO (leverage buy-out).

The store concept was then adapted to the French culture, and Pier 1 Imports, a veritable Ali Baba's cavern where one can find a selection of small pieces of furniture and an array of exotic articles, for example Chinese paper lanterns, bamboo and cane furniture, succeeded rapidly among consumers in France. In 1987, there were already 37 Pier Import stores in France, and the chain was listed on the French Stock Exchange. The sales volume at that time was FF 440 million with a profit of FF 15 million. But, notwithstanding the success of his Pier Import stores, in 1988, François Lemarchand felt that he would like to move on to something different, and therefore decided to sell Pier Import to his executives.

At the end of the 1980s, in California the cult of ecology gradually eclipsed the 'baba cool' trend. In 1989, during a trip to San Francisco, François Lemarchand visited The Nature Company, part of a chain of around 60 stores offering products related to nature and environment, enhanced by a specifically nature-oriented interior store design. This new store concept immediately appealed to François Lemarchand, and all the more so because it is wholly in keeping with the deep interest he has always had in nature. Thus, with the plan of importing this idea to France, François Lemarchand met with the directors of 'The Nature Company' who were interested in holding a minority share in the capital of the future venture. François Lemarchand soon found a company name that perfectly conveyed the concept behind his new project for the French: Nature et Découvertes.

The Nature et Découvertes formula, although sourced in the American experience of The Nature Company, is more than a simple clone. Like its US counterpart, the product mix contains a variety of stones (semi-precious and others), objects made of natural wood, nature books, telescopes for star-gazing, posters, compasses, etc., but this concept is further extended via expositions, workshops, conferences, natural science classes, all of which translates into strong relations with various non-profit associations and, above all, into a 10 per cent donation of company pre-tax profits to a foundation for the advancement of knowledge and respect of nature.

For the full development of this retail concept, each Nature et Découvertes store requires a sales area of approximately 400 m^2, and must be located in city centres or in a shopping mall of a major urban area whose inhabitants are characterized by their strong 'need for nature', and must likewise be located in a favorable cultural and learning context, exemplified by the presence of universities, museums, festivals, etc. However, problems connected with location and availability in shopping malls or in city centres were such that, at the end of 1994, the Nature et Découvertes stores generally have selling areas ranging from 200 to 400 m^2.

During the start-up period of Nature et Découvertes, Mr Lemarchand thought that, if everything went according to plan, the chain could ultimately have stores in most French urban areas of more than 500,000 inhabitants. Even if the number of urban areas deemed 'sensitive to the concept' was limited, Mr Lemarchand knew that he would quickly need to find a considerable amount of capital for development. The initial outlay of FF 100 million would not suffice for this operation.

◇

THE ENTREPRENEUR'S PROFILE

A graduate of one of France's leading business schools, the Ecole Supérieure de Commerce de Paris (ESCP, class of 1971), François Lemarchand built on his initial curriculum by further studies in the field of agriculture and food industry at Harvard Business School. After having lived and travelled in the United States over a four-year period, he returned to France in 1976 and initiated his concept of the Pier Import stores. Admittedly,

François Lemarchand is widely known in the retailing milieu, owing to the remarkable success of the Pier Import chain, which he sold in 1988, precisely when the concept had reached its peak. During his 12 years as head of Pier Import, François Lemarchand and his wife who is a photographer, travelled the world in search of natural craft products.

François Lemarchand is a genuine nature lover, an enthusiast of natural sciences and oceanography. On numerous occasions he has considered leaving the business arena to pursue a life closer to nature. None the less, above all, he is and remains an entrepreneur since, after a two-year hiatus devoted to other activities such as breeding salmon, in 1990 he opted to return as a major player in the business world. Nature et Découvertes might well be, according to Mr Lemarchand's own words, 'a very special' business, due to its concept and to the human dimension surrounding it, but it is still a business.

THE DEVELOPMENT OF NATURE ET DÉCOUVERTES

In November 1990, the first Nature et Découvertes store opened at Eragny, located in the Greater Paris Area. By January 1993, Nature et Découvertes had 16 stores. At the beginning of 1994, the company added five new stores and during that year there were three additional openings, increasing the total number of Nature et Découvertes stores to 24.

The success enjoyed by the Nature et Découvertes formula, leads Mr Lemarchand to review his initial forecasts for store openings. Thus, at the end of 1993, he declared that 'no matter what the sceptics say, there are at least 30 potential sites in France, and maybe more'. In 1994, the figure of 40 Nature et Découvertes stores is most often cited by Mr Lemarchand in his public statements.

ORGANIZATION AND TOTAL NUMBER OF STORES

Table 9.1 shows the development of Nature et Découvertes stores from 1990 to 1994. There were five projected store openings for 1995: Velizy 2 shopping centre in the greater Paris; Metz city centre; Cap 3000 shopping centre in Nice; Rosny 2 shopping centre in the Greater Paris and Calais, representing an increase in selling area of approximately 2,000 m².

Table 9.1 The schedule of store openings

Year	Site of store openings	Selling area in m²	Number of openings	Total stores at end of year
1990	CC Art de Vivre Éragny Cergy Pontoise (RP)	245	3	3
	CC Forum les Halles (Paris)	340		
	Marne la Vallée (RP)	249		
1991	CC Italie Grand Ecran (Paris)	204	8	11
	58 rue de la République (Lyon)	300		
	CC Parly 2 (RP)	188		
	CC Créteil Soleil (RP)	258		
	CC Bourse (Marseille)	315		
	CC Colombia (Rennes)	216		
	Les trois Quartiers (Paris)	201		
	64 rue La Pomme (Toulouse)	288		
1992	Quatre Temps La Défense (RP)	408	5	16
	8 place Général de Gaulle (Lille)	289		
	61 rue de Passy (Paris)	277		
	CC Mériadek (Bordeaux)	225		
	CC La Part Dieu (Lyon)	262		
1993	CC Art de Vivre à Orgeval (RP)	185	5	21
	CC Régional Belle Épine (RP)	328		
	Galerie marchande Auchan (Avignon – Le Pontet)	285		
	Carrousel du Louvre (Paris)	400		
	CC place des Halles (Strasbourg)	400		
1994	CC Nancy–St Sébastien (Nancy)	300	3	24
	CC Toulon Grand-Var (Toulon)	300		
	CC Lille Euralille (Lille)	300		
	Store expansion CC Louvre from 400 to 600 m²	600		

CC = Shopping centre; RP = Greater Paris Area.

MARKETING POLICY AND HUMAN RESOURCE MANAGEMENT

The company and its stores

Always highly visible and wide open to its shopping mall, the Nature et Découvertes stores have progressively become key tenants for shopping centre developers. According to François Lemarchand 'entering a Nature et Découvertes store, gives the feeling of taking a break ... muted, half-light, sounds of surf, subtle scents ...'. The style of the Nature et Découvertes stores are quite different from that of traditional stores. He claims, 'The "museum effect" also explains the low shoplifting rate, despite the store's many fragile and costly articles' (interview with François Lemarchand, *Points de Vente*, No 522, September 1993). According to its founder, a typical Nature et Découvertes store should have a 400 m² sales area to 'allow room enough to breathe, to take time-out, space for a workshop, an area for enjoying tea, perusing a book ...'.

In 1992, the company management attempted to put a halt to the public's 'gift-product image' of the articles on sale at Nature et Découvertes. On this subject, Mr Lemarchand pointed out: 'We are not a gift shop surfing on the ecology wave, but rather a store specialized in the discovery and awareness of the environment.' And, to change the stores' image, he decided to modify the layout of the shelves and their location. The products originally displayed according to themes, for example minerals, botany, etc. are re-arranged according to buying behaviours. Hence, seven different zones are created: garden, sciences, hiking, education, book shop, youth and living with nature at home. Since the start of 1995, the concept has been extended to 10 sections:

1. ornithology and botany;
2. scientific zone, for example astronomy, microscope and biology, etc.;
3. sound and video;
4. book shop;
5. jewellery counter;
6. geology;
7. hiking, for example compasses and clothing;
8. scents;
9. instruments for observation (with some overlap to the scientific zone); and
10. education, for example educational books, games and toys.

From their review of 1994, Nature et Découvertes sought to expand the existing selling area with a view to allocating around 40 m² for organizing various activities for their customers, such as expositions, children's workshops, etc. When such an extension was not feasible, efforts were made to rent a separate room for this purpose in the shopping mall. Along these lines, five such rooms were established in the Nature et Découvertes stores in Strasbourg, Nancy, Toulon, Lille, Paris Carrousel du Louvre shopping mall and in the La Defense shopping centre. Simultaneously, Nature et Découvertes' new orientation involves broadening the concept of awareness of nature by adding colours/painting, shapes/architecture, sounds/music to nature as a source of knowledge.

The product assortment

The typical Nature et Découvertes assortment entails approximately 2,500 SKU (Stock Keeping Unit, the smallest unit of inventory control). Of these 56 per cent are of French origin, 12 per cent from other European countries, 15 per cent from North America and 14 per cent from Asia. The suppliers are often small and medium-sized companies or artisans (33 per cent of the aggregate European purchases). Each year, there is a product review and seasonal themes are established.

An extension of the offer can be observed in the sector of educational articles, books, recordings and games. For example, in the chic Carrousel Louvre shopping mall, the Nature et Découvertes store, at the end of 1994, devoted three store windows to hiking, astronomy and educational toys.

The store

The store design and merchandise display is a keystone to the stores' appeal. Fixtures are in Scandinavian softwood; baskets made of fabric, invite customers to help themselves; sand-filled ashtrays located at the entrance encourage customers to extinguish cigarettes. Everything communicates buying in a comfortable environment. All of the senses should be pleasantly stimulated: sight via the layout and aesthetics of the objects displayed; smell via the fragrance of cedar; sound via gentle, natural music. The store windows play a key role and, each month, all Nature et Découvertes stores depict a selected theme.

The customers are able to circulate freely and comfortably in the stores' different areas and so feel completely at leisure to stop and examine an object or pick it up. Above all, they must be utterly at ease and feel they can take their time to browse and look for the desired article, free of any constraints. In each store, a visitors' book is made available to customers, permitting them to voice their opinion, comment on what pleased them in particular, or suggest improvements.

Sales promotion and media communication

Nature et Découvertes does not use traditional advertising. The primary communication is the store itself, as well as the store's highly protective statement on behalf of our 'so very fragile' environment and planet, which is posted in all of the stores' windows. Folders and brochures inform the public on the programme of educational events and activities being held. A catalogue, sold at FF 15 and reimbursed upon any purchase, is available to customers and serves as a guide to Nature et Découvertes products. The paper bags used to contain the purchases remind customers of the company's mission statement:

> Nature et Découvertes has the purpose of offering quality products to people of all ages, allowing them to observe, understand, participate in, and appreciate the world of nature within an educational and positive framework. We would like our stores to be places of enchantment, harmony and welcome, where our guides can pass on to you their passion for nature and natural sciences. By sharing our enchantment of our planet's beauty and diversity with you, we believe that together, shoulder to shoulder, we can be a little more protective, with each passing day, of this fragile oasis, the planet Earth.

Personnel management

Nature et Découvertes uses an internal school called 'La Source', which is somewhat like a 'University of Nature'. This organization trains the personnel which, according to François Lemarchand, enables 'building a good, healthy atmosphere and a very strong sense of company loyalty'. Training is a high priority with 11 per cent of the personnel expenses devoted to employee training. As a result of personnel training in the company's school, along with the personnel's high level of qualification, many staff have a university degree, an educational function can readily be integrated in the sales process such that the salesperson can give guidance and explanations to the consumer.

Customers and customer activities

In 1994, the average sale per customer was FF 130, compared to an initial FF 120 at the company's start. During the Christmas seasons, this increases to FF 300 per customer, since numerous items are bought as gifts. The Nature et Découvertes clientele is very cosmopolitan, due to the stores' locations in areas with heavy traffic, consisting of a large percentage of foreigners and out-of-town visitors.

In 1993, educational activities for children drew a total of 5,000 participants. The number of participants has significantly increased, since in 1994, over 20,000 individuals took part in the activities. Moreover, 2,000 people, essentially adults, attended the four conferences organized in Paris and Lille by the National Oceanographic Institute, under the auspices of Nature et Découvertes.

Wednesdays, a school holiday in France, and Saturdays are the days with the highest rate of store attendance when customers tend to come with their families. Nature et Découvertes stores are viewed as museums by some, i.e., as places of culture and education; whereas others see them as places where one can spend time agreeably, whether one plans to buy or simply visit.

ANALYSIS AND MANAGEMENT RESULTS

The store premises are rented, but as they are located in prime sites at select shopping malls and city centre locations, their cost is high. Given the seasonal incidence of sales, new store openings generally occur at the end of the third or fourth quarter. At the beginning of 1995, the cost of opening a new Nature et Découvertes store with a selling area of 305 m² was estimated on average at FF 7.5 million (including store layout and eventual purchase of lease rights + costs of opening + financing of the initial inventory). Depending on the town considered, the store's location and its selling area, the investment can range from FF 5 million to FF 10 million. Costs for the store layout per se are estimated at FF 10,000 per square metre.

In 1994, for a sales volume of FF 245 million (VAT not included), the traditional ratios used in the retailing industry show the following results (see table 9.2):

- Gross margin on sales per square metre: FF 21,000 (VAT excluded).
- Sales volume per person employed: FF 1,170,000 (VAT included).
- Sales volume per square metre: FF 46,000 (VAT included).

Furthermore, the stockholders' equity to permanent capital ratio is 0.50.

Table 9.2 Sales and profit in the early 1990s

Year	Number of employees	Sales million FF (VAT excluded)	Net profit (or loss) million FF (VAT excluded)
1991	65	61.6	−10.2
1992	135	129.5	−2.8
1993	193	184.1	6.0
1994	246	244.0	10.5
1995 (forecast)	295	296.0	

Other than François Lemarchand, the company's main stockholders at the end of 1994, were Union Européenne de CIC Finance (12 per cent of the capital, since 1992) and The Nature Company which holds 10 per cent of the capital.

THE ISSUE OF COMPANY DEVELOPMENT

François Lemarchand is concerned with the question of how his company should expand in France since international development is not a priority. Should he retain the same store formula or, as with other store groups, for example FNAC, Darty or Toys 'R' Us, vary his formula by creating stores with smaller formats? François Lemarchand also wonders whether, given the stores' current success and the predictable saturation of sites in urban areas of over 500,000 inhabitants, Nature et Découvertes should not expand by locating stores in smaller trade areas, even if this more or less implies changing the initial formula? But, by doing so, is there not a danger of losing the very factors constituting his company's success?

———— QUESTIONS ————

(1) Should Nature et Découvertes expand to smaller trade areas than those initially planned? If yes, give your supporting arguments. And, given this hypothesis:
   (a) What should be the optimal size and characteristics of the trading areas envisaged?

(b) What should be the desirable size of the stores?

(c) What should be the location of these stores (centre of town, shopping centre or city outskirts)?

(d) What is the typical product assortment that should be offered in these stores?

If not, why not?

(2) What core values does Nature et Découvertes offer to its customers?

(3) How might the product assortment and marketing policy be extended to prevent customers becoming bored with the current store?

—— **10** ——

Shoe Express: A New Concept in Footwear Retailing

LYNN STAINSBY

—— **OVERVIEW** ——

In October 1992, British Shoe Corporation launched a radically new retail format, Shoe Express, in St Helens, England. This case study describes both the contextual background and the decision-making processes involved in the development. In doing so, the case study also highlights the complexity of the UK footwear market, its structure, trends and the importance of key environmental influences on consumer behaviour.

—— **KEY WORDS** ——

Footwear retailing, UK, Consumer research

BACKGROUND AND HISTORY

In October 1992, British Shoe Corporation (BSC) launched a new retail format, Shoe Express, in St Helens, England. The new format represents a new way of shopping for shoes based on a self-service approach, rather than the traditional personal service method common to specialist footwear retailers. Until the launch of Shoe Express, self-service was largely confined, in the UK, to variety stores such as Marks & Spencer, Bhs and Littlewoods, although not in 'boxed by size' display.

By the end of 1995 there were around 300 Shoe Express shops operating in the UK. The introduction of this new concept, its rapid development and future business prospects represent a new management philosophy and strategic direction for BSC. In fact, it represents an investment in the future following the rollercoaster trading conditions which have characterized the footwear market since the recession of the late 1980s and the cost-cutting of the early to mid-1990s, when retrenchment and survival became the overall strategic objective.

BSC is part of the Sears organization and originated as a collection of footwear companies which were assembled in the 1950s and 1960s by entrepreneur Sir Charles Clore. J. Sears & Co was Clore's first acquisition in 1953. The company was a shoe manufacturer and retailer with some 920 stores trading as Trueform and Freeman Hardy & Willis. Over the following decade Fortess (later re-named Curtess), Dolcis, Manfield, Saxone and Lilley & Skinner were all acquired and added to the group. Since then, most of the growth and development has been achieved organically.

During the 1960s and 1970s, BSC was an extremely successful manufacturer and retailer of footwear. Its structure reflected the fashion of the day for centralized operations which capitalized on economies of scale. BSC, in particular, looked to increasing and consolidating its buying power, and adopted a mass marketing approach to serving its customers. At this time, the buyers, whether working for Dolcis, Saxone or Trueform reported to the same director. Similarly, all central facilities were uniform throughout the group. The distribution network serviced a volume business like Curtess in the same way as the smaller, up-market, Roland Cartier. Even the store design team worked throughout the group. A result of this was that many customers had great difficulty in telling one BSC unit from the next. Nevertheless, during this period, BSC used these economies of scale with ruthless efficiency. By the mid-1980s, the organization operated a total of over 2,500 retail outlets (including concessions), making it the largest specialist footwear retailer in the UK. At this time it also had an overall market share, by value, of 24 per cent, far exceeding that of its closest rival, C&J Clark, which had 10 per cent.

However, in the 1980s BSC's marketplace was changing. The company's traditional tactic of depressing the average price of footwear was no longer sufficient to deter competition, when newcomers could identify value-added segments within the mass-market, in which price was not the barrier. During this time, BSC was increasingly being regarded by retail analysts as a

Table 10.1 Financial performance of BSC Holdings plc, 1992–1995

	1992/3	1993/4	1994/5
Sales (excl. VAT) £m	552.2	567.4	618.1
Trading profit	(14.4)	32.9	38.1

Source: Annual Company Reports and Accounts

cumbersome organization, a 'retail dinosaur', trading from too many shops and too many fascias.

BSC responded by selling-off its manufacturing arm and implementing a twin strategy of market segmentation and outlet rationalization. The company was restructured and divided into four sectors, namely: Quality (Saxone, Lilley & Skinner and Manfield), Fashion (Dolcis), Family (Freeman Hardy Willis and Trueform) and Volume (Curtess), in an attempt to target newly identified segments. Each group had its own team of directors, cost structures and profit targets. As well as market segmentation, resources were also pumped into areas like strategic planning and site location. The aim was to change the culture of the company from a 'distribution' to a 'market-led' concern.

By the beginning of the 1990s losses (see table 10.1) forced BSC to implement emergency measures: unprofitable outlets were closed, large numbers of middle and senior management, as well as operational staff, were made redundant and most marketing initiatives were suspended.

A weak performance by the group, at this time, had been expected, but the eventual outcome was considerably worse than had been anticipated. There were several possible reasons for this. First, although the strategy of rationalizing its portfolio of stores, and, thus, sacrificing market share in a bid to strengthen profitability appeared to be sound, the timing was unfortunate in that it coincided with the recession of the late 1980s and the squeeze on consumer spending. In addition to its store closures, BSC also dropped its average prices to encourage sales. This combination of policies had a negative impact on profits. Thus, from 24 per cent market share in the mid-1980s, BSC's share dropped. At the end of the 1980s it was 19 per cent. By 1996 it was about 13 per cent and set to fall further.

Thus, in the mid-1990s, BSC was in transition. New retail formats have been introduced and old ones dropped or sold. Famous shoe brands, Saxone and Curtess, have been dropped in a bid to return the group to a sounder footing. The restructuring of BSC, which has already seen the Freeman Hardy & Willis, Trueform and Manfield brands sold to Stephen

Hinchcliffe's Facia Group, will allow the company to concentrate on Dolcis and relatively new outlets, Shoe City (out-of-town) and Shoe Express (High Street). Market share will inevitably decline in the short term. BSC, which once dominated shoe retailing in the UK, has new agendas to address requiring new directions of development.

$$\Diamond$$

FOOTWEAR RETAILING IN THE UK

Footwear has not been generally regarded as a dynamic retail sector. Part of this can be attributed to the conservative tastes in shoes by British men and women. In addition, several businesses date back to the nineteenth century. Many are family owned and managed and have strong property portfolios. These factors may be some of the reasons for the traditionally sluggish nature of the market. However, recent events are beginning to change this perception.

Footwear retailing also has a number of inherently difficult operational elements. Perhaps the most notable is the necessary commitment to working capital. Although good stock control is a necessary component of any successful retailer's strategy, in footwear retailing it is particularly difficult to achieve. Strict stock control, however, has to be balanced against maintaining service levels. This is difficult to manage because of the amount of styles, colours and sizes that need to be held in the inventory.

Added to the problem of maintaining service levels is the physical nature of the stock. In relative terms, it is quite 'bulky'. It is estimated that an average of 50 per cent of a shoe shop is taken up by storage space. This means that the selling area needs to be that much more productive than in other retail sectors. In practice, it is not so. Sales per square foot for the industry have not increased in absolute terms. In real terms this means that sales densities have been in decline. To put this into perspective, K Shoes in 1990, with a stock turn of 2.5 times, was considered one of the better operators. This contrasts quite sharply with, say, the clothing retailers. Although there are considerable variations amongst the clothing retailers, Etam, for example, had a high ratio of 10.5 times in 1990, and Next had a stock-turn of 7.1.

As a consequence of the above, the specialist retailers do not have a reputation for being innovative or dynamic. The revolution that occurred in the retail market during the 1980s, caused, in part, by the advent of 'life-style' shopping, did not make the same impact on footwear retailing. During this period, UK shoe shops were still regarded as 'dozy', unfocused and catering for 'everybody and nobody'. However, this appears to be changing.

Consumer attitudes and involvement

Consumer research undertaken by the footwear industry indicates that most men and women dislike shopping for shoes. A multitude of frustrations have been identified. In addition to the major criticisms regarding the quality and level of personal service, other problems include: stockouts of certain shoe sizes, limited choice of certain sizes, limited quantity of certain sizes, required size not in stock. When looking for shoes, many women engage in what is known as the 'trawl'. This refers to the behaviour of flitting from one shoe shop to another, comparing styles, sizes and prices.

Two distinct groups of buyers can be discerned in the footwear market: the 'Shoe Enthusiast' and the 'Shoe Functionalist'. The Enthusiast sees shoes as an expression of self-taste, style, discrimination and fashion. They are strongly involved with product and design values. They also tend to have an active, gregarious lifestyle. Overall they are younger, working and have a high disposable income. Although fashion and style conscious in the way that they dress, they are not necessarily concerned with 'high fashion'. The Functionalist, conversely, sees shoes as a means of clothing feet. Comfort and good fit are important (although not always). They tend to have minimum design and fashion values. They also have a 'throw-away' mentality and tend to have practical attitudes towards dress in general. Having a lower disposable income, they are home-centred and concerned with child rearing; their personality/lifestage dictates fewer external interests.

Market structure

The footwear sector in the UK is led by a small number of major chains, with only two companies, BSC and C&J Clark, accounting for just over 24 per cent of the retail footwear market at the end of 1994, as shown in table 10.2. Throughout the 1980s analysts considered that the number of stores within this sector was greater than sector sales could sustain.

In the mid-1990s, the effects of the recession and increased rationalization by the major multiples and specialist retailers have reduced the total number of specialist shops trading to fewer than 10,000 (see table 10.3). Despite these reductions, further closures are considered likely before the retail trade reflects the market's real capacity for shoe stores.

Table 10.2 Retail market shares of footwear, 1992–1994

	1992 %	1993 %	1994 %
BSC	14.8	15.0	13.0
C&J Clark	11.4	11.4	11.4
Marks & Spencer	4.9	5.0	10.0
Barratts/Stylo	2.5	2.5	2.7
Oliver/Timpson	2.3	2.3	1.8
Storehouse (incl. Bhs)	1.6	1.6	1.8
Church & Co	0.8	1.0	0.8
Mail order	8.5	8.2	8.0
Other	53.5	53.0	50.4
Total	100.0	100.0	100.0

Source: Mintel

Table 10.3 Structure of UK Footwear Trade, 1984–1994

	Businesses	Index	Outlets	Index	Employees	Index
1984	3,596	100	11,942	100	85,000	100
1986	3,790	105	11,447	96	80,000	94
1988	3,934	109	12,066	101	82,000	96
1990	4,228	118	13,166	110	85,000	100
1991	3,610	100	11,679	98	74,000	87
1992	3,098	86	10,144	85	67,000	79
1994 (est)	2,890	80	9,620	81	63,500	75

Source: Retailing Inquiry/Mintel

Economic and demographic influences

Developing retail strategy for footwear is complex. Many 'good ideas' are not considered or implemented due to logistical factors and the cost involved in new operating systems. There is also a strong correlation between the health of the economy and footwear sales. Between 1989 and 1992 a combination of economic factors weakened the UK's retail markets. Rising interest rates, high consumer debt and growing unemployment undermined consumer confidence and caused a real decline in overall sales.

The footwear market performed quite badly until 1993. Comparing footwear retail sales with all retail sales, the sector performed considerably

Table 10.4 All retail sales and footwear retail sales, current prices, 1989–1995

	All £bn	Index	% Annual change	Footwear £bn	Index	% Annual change
1990	129.3	100	–	2.84	100	–
1991	135.4	105	+4.7	2.84	100	–
1992	140.5	109	+3.8	2.87	102	+1.1
1993	149.2	115	+6.2	3.07	108	+6.7
1994	153.4	119	+2.8	3.34	118	+8.8
1995 (est)	159.7	124	+4.1	3.51	124	+5.1

Source: Business Monitor

worse than the overall retail market. From 1993, footwear sales staged a recovery (see table 10.4). In 1994, consumer spending on shoes grew by 7.8 per cent in real terms. This buoyancy was attributed to several factors. First, there was an element of pent-up demand after four years of weak growth. Secondly, BSC had finally taken the initiative of developing new store formats, eliminating unprofitable stores and was becoming more pro-fessional with its buying techniques and supply chain management. This encouraged other multiple retailers to respond by investing in upgraded information technology, logistics, supply chain management and store design.

Demographic factors are also a key influence on the market for footwear. Table 10.5 shows the UK population age profile and projected changes to the year 2001. It is widely appreciated in consumer markets that the number of 15–24-year-olds fell significantly from the mid-1980s to mid-1990s. This group is strongly influenced by fashion footwear. Although the footwear sector has developed a strong fashion product offering, the spending power of this group is inhibited by the impact of recession.

The baby boomers of the late 1950s and early 1960s may be more numer-ous, but have become one of the groups worst hit by recession. Price dis-counts and a lower purchasing frequency characterize their buying behaviour. The over 55-year-olds are an increasing part of the population. Believed to be largely unhindered by mortgages and other debt, this group represents an opportunity for many retailers. Some footwear groups are developing a more conservative offering to appeal to this group.

Penetration of footwear buying is slightly higher among women than men. Some 75 per cent of women and 71 per cent of men claimed to have bought shoes in 1992. Interestingly, research shows that men are less

Table 10.5 Age profile of the UK population, 1986–2001

	1986 million	%	1991 million	%	1996 million	%	2001 million	%
0–4	3.64	6	3.88	7	4.02	7	3.93	7
5–14	7.16	12	7.16	12	7.56	13	7.91	13
15–24	9.26	16	8.22	14	7.27	12	7.25	12
25–34	8.02	14	8.95	16	9.16	16	8.13	14
35–44	7.72	14	7.91	14	7.93	14	8.82	15
45–64	12.28	22	12.41	22	13.31	23	13.92	24
65+	8.68	15	9.03	16	9.18	16	9.23	16

Source: OPCS

reserved about buying footwear for themselves in the mid-1990s than they were in the mid-1980s when many would prefer their partner to buy shoes on their behalf.

In addition, while recession has influenced economic forces since the late 1980s, the longer term influence on spending power in the footwear market will be the gradual growth in the number of women in paid employment. Table 10.6 shows that the number of working women is increasing and represented over 46 per cent of the working population in 1994.

Consumers in general have undoubtedly become more 'value' conscious. 'Value-for-money' is now the dominant theme in the footwear market. Interestingly, variety stores such as Marks & Spencer are increasingly perceived as good providers of value-for-money footwear by consumers. Marks & Spencer has been so successful with its footwear strategy that there is a real threat that it will overtake Clark's market position in the short term.

Thus, responding to economic and demographic changes, both in the short term and the long term, is not something that the footwear retailers have, in general, been able to do effectively. In addition to new methods of marketing, many solutions require fundamental changes to the sourcing of footwear, shorter lead-times and new methods of delivery and ordering.

Seasonality

Despite early indications that 1995 was going to be a good year for footwear sales, by the end of the period a downturn in trade was experienced. As with other industries, footwear retailing is significantly influenced by the seasons

Table 10.6 Profile of the working population, 1987–1994

	Men million	% of total	Women million	% of total
1987	14.3	57	10.7	43
1991	14.5	56	11.5	44
1993	13.7	55	11.4	45
1994	13.6	54	11.6	46

Source: OPCS

and the weather. An internal analysis of the average weekly sales for specialist footwear retailers would show significant variances in trading activity throughout a given year. Such trading activity is not always predictable in advance. The British weather is notoriously changeable. The long, hot summer of 1995 actually started in July. This played havoc with the buying patterns of both retailers and shoppers. Summer repeat orders did not happen and manufacturers and suppliers were dealing with their autumn and back-to-school ranges at a time when they would normally have been dealing with summer repeats. This left retailers with shoe stocks that they could not shift and culminated in shops not selling footwear at the predicted levels.

SHOE EXPRESS

The antecedents of Shoe Express

Shoe Express represents a complete departure from traditional retailing. It is the outcome of managerial judgement and primary marketing research which demonstrated that many consumers wanted to find all ranges, all sizes, all colours for men, women and children in a self-service format which would make it easy for them to see exactly what was on offer in their shoe size. Shoe Express customers try the shoes on themselves without assistance, at displays consisting of boxed shoes grouped by size, and, if wanted, they pay for them at the till. Rapid replenishment systems ensure that each pair sold is replaced in the same size and colour. A feature of this concept is that valuable sales space is not used as extensive stock rooms.

The introduction of Shoe Express was one of a series of responses BSC made to the difficult trading and market conditions of the late 1980s and early 1990s. It was recognized that established business and operational methods could not necessarily be relied upon to provide BSC with a viable future. New opportunities in the marketplace needed to be addressed; new directions followed.

In the late 1980s there was a growing concern within the company that the structure of the business did not match the market needs. In the mid-1980s, although BSC dominated the high street with fascias like Curtess, Freeman Hardy & Willis, Trueform, Saxone, Manfield and Dolcis, none was clearly differentiated. Similar merchandise could be found in different chains at different price points. It was not uncommon for consumers to see, for example, a pair of shoes in Saxone that they liked, and then go to Freeman Hardy & Willis to see if the style was also there, at a lower price. Not only was it confusing for the consumer, but also for the BSC buyers. Without a clear understanding of consumer segments, target marketing and positioning, buyers responsible for individual fascias were duplicating ranges. Dolcis was the first footwear chain to adopt a clear, focused offering. Early 1985 saw the launch of a new image for Dolcis, to keep the division in line with up-to-the-minute fashion trends, then for the 15–35-year-olds. By Autumn 1988 all shops had been refitted to reflect the new positioning. Much work was then undertaken to refocus all of BSC's businesses, to aim all existing fascias at distinct segments in the market. The performance of these re-positioned businesses was mixed.

Of particular concern was the performance of Curtess at the value-end of the market. A widely recognized and one time successful chain, then operating from 250 sites, Curtess's performance was disappointing. Although the brand had clear product associations, the chain was not performing to an acceptable level.

Customers' image of Curtess

In the late 1980s, extensive qualitative and quantitative research was undertaken to discover the reasons for Curtess's poor performance, and to explore opportunities for improvement. The research showed that consumers who bought from Curtess did not actually associate themselves with the shops. Instead, they regarded Curtess as a shop for other people, including: under 11s, teens, older teens/early 20s wanting 'tarty stilettos', pressed mums, the elderly, ethnics and the 'hard-up' in general.

An analysis of the research data highlighted a number of possible causes for the decline in sales. These included: a dislike of the physical aspects of the stores, cheapness with no supporting reason to buy, too many sales, boring merchandise, blurred image ('just another shoe shop'), the growing affluence and style consciousness amongst customers, and intensifying competition. Although it was concluded that Curtess had a role to play at the cheap end of the market, to succeed it had to be supported by a clear, non-price discriminator.

In exploring possible solutions to the poor trading results of Curtess, the idea of converting the stores to self-service was put forward. One problem with the overall image of Curtess was the perception of the style of service. Research showed that, although a minority of customers viewed the shop staff as 'young and friendly', the majority regarded them as pushy, ultimately indolent and unhelpful, never there when you need them, and more intent on discussing boys than footwear. Could self-service be a solution?

The image of self-service stores (Curtess)

Pilot self-service schemes were launched in 1989. Six focus groups were held in Manchester, Bracknell and Hinckley to discuss the schemes. The results of this research were encouraging. Most respondents were in favour of self-service, noting also a clearer, cleaner image, particularly for the store interiors. Self-service stores were considered more comfortable places in which to shop. Although the results were encouraging, and also showed that the self-service stores were attracting a slightly more up-market profile, in addition to its traditional customers, consumers did not seem to buy more footwear once inside the stores. Key strategic questions were now asked concerning the continued existence of Curtess. At the same time, BSC's overall profits collapsed and in 1990 changes were made at senior management level. During this period the new managing director cut costs and rationalized the business as a whole. Business development for the 1990s was suspended as survival became the key priority.

New beginnings

The new impetus for business development was triggered by another change in leadership, at Sears plc. In 1992, Liam Strong was recruited from British Airways as the chief executive. It was Strong who encouraged the development of new strategic directions for the whole of the Sears group, including BSC. A new managing director was brought in to the latter, with a brief to win more sales from existing customers in the short term and to take new customers from the competition in the longer term, through better product ranges and new retail formats, based on a deeper understanding of consumer wants. Thus, the time was right to re-visit the idea of self-service. However, Curtess was not regarded as a viable proposition for the future; something different was required.

Payless Shoes USA

The belief in self-service as an opportunity was strongly influenced by the success in the United States of Payless Shoes, a footwear retailer with over 3,500 stores and a target of 4,500 for the United States as a whole, aimed at the value-end of the market. BSC decided to explore the nature and success factors of the Payless business, and a working party was set-up to do this. Contact was made with senior management at Payless Shoes, and arrangements were made to meet-up with their Payless counterparts for a fact-finding exercise.

The Payless Shoes management were very helpful and provided information on aspects of marketing, merchandising, buying and operations. The company is currently sourcing over 20 million shoes a year from South-East Asia, 10 million shoes from Brazil, and the overall mix of leather is about 25 per cent, with much of that representing athletic shoes of some type. In its never-ending pursuit of cost-effectiveness it has cut manufacturing lead-times from 120 to 50 days, from order placement to delivery. The product mix is a combination of core regular lines and quick test lines, where a 1,000 pair run is spread across 50 key stores, to get a quick re-order based on actual consumer response, in order to reduce stock-holding. The company also achieves a 51 per cent margin, after markdowns, and engineer the product from start to finish, working with a restricted number of factories, which have been chosen according to Payless's own studies of work flows, efficiencies etc. One highly automated warehouse in Kansas supplies the entire chain.

The typical store is about 3,000 ft^2, although the company is considering even more intensive use of space, and sells about 42,000 pairs of shoes per year, with an average price of $8.99 per year. Payless's site requirement is a catchment area of 50,000 people, with the original stores being suburban small towns, usually on the edge of town. Recent openings are taking it into a higher-quality market in the malls, which is leading it to upgrade its offer slightly, and also to exploit the volume in the children's market, by creating separate Kids stores in up to 500 locations. Payless's overall stance has been to maintain the price points, and to use its enormous purchasing power to introduce higher-quality products at low prices and still secure the required margin. As a result, they are able to sell footwear for $8.99 in the United States, which would sell for £12.99 in the UK.

Pilot research

Qualitative research commissioned by BSC on the Payless concept was undertaken in the UK. The results were encouraging, and, using their knowledge of the American operation and their early experience in self-service in selected Curtess stores, a totally new retail concept, Shoe Express, was launched in the UK. The brand name was already registered by BSC and seemed to appeal to customers who could identify the name with the self-service approach.

The first opening of Shoe Express was in St Helens, England, at the end of 1992, and early research into the concept conducted in February 1993 was positive. It was decided that marketing research was needed to test the appeal of Shoe Express in its first store and to pilot a research methodology to be applied at subsequent new stores. The initial research method comprised of: three days of user exit interviews (n = 52), one day of non-user street interviews (n = 22) and one day of depth interviews in store (n = 15). Although it was appreciated that the base samples were relatively small, this was condoned for the pilot survey, but it was agreed that sample sizes would be increased in future research.

An analysis of the research showed that the typical Shoe Express user in St Helens was:

- female (87 per cent);
- 25–34 (35 per cent);
- housewife (29 per cent);
- Married (54 per cent);
- with young children (e.g. 21 per cent have a 0–4-year-old, while 21 per cent have a 5–9-year-old);
- shopping on her own (61 per cent) or with another female adult (27 per cent);
- shopping without her children;
- lives 20 minutes from the shop.

The main features of the offering liked were: low prices (27 per cent), limited involvement from assistants (21 per cent), the shoe range and other footwear (19 per cent), sectioned by size (19 per cent) and a wide range (15 per cent).

Qualitative interviews with users walking around the store appeared to confirm the mainly positive response to the Shoe Express concept. For example, users appeared surprised that low prices could also mean 'quality' merchandise. The liking of hassle-free shopping was strongly confirmed and the occasional shelf gaps were condoned because it meant that the stock was moving.

While there were some dislikes, these were fewer, and at lower levels than the likes. The main dislikes were: a confusing layout (12 per cent) and narrow range of choice (12 per cent). Further qualitative probing indicated that confusion could derive from the mass of merchandise, the signing, the display in sizes (rather than by styles) and the lack of staff. It was also noticeable that women's and children's shoes were more important to Shoe Express than men's.

The preliminary findings also showed that 94 per cent of customers said that they would use Shoe Express in the future, primarily because the shoes are cheap (29 per cent), because they often buy shoes (20 per cent), and because they liked to shop around (16 per cent).

Further research

In May 1993, further research was undertaken at the St Helens store, and also two new openings at Warrington and Farnworth. The objectives of this research were to update user profile data and consumer responses to the Shoe Express concept. The research was based on:

- user exit interviews: St Helens 107, Warrington 100, Farnworth 100;
- non-user street interviews: St Helens 22, Warrington 25, Farnworth 22;
- depth interviews in store: Farnworth 18.

According to the findings the average user for all shops was:

- female (90 per cent);
- aged 25–34 (31 per cent – mean age 35 years);
- housewife (67 per cent);
- C2 (39 per cent), C1 (27 per cent);
- married (59 per cent);
- has a child aged 0–15 years at home (59 per cent);
- is shopping as a lone adult (46 per cent);
- lives 10–14 minutes from Shoe Express (39 per cent).

Again, the opinions of consumers towards the concept was favourable. The levels of agreement with statements about Shoe Express, in descending order were (scale 1 = disagree strongly, 5 = agree strongly):

– gives you time to choose	4.6
– gives good value for money	4.5
– makes buying shoes quick and simple	4.5
– makes buying shoes enjoyable	4.5
– will exchange shoes if there are any problems	4.5
– is a shop I would like to come back to in the future	4.5
– suits all the family	4.3
– has a wide range of footwear	4.2
– is a new way to shop for shoes	4.1

Likelihood of visiting Shoe Express in the future

Most respondents were very (62 per cent) or fairly (30 per cent) likely to visit Shoe Express in the future because for them the concept offered low prices with a good range of choice. The small minority who were doubtful about re-visiting or unlikely to re-visit perhaps felt that the concept was 'too cheap'. At that time, however, no major negatives emerged.

Those who were aware of Shoe Express but had not visited the store were few. Most had not visited simply because they were not in the market for shoes at that time; most were prepared to visit it in the future. Overall, the research was very positive, although some improvements to the offering were suggested, such as more store space, more seating, more sizes – such as half sizes, and more widths.

By the end of 1994, about 155 Shoe Express stores had opened. Some were converted Curtess and Freeman Hardy & Willis units, others were new sites. Consumer research conducted in 1994 continued to build on the user profile and attitudinal data already collected. For this, exit survey interviews were conducted at five northern and five southern stores; the overall sample size was 1,074. From this research, key strengths and weaknesses began to emerge.

By the end of 1995, there were about 300 Shoe Express shops in the UK, the target number is about 450. Further research has helped to create a rich bank of data on customers and competitors. Major themes addressed by the research include: customer profile and behaviour, perceptions of store and product values, issues of communication and brand development opportunities.

Shoe Express – strengths

Strengths of the format can be identified as:

- awareness from passing by is strong; the shop frontages appear to gain attention;
- TV advertising at launch has had considerable impact in the South;
- repeat usage/high purchase rate/high penetration;
- spontaneous likes: low prices/the range/self-service (especially at first);
- prompted likes: range, ease of finding, finding size, low prices, space, finding way round, neat and tidy, overall value, no hassle, novel, quick and simple, good staff, few queues;
- children's: range, low prices, style;
- price range: £9.00–£25.00;
- propensity to re-visit – 91 per cent likely.

Shoe Express – weaknesses

Weaknesses of the format are:

- not a popular destination;
- spontaneous dislikes: lack of sizes, but no major weaknesses;
- prompted dislikes (relative weaknesses): quality of footwear, not too enjoyable, can't always find staff when wanted;
- ranges: shoes for teens, fashion (in south), trainers (especially among the young);
- boxes the shoes are sold in;
- children's: range (for some), lack of sizes (for some);
- 'leakage' to a broad range of competition.

Core customer characteristics

An analysis of the data shows that 30.5 per cent of the core Shoe Express customers are female with children from social classes C1, C2 and D. The data also show that 13.2 per cent are married females from the same social classes, without children, 10.8 per cent are males without children and 8.2 per cent are males with children. More specifically, the core customer characteristics are as follows:

- female aged 25–34;
- C2,D (C1);
- low involvement with shoe purchasing;
- focus on children;
- limited disposable income;
- frequent shopper but does not buy very much;
- shops for groceries at Kwik-Save or ASDA;
- husband probably has a blue-collar job;
- probably live in a council house or is first generation to have bought a house;
- has a limited social life based upon TV and magazines (*Chat, Hello*);
- husband reads a tabloid newspaper;
- regular user of public transport;
- probably works part-time;
- buys clothes from Peacocks, Littlewoods and, sometimes, M&S.

Thus, Shoe Express has been successful in attracting a core target of down-market women aged 24–34 with little or no involvement in shoe buying.

Interestingly, the retail concept should be an obvious source of shoes for children. As relevant sizes are grouped together, children could be shown from where to choose shoes without the involvement of shop assistants. The constant problem of asking for second shoes only to find that the child has changed his or her mind has been removed by the self-service concepts. However, although an 'obvious' source for children's shoes, it tends not to be so regarded. Perhaps one reason discouraging some children's buying is the space between the rows of shoes being insufficiently wide to allow pushchairs or prams and children. This is more likely in converted, smaller units. The continuous rows of boxes piled high also means that children can get lost. There is not a 'focused', identified children's area either. There are no games, toys or other sources of interest to keep them amused and contained. Neither is there a foot measurement service or source of advice. Although there is a DIY facility, many parents do not feel qualified to use it. They like professional reassurance.

Perceptions of store and product values

A significant polarising effect between Functionalists and Enthusiasts has been discerned. Although the Functionalists see Shoe Express as a 'fast, easy way for anybody to buy everyday shoes at cheap prices', the Enthusiasts do not relate to the proposition to the same extent, due to adverse reactions to product values and the store atmosphere. For these consumers, Shoe Express is only relevant in the context of functional shoe categories, for example work, casual, beach shoes and driving etc. It is unrealistic to expect Enthusiasts to regard Shoe Express as a potential outlet for special occasions or fashion shoes.

For the Functionalist, the Shoe Express footwear offers acceptable fashion, comfort and quality – 'they will do'. The consumer expects them to last a minimum of 3–4 months. The perceived price range is low, between £5.99 to £19.99, but most would not expect to spend over £20. Although there is a desire for more leather shoes at the middle/upper end of the price spectrum, consumers expect the 'value' proposition to be retained. The Enthusiasts do not expect that fashion or design values can be obtained at these prices and feel that there is too much emphasis on plastic, synthetic, low-quality shoes.

The Shoe Express customers frequent a broad spectrum of other shoe shops (see appendix), although 21 per cent now consider Shoe Express their main store, compared to 14 per cent in late 1993. What is clear is that, at present, there is no national competitor which targets Shoe Express's core customer.

———— QUESTIONS ————

(1) Why did BSC's market position decline during the late 1980s and early 1990s?

(2) How does the footwear retailing through Shoe Express contrast with traditional methods?

(3) Using data from the case study, analyse the prospects for the footwear market in the UK in the late 1990s.

(4) What is Shoe Express's competitive advantage and how can this be sustained?

(5) Using case information, develop a retail marketing strategy for Shoe Express.

Appendix

Characteristics of footwear competitors in the UK

Premium	Fashion	Sensible	Middle of road*	Cheap
Bally Russel & Bromley Jones	Ravel Shelly's Faith River Island Lilley & Skinner Next	Clarks K Shoes M&S	Dolcis Saxone Lilley & Skinner M&S	Shoe Express Freeman Hardy & Willis Curtess Trueform
Classical design. Individual. Quality leather. Product excellence. Attention to detail. £50+	Emphasis on current fashion trends. Changing range. Good quality. Leather. £30+	Few contemporary designs. Solid, substantial product values. Not cheap. £30+	Fashion 'copies'. Reasonable product quality (still leather). For most, equates to value. £20+	Limited fashion element. 'Imitations'. Plastic/synthetic. Cheap and cheerful. Limited life. Less than £20
Sophisticated, elegant. Good taste, sense of style. Career women, any age.	Young, fashion-conscious women. Men.	Children (pre-teens). Older 'traditionalist'. Tweed skirts/twin sets.	Family values. Teenagers/young singles on a budget.	Shoe Functionalist. Those on a tight budget. Functional, or 'throw away' shoe categories.

*Includes a mix of comfortable, sensible, classics and fashion.

11

The Benetton Nebula

FRÉDÉRIC FRÉRY

─────── OVERVIEW ───────

Benetton, the number one in the European garment industry, represents the ultimate form of network firms and transactional corporations. Almost each step of its value chain, from design to production, and to distribution, is externalized with small and medium-sized firms. Instead of financially integrating production and distribution facilities, the Benetton group uses alternative obligational linkages: brand name capital, cultural proximity and logistics integration. As a result, Benetton's retailing system appears to be very specific, for it is neither fragmented nor franchised. However, it is not yet clear that this structure constitutes a model for a different retailing approach, even for Benetton's own diversifications.

─────── KEY WORDS ───────

Retailing, Italy, Clothing, Network, Transaction costs, Quasi-integration

HISTORY OF BENETTON

Within 25 years of its creation, the Benetton group has become number one in the European clothing industry and the world leader in the field of knitwear. Benetton is frequently presented as the archetypal network structure. A structure whose value chain is made up of a series of transactions between financially independent companies.

Benetton's success is typical of the Italian miracle in the 1950s. The Benetton family is native of the traditionally poor farming area of Treviso, a city of 90,000 inhabitants located 50 kilometres north of Venice. After the early death of their father, Luciano and Giuliana Benetton left school in order to help their mother, an embroideress. Luciano, aged 14, became a salesman at Dellasiega's, a ready-to-wear store in Treviso, while his sister was hired as a worker in a hosiery factory.

In 1955, they bought a knitting machine. Legend has it that Luciano had to sell his accordion and his brother's bicycle in order to obtain the 300,000 lira which were necessary. This machine enabled Giuliana, with the help of her younger brothers Gilberto and Carlo, to produce at home five models of woollen sweaters using the brand name 'Très jolie'. Luciano, aged 20, sold these sweaters after work. The 'Très jolie' style at affordable prices, good quality and in vivid colours were distinct from the black, dark blue, grey and white colours which were used in the area at that time. Local young consumers quickly adopted these new stylish products. In 1956, the Benettons bought a second machine, set up a workshop close to the family house, hired some young workers from the surroundings, and launched two other brand names, 'Lady Godiva' and 'Dorval'. Some time later, after a trip to Scotland, Luciano developed a wool treatment technique which enabled production of cashmere-like softness. In 1964, a friend of the family opened the first shop, named 'My Market', in the village of Belluno, located near Venice. This small 40 m² shop was an immediate success and set the style for the future shops, namely exclusivity, attractive decorations, and product accessibility.

The 'Maglificio di Ponzano Veneto dei Fratelli Benetton' company was established in 1965, with the takeover of a knitwear company in Ponzano Veneto, a small town a few kilometres from Treviso. Today, the Benetton headquarters are located in Villa Minelli, a seventeenth-century mansion, in the same city. Luciano became president and sales manager, Giuliana was the designer, Gilberto (then employed at the Treviso Craftsmen Association, where he dealt with accounting and tax issues) was finance manager and

Carlo was operations director. The factory was equipped with old machinery. As they had been bought at a low price these machines proved to be very profitable after some alterations were made. To modernize the premises Luciano turned to Toba Scarpa, an architect who eventually designed the shops. The Benetton logo, a white stitch on a green background, was designed in 1966.

In 1968, three independent shops opened in Italy, and in 1969 the first shop outside Italy opened in Paris. The general concept, the style of the clothes, the organization of production and distribution, was then set. In 1972, a range of denim clothes was created after the opening of a second factory in Resano. In 1975, a collection of cotton sweaters was launched, when the Cusignana factory came on stream. The company changed its name in 1975 and became the 'Maglierie Benetton di G. Benetton e C.'. In 1976, 80 per cent of the production was externalized, and there were 600 shops in Italy with 80 per cent of exports being shipped to France. In 1978, the company became 'Benetton S.p.A.' (the name 'Benetton Group S.p.A.' appeared only in 1985). Since the end of the 1970s, Benetton shops have opened at the rate of one a day.

From 1982 to 1997, there was an average annual growth rate of sales of more than 14 per cent. Figure 11.1 shows the growth of sales.

Profit over the same period increased at an annual rate of over 19 per cent as is shown in figure 11.2.

In 1997, the Gruppo Benetton, which had adopted the slogan 'United Colors of Benetton' as its corporate name, was present in 110 countries, employed 6,000 people directly, provided work for an additional 70,000 and had 14 factories. The group sold its 50 million customers 83 million items (7,500 models) in its 7,000 sales outlets (1,900 in Italy, 300 in France, 2,400 in the rest of Europe, 2,400 in the rest of the world). Seventy per cent of its turnover was exported. It was quoted on the stock exchanges of Milan, London, Frankfurt, New York and Tokyo. It is present now in India and Pakistan (70 shops), and China (almost 50 in Beijing, Nankin and Shanghai, with a 1998 target of 300). Figure 11.3 shows the geographical distribution of sales. Figure 11.4 shows the structure of the organization.

DIVERSIFICATION

The Benetton Group includes three brand names: United Colors of Benetton (for customers aged 15–25), 012 (children) and Sisley (customers aged 25 and more). The group has several licensing agreements generating a global income

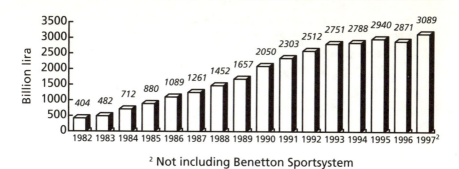

² Not including Benetton Sportsystem

Figure 11.1 Evolution of Benetton sales

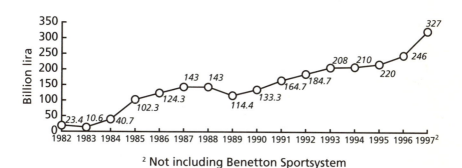

² Not including Benetton Sportsystem

Figure 11.2 Evolution of Benetton profit

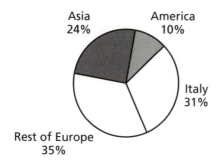

Total: LIT 2,871 billion

Figure 11.3 Geographical distribution of Benetton sales in 1994

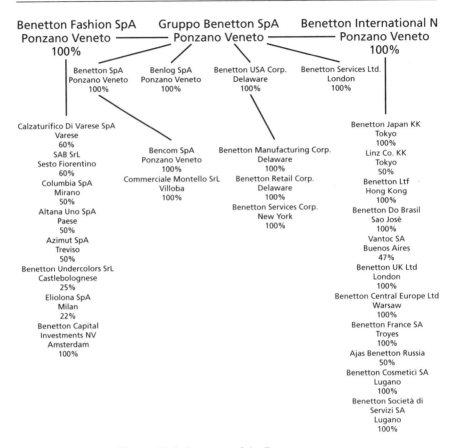

Figure 11.4 Structure of the Benetton group

of LIT 560 billion in 1996. These agreements cover cosmetics (including the *Colors* et *Tribù* perfumes), watches (with Bulova, Timex and Junghans Uhren), pagers (with Motorola), glasses (with Polaroid), linen (with Eliolona), underwear (with the Korean company Tae-Chang), shoes (with the acquisition of Calzaturificio di Varese), stationery, toys, nappies, condoms and even cars. In 1996, Renault produced a Benetton limited edition of its Twingo microvan.

In the mid-1980s, Benetton began a first wave of diversifications, in order to invest the profits generated by the textile activity. Their first attempt consisted of financial diversification with the creation of a venture capital company with Merril Lynch, and investment in three banks (Banca del Friuli, Banca di Trento e Bolzano and Credito Industriale de Sammarinese). However, after the 1987 stock market crisis, the group withdrew from these activities. It still holds a stake in insurance companies, with 50 per cent of

Assicurazioni Prudential, and 0.36 per cent of Generali. It also has loan, factoring and leasing activities for its subcontractors and distributors, through a 70 per cent stake in In Factor SpA, a company formed in 1984 with the Banca Nazionale del Lavoro and Banca Cattolica del Veneto.

The second wave of diversification took place in 1989 through the holding company Edizione. This holding company is 100 per cent owned by the four brothers and sisters, and is the core of the group. Benetton diversified in sports, via its Benetton Sportsystem (BSS) subsidiary, through the acquisition of Nordica ski shoes, Prince and Ektelon rackets, Langert and Nitro golf equipment, Kästle skis and mountain bikes, Asolo mountain shoes, Killer Loop snowboards and Rollerblade skates (which contribute 36 per cent of the 1995 sales of BSS). Benetton has also invested in sport clubs, including Treviso basketball, rugby and volleyball teams, the motor-cycling Benetton-Honda team and the Formula 1 racing team. Benetton Sportsystem, with 1996 sales of LIT 1,246 billion and loss of LIT 14 billion (due to the acquision of a further 40 per cent stake in Rollerblade), is the world's number six manufacturer in sports equipment, and is quoted on the New York Stock Exchange (55 per cent of its sales are in the United States). As the CEO of BSS, Gilberto Benetton, unveiled an ambitious development plan in sports garments, with a target of LIT 250 billion in 1998, in order to take advantage of its parent company's resources and capabilities. In 1998, Benetton Sportsystem was merged into Benetton Group S.p.A. in order to develop synergies with the garment business. A new network of shops, Playlife, was established in order to sell sportswear and accessories.

During this second wave of diversification, Benetton also invested LIT 460 billion in real estate (50 per cent in Italy, 20 per cent in the rest of Europe, 30 per cent in the United States). Moreover, its industrial investment subsidiary, 21 Investimenti, bought 50 per cent of E Group, a company which sells top quality food products (including olive oil, ice cream and coffee), 37.5 per cent of Domino, which manufactures jaccuzzi baths, 50 per cent of TWR, an English automotive engineering company, a stake in Enervit (health food) and the English car manufacturer Lotus, bought in 1995 for almost LIT 90 billion.

The third wave of diversifications, by far the largest one, took place at the end of 1994 with the take-over of the publicly owned group SME, which includes Generale Supermercati (GS) supermarkets and Autogrill highways restaurants. Edizione Holding provided 32 per cent of the required LIT 2,000 billion, and the rest came from Leonardo Finanziara (a company owned by Leonardo Del Vecchio, the founder of Luxottica), from the Swiss Mövenpick catering group and from the CREDIOP bank, a subsidiary of the San Paolo group from Torino. On the one hand, with 7,440 employees in 243

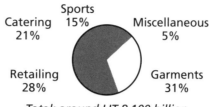

Total: around LIT 8,100 billion

Figure 11.5 Distribution of Edizione Holding sales in 1997

supermarkets, a turnover of LIT 3,000 billion in 1994 and a LIT 50 billion profit, the GS group is number three in its sector in Italy, with 13 per cent of the market. On the other hand, with 6,460 employees in 311 restaurants located on the Italian roads and highways, Autogrill has sales of LIT 1,330 billion and makes a LIT 40 billion profit. But Benetton did not stop here, and in December 1994, with Del Vecchio again, it bought the Euromercato hypermarkets chain (1994 sales: LIT 1,250 billion). For the first time in its history, Edizione Holding had to go into debt in order to obtain the LIT 800 billion which were necessary for these operations. However, these debts should be reimbursed quickly as the companies are very profitable.

Through a total of 350 supermarkets and seven hypermarkets, Benetton has become the number two in Italian retailing, after the co-operatives, with a turnover of LIT 4,000 billion. Therefore, the size of the group has doubled, and garments are no longer its main business, accounting for approximately only 31 per cent of sales. Figure 11.5 shows the distribution of Edizione Holding sales.

Luciano Benetton himself acknowledges that these various diversifications present very little synergy. The experience gained through the selling of clothes could benefit the retailing activity, but the logic remains different: small shops on the one hand, hyper and supermarkets on the other. In fact, Edizione holding seems to be more a conglomeration of financial interests than a coherent industrial group, perhaps because Benetton are reluctant to use vertical integration, which would come into contradiction with the foundations of its successful strategy in the garment industry.

Last but not least, through their Edizione Property subsidiary Benetton owns 900,000 hectares in Patagonia, 1,800 kilometres south-west of Buenos Aires, where 280,000 merinos sheep graze, as well as a cotton plantation in Texas. Incidentally, Benetton is the largest consumer of wool in the world, purchasing more than 70 tons a day. The personal fortune of the Benetton family is one of the biggest in Italy, and Luciano was elected a Senator of the Italian Republic between 1992 and 1994.

The structure of Edizione Holdings is shown in figure 11.6.

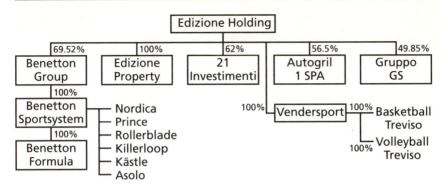

Figure 11.6 Interests of Edizione Holding in April 1998

THE BENETTON SYSTEM

Benetton's strategic intent is 'to put fashion on an industrial level'. Its success is based on a creation, design and distribution system which enables it to be, with McDonald's, one of the largest international transactional structures. The entire supply chain is concerned with externalization. This system is based on the 'short circuit' principles, and was optimized in the early 1980s by Aldo Palmeri when he replaced Elio Aluffi, an engineer, as CEO of the group. Palmeri was a former top executive at the Italian ministry of industry, and a deputy director of the Bank of Italy. Its manufacturing organization enables Benetton to maintain essential reactivity in a business dealing with fashion, while reaching the same efficiency as a large industry. However, the implementation of this system was expensive. Until 1992, Benetton's debt was equal to its net capital.

Creation: a seller of colours

Originally, a technical breakthrough, a garment-dyeing technique invented by Luciano and a dyer from Treviso in 1963, was the start of Benetton's development. Traditionally, in the entire knitwear industry, woollen sweaters are knitted with coloured yarn. This can be very risky if the colour chosen is no longer fashionable when the products reach retail store shelves. More-over, it is impossible to anticipate the customer's response. In order to avoid this drawback and to increase responsiveness Benetton woollen sweaters are knitted with uncoloured natural grey yarn. They are dyed just before shipping time, according to the prevailing tastes at the moment of the sale. This process is slightly more expensive, but it enables Benetton to manufacture and store 'neutral' products which are finished only a few weeks before they are sold. Of course, this works only with solid colour wool or cotton clothes, it does not work with patterns. Therefore, Benetton's style does not rest on the cut of clothes, which is very classical and renewed almost every year, but on vivid plain colours. Hence the pun 'United Colors of Benetton', which signals both a multi-racial philosophy and the absence of patterns. In 1992, Benetton knitwear used 60 different shades and casual garments 150.

The design of the 4,000 models of the two annual collections (February to June, and September to December) is managed by Giuliana Benetton, and comes from two different sources:

1　a group of 25 designers who are hired for 2–3 years only, to enable continuous innovation;
2　an international pool of 200 freelance creators who are used through a bidding system in which Benetton pays only those who are selected.

This system guarantees maximum creativity at minimum cost, even if Benetton clothes, according to Luciano's orders, must remain simple. Each new clothing item project is handmade in a few hours by a team of four dressmakers, and tried on a model. Giuliana Benetton herself makes the decision to manufacture or not. Then, the accepted clothes are introduced in a CAD/CAM system to automate manufacturing. The factories which are close to the headquarters are linked to them by a fibre optic network and equipped with laser cutting machines which can produce 15,000 units in 8 hours, with only a 15 per cent cloth waste. Therefore, a new model can be produced in half a day. Now, some of the designers work directly on computer screens.

Production: maximum subcontracting

Very quickly, the garment-dyeing process, which only concerns knitwear, enabled Benetton to subcontract standardized manufacturing steps (knitting, assembling, finishing). Benetton only keeps the really strategic steps, which are dyeing, which requires an investment of more than LIT 10 billion which is out of reach for subcontractors, and quality control. This approach was facilitated by the introduction of CAD/CAM, which strongly reduces the risks of discrepancy between specifications and output. All in all, an average 80 per cent of Benetton's manufacturing is externalized. Table 11.1 shows the breakdown depending on production steps

Table 11.1 Extent of externalization of Benetton production

Step of production	Rate of externalization (%)	Number of subcontractors	Exclusive subcontractors (%)
Knitting	99	70–80	90
Assembling	100	100	100
Preparing	70–75	3	100
Dyeing	0	0	0
Finishing	95	20	100

Subcontractors

Benetton works with roughly 450 subcontractors (only 200 for woollen sweaters), 85 per cent of whom are located in the Venice region, 10 per cent in Emilia-Romagna, and 5 per cent in Lombardia. These subcontractors hold 80 per cent of the overall production capacity, and they even directly manufacture 60 per cent of the models. They are often small companies, which take advantage of very favourable Italian legislation. Their average payroll is between 20 and 40 employees, but some companies employ more than 100 people, and generally subcontract with smaller firms. In total, these subcontractors employ 25,000 people, whereas Benetton, with only one thousand employees in manufacturing, could not produce more than 2 to 3 per cent of its products in its own factories. Benetton's wage costs only represent 6.5 per cent of its overall expenses, against an average of 25 per cent in the Italian textile industry as a whole.

Benetton supplies its subcontractors with the raw materials, gives them all the manufacturing procedures, generally in a computerized form, and collects their production through its fleet of lorries. Each year, less than one out of ten subcontractors is excluded from the network because of quality defects. Benetton carries out three quality checks successively: one when the lorry arrives, a second during storage, and a third before shipping. All in all, 1 per cent of the products are rejected. Moreover, an audit team may be sent to the subcontractors who cannot reach the required quality standards.

Eighty per cent of the subcontractors work exclusively for Benetton. The entire availability of their production capacity is an implicit selection criteria, even if in theory they are not committed to exclusivity. As self-employed entrepreneurs, they readily accept to work overtime, which makes it possible to optimize the flexibility of Benetton's 14 own factories: seven around Treviso (Ponzano Veneto, Resano, Cusignana, Monzambano,

Fontane, Quattro Castella and Castrette), two in France, one in Spain, one in Scotland, one in Argentina, one in Brazil and one in the United States (South Carolina). The group's most recent factory, located at Castrette, 18 kilometres from Ponzano Veneto, is directly linked to the headquarters by fibre optics. With its 40,000 m^2, this LIT 110 billion factory can produce 15–16 million pieces annually with only 320 employees, whereas a unit this size generally requires 800. It is nicknamed 'Golden Gate II' because its structure is suspended from 30-metre high poles.

The executives of all factories personally know the subcontractors, and they give them information and advice every day. In 1985, Benetton even sold two of its preparing workshops to their managers, who became new subcontractors (extrapreneurs). Conversely, since 1992, in order to improve the technology of its subcontractors, Benetton has not hesitated to invest in their capital. In 1994, the group owned from 40 to 60 per cent of the capital of one-third of its subcontractors. At least once a year, the contractors must inform Benetton about the availability of their resources (machines and employees), and they must accept its control visits. In return, they receive advice and financial support, as well as the right to use the Benetton computerized network for their own administrative needs. Moreover, Benetton guarantees the use of their entire production capacity, as well as the on-time payments.

Prices are negotiated, and generally are based on an assumed cost structure as follows: 10–15 per cent for equipment, 10 per cent in financial costs, 60–70 per cent in wages and a 10–15 per cent margin for the contractor. However, all these are purely oral agreements, except for orders and work contracts.

Logistics

Seventy-five per cent of the European production passes through the 20,000 m^2 of 'Charlie', the Castrette fully automated warehouse which deals with 30,000 parcels over 21 hours a day with the remaining three hours dedicated to maintenance work. The computerization and robotization of this logistics hub, which was opened in 1985, has been subcontracted to Comau, a subsidiary of the Fiat group. Parcels containing end products (an average of 30 pieces in each parcel) are labelled according to their destination. Some come from the Castrette factory via an underground conveyor belt. Once they reach the warehouse, the parcels are sorted out by a barcode laser reader and automatically sent, through a system which is similar to those used in airports to convey baggage, to an area dedicated to each customer

(15-metre high shelves with a surface area of 7,000 m^2). There they wait an average of two weeks until the order is complete, and then a picking robot brings them to the lorries and wagons. Railroad cars enter the warehouse directly. This system, which is supervised by only 20 people, has cut transportation costs by 20 per cent which now accounts for approximately 5 per cent of turnover, and has cut delivery time by five days. More than 50 per cent of the goods are transported by train.

Suppliers

Benetton uses a small number of suppliers and concentrates its purchases. Piobesi for cotton and Marzotto for wool account for more than 50 per cent of Benetton's needs. Benetton issues orders for the entire season two months before its competitors, which makes it easier for the suppliers to plan their production. In return, these suppliers grant a 5 per cent discount and payment at 120 days, which is better than the standard in the industry. Approximately 10 per cent of the wool used by Benetton comes from its own Patagonian flock. The extent of this vertical integration is unlikely to increase in the near future.

In addition to this structure, there is a network of joint venture factories in countries where imports are hampered by local regulation: Japan, China, Egypt, Turkey, Mexico, India and Cuba.

$\Diamond$

RETAILING: A FRANCHISING OF SORTS

The 7,000 shops which distribute the Benetton products all around the world strictly conform to the instructions of Luciano Benetton and Toba Scarpa, the architect. Areas, typically from 30 to 100 m^2, and layouts are standardized, which enables a reduction in the cost of each new installation. The shop is small because customers must feel packed into it. All the goods must be seen from the shop window and it must be possible to touch and try on all the merchandise. There are 12 authorized layout models, all reproduced in the Ponzano Veneto headquarters basement, in an artificial street. The most common shop design measures 3 by 12 metres, with two rows of 2.4 metre high shelves, and two fitting rooms. All the furniture must be ordered from the same supplier in Treviso.

These shops, however, do not belong to Benetton but to independent owners who are linked to the company by a simple verbal agreement. This agreement, even if it presents some similarities with a classical franchising contract, is not franchising proper. The difference is that Benetton does not receive a fee for the use of its name, nor a royalty based on the retailers' profit, but sells its products to them, at a so-called 'reasonable' price. In addition, Benetton owns some large 'megastores' (from 400 to 1,600 m^2) in Milan, Rome, New York, Düsseldorf and Paris, as well as approximately 30 smaller shops, which were bought during the first stage of its development in the 1960s and 1970s. Moreover, in the United States, a classical franchising system, with written contracts, was adopted for legal reasons, and in France there are distribution companies between Benetton and its shops.

Shops

Benetton preferably selects young entrepreneurs without experience in the ready-to-wear business, lets them use the brand name and fixtures, but does not guarantee an exclusive territory. In some streets of Milan, there are five Benetton shops. Benetton offers to its retailers a full range of financial services (loans, leasing, factoring, insurance, etc.), checks the quality and originality of the assortment and designs the advertising campaigns (mainly posters) at a cost of 4.7 per cent of the group's annual turnover. Benetton advertising is the same all over the world. It is entirely insourced with the inside specialist Oliviero Toscani, and then distributed through only one agency located in Milan, J. Walter Thompson. Whereas in the 1980s Benetton advertising was based upon brotherhood and anti-racism, it has become more and more provocative since 1991, with the use of images such as a dying AIDS victim, an oil-drenched gull, boat people or South African mercenaries. This new approach has had a positive effect on sales.

However, after the AIDS campaign in September 1993, with images of human bodies displaying a 'H.I.V. Positive' tattoo made with the violet ink used in slaughterhouses by veterinary services, and the Bosnia campaign in January 1994 showing the blood-soaked and bullet-pierced uniform of a dead Bosnian Croat soldier, the French minister of humanitarian action, Lucette Michaux-Chevry, asked the French people to 'tear off Benetton sweaters from those who wear them'. Protest and boycott associations were created, such as 'United Boycott'. Some of these associations even include some Benetton shop owners, who worry about the negative effect on sales of this type of advertising. One hundred and fifty retailers in Germany and 30 in France have joined these associations, and some of them even refuse to pay for the products delivered by Benetton, as a compensation for their losses. However, until now, global turnover keeps on increasing and these rebel retailers have always been sentenced by the courts.

Yet, the international reputation of Benetton remains comparable to Coca-Cola's. Apart from its controversial advertising campaigns, this reputation is enhanced by sponsorship, for example in sports, by the publication of *Colors*, the company magazine with a print run of one million copies in six languages, and also by selling articles to fashion magazines via the specialized Inedito subsidiary, located in Paris.

In return for this promotion, retailers are committed to distribute only Benetton products, to scrupulously follow Benetton's instructions concerning computerized orders and merchandising, even lighting and music are specified. Retailers must reach defined sales levels and accept the retail prices defined by Benetton. Products are delivered to the shops with printed price labels, and the amount of each transaction is automatically transmitted by computer to Ponzano Veneto. To join the network, a new retailer must pay from LIT 30 million to LIT 1 billion, to pay for the premises, the fittings, the furniture and the products. Shops generally make a gross profit margin of 45–50 per cent, and their expenditure includes loans repayment (10 per cent), wages (9–12 per cent), overheads (3 per cent), credit cards handling costs (4 per cent), and electricity (2 per cent).

In 1992, with the international crisis faced by the textile industry, Benetton changed its pricing policy. Prices were reduced by between 25 and 40 per cent, depending on the country, between 1993 and 1995. This resulted in a slight growth in sales resulting from a strong growth in volumes sold from 57.29 million units in 1993 to 64.5 in 1994. Moreover, the number of shops stabilized at around 7,000 worldwide. In some countries there are new openings and in others closures, for example, half of the 600 French shops closed between 1990 and 1995. There is, however, a move towards specialized shops with some specializing in shirts, jeans or skirts, which accounted for 25 per cent of sales in 1994, which is double, the proportion in 1992. Benetton, in addition, is encouraging retailers to open 'megastores' of 300 to 500 m^2, which offer a much wider range of products than classical shops. Such megastores have opened successfully in Paris, London, New York, Barcelona, Lisbon, Frankfurt, Munich, Berlin, Vienna, Prague, Budapest, Bucarest, Sarajevo, Riyad and Jeddah.

Agents

Besides computerized communication, the link between Benetton's headquarters and shops relies on 84 independent agents who select and train retailers, and choose the location of shops. These agents, who are encouraged to own some shops themselves, are not Benetton employees. They receive a 5 per cent commission on the purchase made by the shops they supervise, in addition to their share of profit from the stores they own. Therefore, some of them earn more than $1.5 million a year. According to the fashion and climate of their territory, agents gather in Ponzano Veneto to choose from the two yearly collections and then present their selection to the 50–100 shops they supervise in a 30–40 day round.

Each shop owner is responsible for the assortment presented to customers, and chooses the assortment eight months in advance, except for colours. All the orders are centralized by the agents, computerized, sorted by material, colour and delivery date, and then sent to headquarters. Products are directly delivered to the shops and paid to Benetton 90 days later. Benetton then pays their commission to the agents. Modifications and reassortments are possible during the season, but Benetton never takes back unsold articles. Shops are expected to maintain storage facilities, because the products are delivered just before the beginning of each season. Consequently, shops must have a storeroom large enough to accommodate 30 to 40 per cent of a season's sales. Since shops are linked by the computer network, exchanges are possible through the agents. The logistics system is organized so that fewer than three weeks pass between a reassortment order and delivery. Moreover, Benetton always tries to be in a position to organize clearance sales when other companies are introducing their new models.

Furthermore, agents hire assistants in order to visit each shop at least once a week (the 84 agents hire 800 employees altogether), and they behave as 'fashion observers'. They have to perceive and translate evolutions in customer tastes and attitudes in their territory. They communicate the early signs of changes in fashion to Ponzano Veneto, which are later confirmed by the daily transmission of sales from each shop.

Lastly, the agents are connected to the factories through a system of Electronic Data Interchange (EDI). Benetton outsources this system with General Electric Information Services. This value-added network is compatible with roughly 100 different computer languages and platforms. The network uses mainframes, initially three Siemens 7865 in Italy and one Olivetti 5330 in France, and now IBM 3090–300, ten nodes of mini systems and workstations, and terminals which act as computerized cash registers in the shops. Figure 11.7 shows the retailing system.

Agents are rigorously selected by headquarters, and it appears that most often they are friends of the Benetton family, or at least natives of the Treviso region. This poses some problems of adaptation to local tastes in

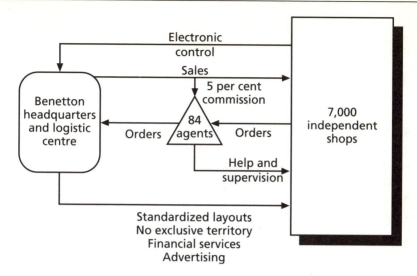

Figure 11.7 The retailing system of Benetton

some countries, and particularly in the United States. Benetton did not hesitate to terminate its relationship with 300 of its 700 American shops between 1989 and 1992, because they were not properly advised by some agents and were unable to compete with local companies like The Gap or Limited. In 1995, there were only 200 Benetton shops left in the United States, which were mainly concentrated in California, Boston and New York. These American shops only accounted for 8 per cent of the total sales of the group. This failure in the United States is a disappointment for Benetton, even if signs of revival are appearing.

In the future, Benetton headquarters could try to set up an alternative retailing structure, to suit local tastes and habits. Another possibility is to bypass agents, because some of them have gained too much power. The massive diversification in large retailing at the end of 1994 could be a forerunner of this change.

◇

TOWARDS A BENETTON MODEL?

The Benetton system constitutes a model of structuring the value chain through maximum externalization, subcontracting almost all design, production and distribution. Numerous companies have already followed this example.

Stefanel

Benetton is imitated by its main Italian competitor, Stefanel (1994 sales of LIT 576 billion and profits of LIT 13.2 billion). This company was formed in 1959 by Giuseppe Stefanel in Ponte di Piave, in the eastern part of the Treviso region, 40 kilometres from Venice. Benetton has been its explicit model, and competitor, since 1982, and in the 1980s Stefanel was very similar to the Benetton of the 1970s. In 1994, Stefanel employed fewer than 500 production people and outsourced its manufacturing to more than 100 workshops which had more than 5,000 employees altogether. Stefanel has 700 shops, with 100 to 150 opening each year. It aims at older customers than Benetton.

Camaïeu

Camaïeu was formed in 1985 in Roubaix (300 kilometres north-east of Paris) by four former executives of the powerful retailing group Auchan. Camaïeu's 1995 sales topped FF 2.5 billion (FF 500 million in 1990 and FF 1 billion in 1991). Distribution was based upon 440 shops (cf. 150 in 1991, 330 in 1993), two-thirds of which were franchized. Seventy per cent of production was outsourced with subcontractors from Roubaix, Cholet, Troyes and Roanne, and since 1995 logistics has been based in a computerized 22,000 m^2 warehouse.

Others

The Benetton model is also imitated in the United States by The Gap and Limited, in Hong-Kong by Giordano (1,000 points of sale, a turnover of HK$530 million and profits of HK$51 million in 1995), in Spain by Mango and in France by Etam and Celio.

However, imitators generally do not surpass the original. Due to its limited diversification, both geographically and in terms of product range, and capital shortage, Camaïeu suffered more than Benetton from the textile crisis of the mid-1990s and the accompanying drop in prices. In 1995, profits were almost nil, and in 1996 the Mulliez group took over the 105 men's wear shops. The 1996 turnover of the remaining women's wear shops (including 111 franchisees) was FF 1.3 billion. Similarly, Stefanel lost LIT 69.4 billion in 1995, and 150 of its shops closed.

Even as it is imitated, Benetton is still the best user of its own model. This is because not only has Benetton designed it, but also because it was the first to implement it, which allows it to capitalize on greater experience in managing logistics, the relationship with subcontractors, the network of agents and the brand image. So far, no imitator has been able to attain this level of knowledge.

Appendix

Consolidated statement of income of the Benetton Group

On 22 July 1997, Benetton Group S.p.A. acquired 56.767% of the capital stock of Benetton Sportsystem S.p.A., the parent company of some of the most important companies in the world of sport. The following chart highlights the data of the Benetton Group (B), homogenous and comparable with 1996 (C) and the data inclusive of the Benetton Sportsystem Group's data relating to the second half 1997 (A).

(in billions of lire)

	1997(A)	%	1997(B)	%	1996(C)	%	Change	%
Total sales	3,636.8	100.0	3,089.5	100.0	2,871.1	100.0	218.4	7.6
Cost of sales	2,105.5	57.9	1,748.3	56.6	1,716.6	59.8	31.7	1.9
Gross margin	1,531.3	42.1	1,341.2	43.4	1,154.5	40.2	186.7	16.2
Selling and general expenses	1,031.7	28.4	810.5	26.2	752.8	26.2	57.7	7.7
Income from operations	499.6	13.7	530.7	17.2	401.7	14.0	129.0	32.1
Net income from currency hedging and exchange differences	86.5	2.4	72.5	2.3	117.2	4.1	(44.7)	(38.1)
Interest income (expense), net	(7.8)	(0.2)	7.7	0.3	(12.6)	(0.4)	20.3	n.s.
Other expense, net	41.6	1.1	28.1	0.9	49.1	1.7	(21.0)	(42.6)
Income taxes	236.4	6.5	246.5	8.0	206.6	7.2	39.9	19.3
Minority interests	10.2	0.3	9.5	0.3	4.9	0.2	4.6	93.9
Net income	290.1	8.0	326.8	10.6	245.7	8.6	81.1	33.0

Ratios

	1997(B)	1996(C)
Income from operations/total sales	17.2	14.0
Income from operations/total capital invested	24.4	23.5
Net income/total sales	10.6	8.6
Net income/stockholders' equity	15.8	13.5

Financial position

(in billions of lire)

	31.12.1997(A)	31.12.1997(B)	31.12.1996(C)	Change
Operating capital	1,648.0	1,236.7	1,136.7	100.0
Total capital invested	2,741.5	2,179.0	1,712.4	466.6
Net borrowing/(liquidity)	508.8	74.2	(133.0)	207.2
Stockholders' equity	2,030.5	2,068.3	1,820.8	247.5
Minority interest	202.2	36.5	24.6	11.9

Consolidated Cash flows

(in billions of lire)

	1997(A)	1997(B)	1997(C)
Self-financing	804.1	789.5	667.8
Increasing in operating capital	(124.1)	(164.3)	(32.9)
Investments in operating activities, net	(91.9)	(84.7)	(91.2)
Other investing activities	(327.3)	(440.4)	1.4
Dividends paid	(90.5)	(90.5)	(79.0)
Income taxes paid	(213.6)	(207.3)	(175.8)
Net cash provided	(43.3)	(197.7)	290.3

Acknowledgement

I gratefully acknowledge Marc Dupuis, Pierre Morel and three anonymous reviewers for their useful comments.

——— QUESTIONS ———

(1) Using the information contained in the case study, draw and comment on Benetton's value chain. What are the conditions of success, the advantages and drawbacks of this structure?

(2) How can Benetton control its partner companies without owning them? Upon which alternative to financial integration does this organization rest?

(3) Does your analysis of the diversification strategy led by Benetton lead you to believe that its structure constitutes a transposable model?

Further reading

Website: www.benetton.com

Benetton, L. and Lee, A. 1990: *Io e I mei fratelli*. Sperling & Kupfer.

Benetton, L. 1995: *Franchising: How Brand Power Works*. Benetton Document.

Biela, M.C., Bui, C., Fournier I. and Lhez, C. 1992: *Lien entre la structure et la stratégie du groupe Benetton*. ESCP-INT paper.

Commiot D. 1993: Le facilities management, une sous-traitance à risques. *L'Usine Nouvelle*, 2413, 3 June, 32–3.

Commons, J.R. 1934: *Institutional Economics*. Madison: University of Wisconsin Press.

Conte, N. 1992: Camaïeu voit la vie en bleu. *Le Figaro économie*, 15 November, 10.

Dapiran, P. 1992: Benetton – Global logistics in action. *International Journal of Physical Distribution & Logistics Management*, 22(6), 7–11.

Donaton, S. 1991: Magazine floodgate opens: marketers turn to publishing for more clout. *Advertising Age*, 62(53), 16 December.

Gérard, A. 1995: Benetton: pendant la pub, la dégringolade continue. *Le Nouvel Économiste*, 1015, 22 September, 68.

Gold, J.S. 1992: Lost in translation. *Financial World*, 161(14), 7 July, 22–4.

Heskett, J.L. and Signorelli, S. 1984: *Benetton*. Harvard Business School Case 9-635-014.

Horwitt, E. 1990: Globalization: key to corporate competition. *Computerworld*, 24(34), 20 August, 45, 48.

Jarillo, J.C. 1993: *Strategic Networks. Creating the Borderless Organization*. Oxford: Butterworth-Heinemann.

Jeudy, E. 1998: Benetton frappé de furie expansionniste. *Le Nouvel Économiste*, 1095, 16 January, 72–3.

Lacube, N. 1992: Pendant les provocations, les affaires de Benetton continuent. *La Tribune de l'Expansion*, 8 February, 8.

Lafont, J. and Lagoutte, C. 1995: Les nouvelles couleurs de Benetton. *Le Figaro Économie*, 15828, 10 July, 3–7.

Lafont, J. and Papazian, C. 1992: Benetton: les recettes d'un marchand de couleurs. *Le Figaro Économie*, 14871, 15 June, 3–8.

Lappen, A.A. 1988: Messenger of the Gods. *Forbes*, 141, 21 March, 50–151.

Lauvige, O. 1994: Benetton invente une usine suspendue au service du juste-à-temps. *L'Usine Nouvelle*, 2446, 3 March, 2–93.

Lazzarato, M., Moulier-boutang, Y., Negri, A. and Santilli, G. 1993: *Des entreprises pas comme les autres, Benetton en Italie, le Sentier à Paris*. Paris: Publisud.

Le Berre, A. 1993: Facilities Management: une offre riche mais disparate. *Zéro Un Informatique*, 1252, 12 March, 21–2.

Leboucq, V. 1995: Benetton Sportsystem vise une entrée en Bourse. *Les Échos*, 16928, 28 June, 14.

—— 1995: Luciano et Gilberto Benetton: nous étudierons d'autres développements dans la distribution. *Les Échos*, 20–1 January, 11.

Leboucq, V., Legras, E. and Queruel, M. 1992: Le textile et l'habillement condamnés au circuit court. *Les Échos*, 16214, 2 September, 11–14.

Legras, E. 1992: Benetton: la réussite bâtie sur des réseaux mondiaux. *Les Échos*, 16214, 2 September, 11–13.

Levine, J. 1991: Self-made press lords, *Forbes*, 148(13), 9 December, 302–4.

—— 1996: Even when you fail, you learn a lot. *Forbes*, 11 March, 58–9.

Lorenzoni, G. 1991: Benetton. In Fontana, F., Nicoletti, B. and Lacchini, M. (eds), *Casi di Organizzazione*. Giapichelli, Torino.

Lorenzoni, G. and Baden-Fuller, C. 1994: Benetton. In Roos, J. (ed), *European Casebook on Cooperative Strategies*. New York: Prentice Hall.

Martin, J. 1989: Italy: IS strategy – Benetton's IS instinct. *Datamation*, 35(13), 11 July, 68-15–68-16.

O'Leary, N. 1992: Benetton's true colors. *Adweek*, 13(34), 24 August, 26–31.

Oddo, G. 1993: Intervista a Luciano Benetton: la mia seconda pelle é il mercato. *Mondo Economico*, 41, 9 October, 84–7.

Ody, P. 1987: How effective is your adverstising?. *Retail and Distribution Management*, 15(1), 9–12.

Pepper, C.B. 1989: Fast forward. *Business Month*, 133(2), February, 24–30.

Peyrani, B. 1991: Benetton-Stefanel: duel de pulls. *Le Nouvel Économiste*, 818, 1er November, 35.

—— 1992: United System of Benetton. *Le Nouvel Économiste*, 872, 4 December, 20–1.

—— 1995: Les nouveaux habits des Benetton. *L'Expansion*, 498, 3 April, 9.

Rossant, J. 1990: Benetton strips back down to sportswear. *Business Week*, 5 March, 42.

Scemama, C. 1994: Benetton a mal à sa pub. *L'Express*, 25 August.

Schuman, M. 1993: Unraveled. *Forbes*, 151(11), 2 May, 97.

Schepherd, J. 1993: Entrepreneurial growth through constellations. *Journal of Business Venturing*, 6(5), September, 363–73.

Segond, V. 1996: Stefanel essuie sa première perte. *Les Échos*, 18 March, 12.

—— 1996: Giordano vise 1000 point de vente en Chine en 2000. *Les Échos*, 18 March, 12.

Shao, M. 1991: Everybody's falling into the gap. *Business Week*, 3232, 23 September, 36.

Signorelli, S. 1985: *Benetton (A)*. Harvard Business School Case, 9–685–014.

—— 1986: *Benetton (B)*. Harvard Business School Case, 9–685–020.

Tabet, M.-C. 1995: Camaïeu file un mauvais coton. *Capital*, 50, November.

Thérin, F. 1994: Comment Benetton s'est joué de la crise. *Le Nouvel Économiste*, 937, 18 March, 58–9.

——. 1994: Comment Benetton s'est attaqué au marché sportif. *Le Nouvel Économiste*, 928, 14 January, 8–59.

Vallée, A. 1992: Camaïeu ou la culture d'entreprise au service de la flexibilité. *Entreprise et Carrières*, 16 January, 8–9.

Vidal, F. 1990: *Le management à l'italienne*: Paris: Intereditions.

Wasmes, A. 1993: Benetton: croissance de 8% en 1992. *Les Échos*, 26 January.

—— 1994: Benetton entre dans la restauration. *Les Échos*, 4–5 November, 5.

—— 1995: Habillement: le groupe Benetton entend développer ses ventes de vête-
ments hors d'Europe. *Les Échos*, 16903, 22 May, 16.

Zottola, L. 1990: The United Systems of Benetton. *Computerworld*, 24(14), 2 April,
70.

12

Häagen-Dazs

MARC DUPUIS AND ÉLISABETH TISSIER-DESBORDES

OVERVIEW

Introduced in Europe and in France at the end of the 1980s, Häagen-Dazs, the premium ice-cream brand, is faced with the growth of price-oriented mass retailing. At the same time, Häagen-Dazs has to manage many channels including franchises. How can it develop its brand in Europe without losing its premium positioning? The pedagogical aim of this case study is to train the students in the decision-making process of multichannel management in an international environment.

KEY WORDS

Retailing, Marketing channels, Brand policy, Pricing

THE PROBLEM FACING HÄAGEN-DAZS

At the beginning of 1995 in London, a meeting took place at the office of the Häagen-Dazs Manager for Europe. Present at this meeting in the London fog were the Marketing Manager for France (**M.M.**), the Manager for Europe

(**M.E.**), the Manager for Retail Operations (**F.M.**) and the Sales Manager (**S.M.**).

M.E. [opened the meeting] Let me quote to you an article published in the French press.

> The situation of Häagen-Dazs in France is more than worrying. Turnover in France, which accounts for 30 per cent of the total European turnover is way off the mark. The forecast turnover for 1995 was FF 2 billion. The actual turnover in 1994 was about 1 billion. The plant, opened in 1992 to supply the whole of Europe, works at only one-third of its capacity. In five years, the firm succeeded in winning only 2.5 per cent of the market in volume, that is to say half the forecast. Germany had sales of 100 million DM, a third of what was forecast. The situation is also disappointing in Italy. Belgium incurred heavy losses.

These are the journalist's views. You know how these people enjoy describing situations as alarming! They do not always take care to check their information, though. But there is probably some truth in what they claim. Our results in France are not what we expected them to be when we started there in 1990.

M.M. You're absolutely right to draw our attention on the seriousness of the situation, but we have to consider Häagen-Dazs' assets. Indeed, this situation is partly due to circumstances which are beyond our control; don't forget that consumption has decreased because of the economic slowdown. In difficult times, consumers tend to cut non-essential purchases first. Nevertheless, we have met with great success. Our turnover increased fivefold between 1991 and 1992. Whereas our retail network was nil in 1991, we now boast 5,500 retailers and we are present in 100 European towns! Today Häagen-Dazs is the leader on the market of 500 ml ice-cream tubs, a segment we launched less than five years ago!

Our real problem today is to adapt our communication to our strategy. As soon as we entered mass distribution, word-of-mouth became inadequate as a means of communication in front of fierce competitors. A big increase in our communication budget is necessary if we want customers to be more aware of our brand and if we want our brand to be a must with mass retailers, in particular on the market of premium ice-cream in tubs.

F.M. Indeed, our network has grown tremendously with our strong presence in mass retailing outlets. But how can we remain credible with our own franchisees when a few mass retailers pare our gross margins to the bone in order to be competitive in their business. Can we explain to our customers in one of our shops that they should pay FF 35, while they can find the same at half price (promotion) at Mammouth? We must overhaul our pricing policy, or else.

S.M. It is true that a mass retailer, Mammouth, decided to cut prices by buying products in UK, taking advantage of the devaluation of the pound. This way they offered 500 ml Häagen-Dazs tubs at FF 17. But didn't we bet on a sales increase in France, where competition is mainly a price struggle? Don't we have to think about our product range anew and to differentiate our offer by network? Remember why we decided to enter mass distribution: today everybody pushes his or her cart in hypermarkets, not only low-wage earners; executives do the same.

M.E. Ladies and Gentlemen, you know the principles which underpin our action: analysis, decision and action. We will be judged on the relevance of our diagnostic and above all on our results. I ask you to give me your conclusions within one month together with your action plan for the next three years.

BACKGROUND

Everything had started well, Reuben Mattus was a Polish immigrant who arrived in the United States in the 1920s. During a trip in Denmark, he tasted excellent ice-cream and decided to adopt a Scandinavian name, Häagen-Dazs, for the ice-cream he would produce from then on. His product was perceived as high quality. It featured in particular a high fresh cream content, no additives or artificial flavours and a 15 per cent air rate, compared to the industry average of 40 per cent. Sales increased steadily but remained confined to a limited market. In 1979, Reuben Mattus's daughter opened a tea-room in the Bronx where she sold only her father's ice-cream. Products were distributed by only a few supermarkets, restaurants and specialized shops in the Bronx.

Häagen-Dazs became a major brand with the arrival of the food giants. In 1983, American Pillsbury bought Häagen-Dazs and decided to develop the brand abroad, first in Japan and the Far East, then in Europe, with a first shop in Germany in 1987, followed by a shop in England in 1989 (see table 12.1). In that age of mergers and acquisitions, in 1989, the British company Grand Metropolitan Foods (Brossard, Burger King) bought Pillsbury, and decided to boost the development of the brand in Europe. In 1990,

Table 12.1 European development

Date of setting up	Country	Number of shops (1995)
1987	Germany	14
1989	UK	21
April 1990	France	45
July 1991	Belgium	5
April 1992	Denmark	1
May 1992	Sweden	2
June 1992	Italy	8
July 1992	Spain	48
May 1993	Netherlands	1
June 1993	Switzerland	3
June 1993	Ireland	1

Häagen-Dazs opened its first shop in a stylish neighbourhood in France. In 1992, the firm opened a plant in Arras in France, with a production capacity of 61 million litres of ice-cream per year at a cost of FF 350 million. In 1990, the firm had a turnover of FF 6 million; in 1991 it was FF 80 million, in 1992, FF 200 million, in 1993, FF 285 million and in 1994, FF 370 million.

Marketing Issues

The market: do the French like ice-cream?

In 1992, consumption in France of ice-cream was 320 million litres, a FF 10 billion market. France accounts for over 10 per cent of the European market of 3 billion litres (see table 12.2) The ice-cream market has grown by 8 per cent a year since 1985. Nevertheless, the average French consumer eats four times less ice-cream than the American counterpart (see table 12.3). French consumption accounts for 70 per cent of sales in volume, but only 50 per cent in value. Sales are very seasonal, and for many brands children bear the strongest influence.

Brands: a struggle between giants

Häagen-Dazs' main competitors are Motta (Unilever Group), the French market leader with a 20 per cent share, Gervais (Nestlé Group) with 17 per

Table 12.2 Development of ice-cream consumption in France

1985	1988	1989	1990	1991	1992	1993	1994	1995
211 L	264 L	303 L	313 L	315 L	320 L	320 L	355 L	360 L

Source: Häagen-Dazs

Table 12.3 Ice-cream consumption per capita in 1994

Country	Consumption in litres
United States	22
UK	8
France	6
Germany	7
Sweden	14
Denmark	10
Italy	6
Spain	4

cent, and Miko with 15 per cent. Häagen-Dazs accounts for only 3 per cent in volume but for 10 per cent in value. Nevertheless, Häagen-Dazs' market share in super premium ice-cream is more than 80 per cent. In 1993, Unilever and Danone created a partnership to launch Yolka, a frozen yoghurt (nine flavours) aiming at 10 to 15 per cent of the market share in 2000. Launch costs reached FF 100 million. Ben and Gerry's, the American ecology brand, should be launched in France soon.

Private labels have become more and more important: 30 per cent of products on the shelves, 26 per cent of sales in volume (30 per cent at Auchan's, 40 per cent at Monoprix's) are now in private label products.

Products: a huge increase in the variety of flavours and sizes

Ice-cream sizes are more and more varied with tubs containing 2 litres, 1 litre, 500 ml, 130 ml (Motta's Mirage), 100 ml, sticks, etc. Two litre tubs, which accounted for 80 per cent of the market in 1980 now account for less than 10 per cent, while 1 litre tubs account for 80 per cent of sales in volume.

Table 12.4 Percentage of households buying ice-cream in different packaging

TOTAL Ice-cream	81%
Tub	55%
of which <1 litre	14%
Leisure	63%
of which stick bars	47%
of which cones	44%
of which bars	15%
Family ice-cakes	39%
Individual specialties	31%
Ice-cream logs (Christmas specialties)	24%

Source: Secodip

Häagen-Dazs products comprise:

- 2.5 l tubs;
- 100 ml tubs;
- 90 ml and 74 ml sticks (1 or 3-pack);
- 500 ml tubs, classic flavours, sorbets, frozen yoghurt or Exträas.

New products for 1995 were:

- 100 ml tubs: cookies;
- 500 ml tubs of mango and vanilla fudge flavour;
- 2.5 l tubs: praline and caramel, coffee, strawberry, chocolate, vanilla fudge flavours;
- 100 ml, 500 ml, 2.5 l tubs: Bailey's;
- 90 ml sticks: peanut brittle and vanilla milk;
- 74 ml sticks: daiquiri.

Table 12.4 shows household buying patterns for major package sizes in the ice-cream market.

Prices

In 1993, the price of a 500 ml Häagen-Dazs tub was FF 30; Häagen-Dazs Exträas, FF 32; Motta, FF 31; Miko, FF 27 and Pilpa, FF 25. In 1994, Mammouth, a major retailer, decided to cut prices by buying products from the

UK, thus taking advantage of the devaluation of the pound. This way they offered 500 ml Häagen-Dazs tubs at FF 17.

Promotion: from word-of-mouth to mass-media

Promotional spend on this market increased from FF 43 million in 1985 to FF 236 million in 1995. Television accounts for 80 per cent of spending. Point of sales sampling increased greatly. Each firm organized about 2,000 'animation' days a year in hypermarkets, at a cost of FF 5 to 6 million. Häagen-Dazs tries to create a 'boutique ambiance' on hypermarkets premises, with maxi-events, where customers can taste all the flavours and is also present in prestigious locations such as the 'Village' of Roland-Garros, the Paris Opera, the Cannes and Avoriaz Festivals, the Lancôme Trophy and the Monaco Grand Prix. Häagen-Dazs also developed partnerships with top of the range retailers, delicatessen stores and fashionable restaurants.

In terms of merchandising, Häagen-Dazs offers point-of-sales freezers adapted to every kind of retail format. The freezers come in four sizes: counter top, freezer, showcase, square. Häagen-Dazs also offers point-of-sales promotion material: leaflets, stickers and display shelves.

Distribution: from stylish shops to everyday low-price hypermarkets

The share of mass retailing in the total of retail sales is growing regularly and this reflects onto ice-cream sales (see table 12.5). In France, Häagen-Dazs started its French retail operations in 1990 simultaneously at Monoprix (a variety store), Picard Surgelés (freezer center chain) and in food-service. Later, the brand decided its products would be distributed in mass retailing outlets. Häagen-Dazs' distribution through mass retailing has developed as shown in Table 12.6.

With 45 shops in France, 6,500 points of sales (hypermarkets and super-markets), 3,000 food-services, Häagen-Dazs has set an objective of 5 per cent in volume of the ice-cream market.

Four distinct retail formats of franchise shops have been developed simultaneously: flagships, shops, take-outs and kiosks.

Franchising is a commercialization system which allows the creator of an unique concept to transfer it to independent retailers who benefit from the brand awareness, its know-how and its products. According to its promoters, Häagen-Dazs' franchise is based on:

Table 12.5 Volume of ice-cream sales (in %) per distribution channel

	1982	1983	1984	1985	1986	1987	1988	1989	1990	1991	1992	1993	1994	1995
Mass Retailing	61	63	67	68	68	69	70	72	72	73	73	74	77	78
Home		19	17	16	17	15	15	15	15	15	15	15	15	14	13
Freezer-Centre	13	13	14	13	13	13	12	12	12	12	11	11	9	9
Miscellaneous	7	7	3	2	4	3	3	1	1	0	1	0	0	0

Source: Secodip

Table 12.6 Percentage of hypermarkets and supermarkets selling Häagen Dazs products

Year	Total	Hypermarket	Supermarket
1991	25	37	—
1992	56	83	47
1993	78	93	65

- the sale of a unique product, defined by the quality of ingredients and its production method;
- the participation in the growing market of super premium ice-cream;
- a well-known international top range brand;
- the assistance of the Häagen-Dazs team before and after the opening of the shop;
- the European shop concept and design for the four outlet types (see table 12.7);
- a global network of franchisees;
- a favourable financial deal for the franchisee.

As a counterpart, Häagen-Dazs' franchisees are selected on the basis of the following criteria:

- motivation and identification of the franchisee with the brand;
- understanding and approbation of Häagen-Dazs' development strategy;
- experience in catering;
- access to the necessary capital to finance 100 per cent of the shop;
- access to a stylish location in a town (or location) targeted by Häagen-Dazs.

The 'flagship' is Häagen-Dazs' most sophisticated concept. It includes both take-out selling (minimum area 80 m^2) and tea-room service (minimum

Table 12.7 The four distinct retail formats of franchise shops

	Sales area (m²)	Turnover (MF)	Investment (MF)	Entry fees (MF)
Flagship	120	50–100	30–60	12–18
Shop	4–10	1.5–7	0.7–4	0.5–1.5
Take-out	>1.5	>1	>0.5	>0.35
Kiosk	0.250	0.150	0.150	0.50

(MF) = million French francs.

30 seating capacity). Flagships are always situated in a first category location in the national and regional European capitals.

Häagen-Dazs' managers had analysed the product life of retailing formats in France and noticed the strong growth of mass distribution in the food market. Moreover, some mass retailers wanted to include top of the range brands in the range they distributed. How could Häagen-Dazs follow this evolution without losing its image of a top range brand? This dilemma was partially solved by the setting-up of freezers with the brand's colours in 30 per cent of Häagen-Dazs' points-of-sales. But Häagen-Dazs still had to defend its top of the range price policy. Häagen-Dazs argued that, to be credible, a top of the range brand needed a high price and that selling a top brand at higher prices improved the retailer's margin thus allowing the retailer to compensate its low margin on low range brands. Price sensitivity surveys carried out for Häagen-Dazs showed a quite large area of uncertainty on that kind of product.

To succeed in being present in mass distribution is a long-term issue. Retailers have a wide selection of brands: 'There are about 2,500 ice-cream references, and we can carry only an average of 130', explains a Carrefour buyer.

Acknowledgement

The authors would like to thank Isabelle Garric, Marketing Manager of Häagen-Dazs France for her help and useful remarks, as well as Patrick Cohen, Jérôme Lemaire, Virginie Lampaert and Judith Lecardonnel, students of the Marketing & Communication Master Program at the ESCP. They also thank Pierre Morel and Héléna Magis for help in translating the case study.

QUESTIONS

(1) Analyse the reasons which led Häagen-Dazs to be present in mass distribution networks: what other strategies were possible? Discuss the advantages and disadvantages of these strategies.

(2) Analyse the chief strengths and weaknesses of the competition on the ice-cream market, using the Porter model.

(3) What would you recommend in order to improve Häagen-Dazs' situation?

(4) How would you respond to the challenge thrown down by the Manager for Europe?

―――――― 13 ――――――

Coop in Italy and the Low Price Challenge

ENRICO COLLA

―――――― OVERVIEW ――――――

In 1993, following the onset of the recession and the resulting changes in consumer behaviour, hard-discount retailing of food was developing in Italy. Coop, the leading grocery retailing group, analyses the strategic decision to enter the sector, which mushroomed in 1994. This case study examines the mission, structure and strategy of Coop and provides elements for evaluating the factors for and against diversification through a comparison of the key success factors in the hard discount sector with the strengths and weaknesses of Coop. The analysis of the Coop group and the hard-discount sector also allows a discussion of entry strategy and particularly of decisions regarding organizational structure, positioning and the retail mix.

―――――― KEY WORDS ――――――

Cooperative, Discount, Strategy, Structure, Diversification

THE COMPETITIVE SITUATION

Ivano Barberini, chairman of Coop/ANCC was reflecting after dinner, one early Summer evening in 1993, on the recent environmental and competitive changes in the food retailing business in Italy. His reflections were prompted by a report he was reading on demand trends and consumer behaviour:

> As in most of the rest of Europe, the early 1990s in Italy were marked by an economic crisis and by a slowdown in the growth of consumer spending. There was consequently a radical change in consumer behaviour during these years as a result of greater economic difficulties, the climate of political and social instability, the increase in unemployment and threats to the maintenance of old-age pension levels. Studies conducted in the early 1990s suggest that many consumers have changed their habits: they choose less expensive stores and less costly brands, purchase a larger quantity of private-label merchandise and show greater interest in promotions. They demonstrate greater scepticism regarding the price–quality ratio of food products and, when they do not find their favourite brand in their supermarkets, they increasingly prefer to replace the brand than change supermarkets. Consumers are therefore less sensitive to manufacturers' brands, and these brands, although still dominant, are beginning to lose market share to private-label products or exclusive brands of hard discount chains. In addition, consumers are responding less to advertising messages, conveyed primarily through television, and are increasingly inclined to avoid advertising by channel-hopping, which damages chiefly brand-name products. Loyalty to retail outlets and chains has increased, however, along with the willingness to purchase private label products.

The reader was fairly familiar with these considerations and considered them mainly a confirmation of information already available. None the less, Barberini continued reading the report, which was now dealing with the so-called 'trading-up of Italian retailing in the 1980s':

> In the 1980s no limited-assortment discount formula was created in Italian retailing. The numerous outlets with characteristics similar to this format created at the start of the decade underwent an evolution in subsequent years that made them more similar to supermarkets than hard discounts. In the early 1990s the strategic orientation of the

principal supermarket and hypermarket chains was still focused on quality and service rather than on price. This was due in part to the positive economic climate, which reduced consumer attention to the pricing factor, and in part to the low level of competitive intensity in the industry. This lack of competitive pressure was in turn caused by the limited growth of modern retailing and thus the low level of direct competition between the various chains.

Regarding supermarkets, their growth rate was high in the years to 1993, and their share of the total grocery market in 1993 was 37.9 per cent, reaching levels close to those of the other European countries. As a result of hypermarket growth, the principal chains gradually modified their offerings to avoid overly vigorous price competition. They therefore focused increasingly on perishables and service departments, and the new stores opened by the major food retailers tended towards larger selling areas with strong non-food assortments. Hypermarkets developed much more slowly in Italy than in the other European countries. They still numbered less than 150 in 1993, and their share of the grocery market was 5.7 per cent. Their characteristics were also somewhat different from the original French model, which was based on a strong low-pricing orientation. The average Italian hypermarket was smaller, with a narrower but deeper assortment, particularly in perishables, and a high level of customer service.

One consequence of all this was that in the early 1990s there was a greater differential in Italy than in the other European countries between the prices of brand-name products and those sold in the foreign hard discounts.

Barberini had now accepted the basic thesis of the report which sought to demonstrate that there is ample room in the Italian market for limited-assortment hard discount stores. He therefore decided to read on: it was only one o'clock in the morning and he wasn't sleepy yet.

These factors favoured the forms of retailing based on low price strategies and thus cost leadership, such as limited-assortment discount stores (hard discounts), which developed rapidly during this period. Competition was fierce in this formula, and the cost differential was achieved mostly through effective purchasing, as well as in low operating overhead.

The initiative was taken by the German chain Lidl, second in Germany behind Aldi but first in the French market. The expansion of hard discount in the late 1980s and early 1990s characterized other

European countries, such as the UK and France. In Italy, Lidl's initiative was immediately echoed by several Italian chains, generally belonging to medium-sized firms associated with voluntary unions or purchasing groups, while the principal Italian chain operations followed a wait-and-see policy.

In the initial phase, the majority of these chains opened stores with characteristics quite similar to Lidl's. It was estimated that the number of outlets might increase by around 1,000 units during 1994 (there were 312 in 1993), mostly through the restructuring of small supermarkets. Their market share would thus increase to 5 per cent of the grocery category by December 1994, a figure expected to double within five years.

Barberini began to read the report with greater attention, as it shifted from an analysis of the past to the description of a rather disquieting future:

Such explosive growth of the discount formula will also take sales away from the supermarkets, especially the small ones, as well as the hypermarkets and will thus help intensify price competition. Indeed, it will cause a reduction in the prices of branded products and consequently the prices of private-label products, which are linked to them. This will exert pressure on the margin and profit levels of the retail companies, which are also likely to decrease in coming years.

The principal Italian supermarket and hypermarket chains will also react to the new challenges with a series of strategic initiatives:

- diversification into limited-assortment discount to exploit the opportunities in this format;
- accentuated development of hypermarkets, which will gradually grow and double the number of units in the 1990–5 period.

As a result of the growth of supermarkets and hypermarkets, the total number of foodstores will decline until it drops below 300,000 in 1995. This is still double the number in the three principal European countries, proportional to population.

Modern self-service retailing may thus capture 65 per cent of the grocery market in Italy by 1994, and the market share of chain operations (multiples plus major independents) will reach 29 per cent, while buying groups will have 20 per cent and voluntary groups 16 per cent (Nielsen projections). Cooperation (including mass retailing) will continue to be the second group (in selling area) both in supermarkets and hypermarkets.

The forecasts are still moderately positive for supermarkets as well, considering that their market share of the grocery category was 39 per cent in 1994. In coming years the number of supermarkets restructured into hard discounts will certainly be greater than new openings, while the new outlets will be chiefly large supermarkets with nonfood assortments.

– The quest for economies of scale and standardization will result in an increased concentration of retail outlets and chains: in 1995, 10 per cent of the outlets will account for 78 per cent of total sales, versus the 62 per cent measured in 1990. The market share of the top ten retailers will equal 43 per cent in 1995, versus a European average of 60 per cent. New central buying offices will undoubtedly be created among medium-sized chain operations in an attempt to gain greater bargaining power with suppliers and obtain better purchasing conditions.
– There will be a significant increase in so-called budget price products, i.e., those with the lowest prices in their classes and at the same level as hard discount products. All the principal chains have added a number of these items, primarily to keep customers from patronizing the hard discounts. Budget pricing has not always achieved the desired result and, in some cases, has even helped lower the average margin on sale without increasing sales volume.
– To offset the overall reduction in margins, companies will introduce a series of cost reduction measures through the rationalization and improvement of logistic systems, a reduction in the number of warehouses and their organizational and operational restructuring, often through the introduction of new information technologies. This logistic rationalization will be followed by forms of co-operation with suppliers, as occurred abroad. In the United States, the ECR (Efficient Customer Response) program was developed: its objective is to reduce inefficiency in the manufacturer–retailer interface regarding logistics, administration and promotions.
– The quest for differentiation by chains that do not stress only cost leadership will also be manifested by the development of private-label products, an increase in items and better quality control in the perishables departments, as well as a few classes of non-food products, particularly toiletries and household products.

The report ended on this note, thus suggesting, Barberini thought, a series of threats but also opportunities for the Coop group.

Hard discount, for example, was presented in the report not as a transient phenomenon linked to the economic crisis, but as a structural fact of the economic system, the result of its modernization. Therefore, it could permanently usurp a part of the Coop's market share if it failed to react. Alternatively, the Coop group could itself penetrate the hard-discount business, as many managers in the movement had been suggesting for some time. They would be entering late with respect to the competition, but being late could also bring some advantages.

The report seemed to suggest that, apart from a possible entry into hard discounting, the Coop had other strategic alternatives for coping with the new competitive situation. The example of other countries (especially France and Germany) demonstrated, unfortunately, that consumer co-operatives could suffer setbacks if they failed to react to the new challenges.

Barberini was convinced, however, that the Italian situation was different and that Coop had the capabilities and resources necessary to avoid such a negative outcome. Thus, having finished reading the report, he finally fell asleep.

$$\diamondsuit$$

STRATEGIES AND STRUCTURES OF THE COOP GROUP

Several months later, during 1994, some ANCC executives met with a group of trade journalists and financial analysts. Barberini was one of the participants. The meeting opened with a brief report on the economic and financial situation of the movement, which seemed highly positive: 'The Coop group emerged from the modernization of Italian retailing, which occurred between the late 1980s and early 1990s, as the leading group, at least from the quantitative standpoint. In 1994, it was composed of 320 co-operatives that operate a network of 1,165 outlets with 724,000 m^2 of sales area [see table 13.1]. The employees numbered 31,807 and the shareholders 2,907,000. Turnover totaled L. 11,230 billion, with a 6 per cent share of all marketed food consumption. The economic and financial results of the principal co-operatives were positive during this period and continued to be positive in the first half of the 1990s. In 1994, the total net earnings of the Coops amounted to L. 40 billion, representing more than 3 per cent of sales.'

'The net results of many co-operatives, however, show signs of weakening with respect to the high levels achieved in the more recent past. This is particularly evident in the smaller co-operatives,' one analyst noted.

'This fact,' someone responded immediately, 'which is very limited in scope, is the result of the changes during the 1990s in consumer behaviour

Table 13.1 The co-operative network in 1994

	Large	Medium	Sub-total	Small	Total
Number of Coops	9	7	16	304	320
Number of stores	474	136	610	555	1,165
Sales area (000 m²)	524	75	599	125	724
Members (000)	2,242	315	2,557	350	2,907
Employees:					
– firms and stores	23,224	2,408	25,632	4,080	29,712
– consort. and association					2,095
Total					31,807
Sales (billions of liras)	8,782	1,000	9,782	1,448	11,230

Source: Coop/ANCC

and in the competitive situation in retailing. Profitability was in any case at high levels.'

'This is true,' commented a journalist, 'but it is also true that the major co-operatives located in the central regions generate profitability levels above 5 per cent of sales. The co-operatives operating in regions with fiercer competition, like Coop Lombardia, however, achieve profitability levels that are below 2 per cent. The level is even lower for the smaller co-operatives.'

'This is precisely why,' the ANCC executive concluded, 'the smaller co-operatives will soon merge into larger units, which will permit them to achieve greater economies of scale and improve profits.'

'Your organizational structure is still quite different from that of your mass retailing competitors,' observed a journalist from *GDO Week*.

A group manager then offered a complete presentation of the group's organizational structure. 'It's true that the total number of co-operatives is rather large, but in reality the 16 largest in the group accounted for 87 per cent of total 1994 turnover and the vast majority of the modern sales outlets, which total 414, are supermarkets (395) and hypermarkets (19).

Ours is thus a group of medium-sized organizations, each of which has less turnover than the major Italian chain store groups, for example GS, Esselunga, PAM, but more than those associated with the buying groups and voluntary groups. Look at the figures [see table 13.2].'

He continued: 'Each Coop is a relatively autonomous organization, since it manages a local retail network and has its own financial resources and logistic structures. At the same time, it belongs to a group which performs certain important common functions through its centralized structures. The retail networks of the co-operatives include supermarkets and hypermarkets.

Table 13.2 Network of large and medium-sized stores in 1994

Format	Number of stores	Per cent of stores	Sales space (000 m²)	Per cent of sales space
Iper	19	3.1	111.8	18.7
Large Super	127	20.8	219.0	36.6
Small Super	268	43.9	218.8	36.5
Superette	124	20.3	37.4	6.2
Others	72	11.8	12.0	2.0
Total	610	100.0	599.0	100.0

Source: Coop/ANCC

The latter, introduced more recently, often represent internal divisions of the co-operatives but sometimes are managed by consortia or by joint-stock companies controlled by a Coop.

Warehouses for the storage and physical distribution of the goods have almost all been integrated into the individual co-operatives that use and manage them. In some cases the logistic structures are shared by several co-operatives, which then undertake joint management.

Other group structures operate nationally on behalf of all the Coops. The principal structure of this type from the economic standpoint is the Coop Italia consortium, which is essentially responsible for the following functions: definition of "blanket" contracts with suppliers, promotional activities of a national nature, management of the products sold under the Coop trademark and all activities of product quality control, including the laboratory.

Coop Italia thus determines the general economic conditions for purchasing the products in the assortment, on the basis of which the individual co-operatives or consortia of co-operatives then make their purchases. In cases where a number of co-operatives have formed a consortium to manage common logistic structures, it is the consortium that conducts purchasing operations on the indications of the member co-operatives. Until 1980 there was only one Coop Italia, which was concerned almost exclusively with food products. In that year, Coop Italia non-food was created to manage purchasing activities, coordinate the commercial policies of the co-operatives and perform quality controls for this category of products.

Another national entity is INRES, which coordinates the physical construction of the network, designs the outlets and conducts the important activity of equipment purchases for the outlets.

All the Coops belong to ANCC, the National Association of Consumer

Cooperatives, which in turn belongs to the National League of Cooperatives and Mutual Companies. The ANCC is the centre for development of strategy common to all the Coops regarding diversification, selling policy, political and social activity and initiatives to safeguard consumers and the environment. The decision-making organ for these matters is the Board, formed of the president and vice-president of the ANCC and the chairmen of Coop Italia food and Coop Italia nonfood.'

$$\diamondsuit$$

EVOLUTION OF THE STRUCTURES

'All this is very fine' retorted a sector analyst, 'having the organisation is one thing, but responding to the changes in the market is quite another. Have you really changed?'

'Look', responded a manager in a rather heated way, 'we've changed more than most Italian retailers. Let me tell you. The commercial strategy pursued by the Coops underwent a transformation in the early 1980s, when it was decided to commit the entire system to the development of modern food retailing by "integrated" supermarkets and hypermarkets. Before then, the foundation had already been laid for such a decision through the radical restructuring of the co-operatives and the sales networks. Growth has proceeded even more rapidly since the 1980s, along with the restructuring of the co-operatives and the rationalization of the sales network. Just look at these figures [see tables 13.3 and 13.4]. In ten years, the total sales area has doubled and the modern component, supermarkets and hypermarkets, has become predominant. How's that for change?

Coop first concentrated its investments in supermarkets and considerably expanded the network, chiefly through direct development and only to a small extent through the acquisition of smaller retailers. Then, in 1988, it began devoting even greater attention to hypermarkets and shopping centres. With the development of hypermarkets, the Coops were able to penetrate the big city markets. Change – we've done nothing but change for decades now!'

'Ok, ok, keep cool, but what are the orientations for future geographical development?', asked a journalist from *Mark Up* at this point, 'do you plan to increase your penetration in the southern regions?'

'Coop,' was the reply, 'has the largest market share of food products in Italy (around 6 per cent). This share will grow in the next four or five years, given our development plans, which include the opening of 25 large supermarkets and 29 hypermarkets during this period. It is true that our national

Table 13.3 Evolution of Coop

	1965	1973	1982	1990	1993	1994
Number of Coops	1,287	956	593	341	330	320
Number of stores	3,869	2,793	1,486	1,162	1,150	1,165
Total sales (billion lira)	123	241	2,184	7,458	10,680	11,231

Source: Coop

Table 13.4 Major Coop's development programme 1995–1998

Format	Number of stores	Total (m^2)	Average (m^2)
Hypermarkets			
more than 4,000 m^2	22	140,270	6,376
2,500–4,000	3	10,500	3,500
Supermarkets			
large	9	14,150	1,561
small	22	19,919	996

Source: Coop

share conceals a highly regional concentration. The co-operatives hold clearly dominant positions in three regions of central Italy (Tuscany, Emilia Romagna and Umbria), characterized by high levels of consumption and moderate levels of modernization. In the north, they are leaders in Liguria, a small region with little modernization, but also hold significant positions in other regions (Piedmont, Lombardy), where the levels of consumption and modernization are both high. On the other hand, they have a scant presence in the southern regions, some of which are extremely interesting because of their good levels of consumption and their limited degree of modernization.

Development in the regions of lesser concentration, and particularly in the south, is important and has yet to be achieved. In effect, development in the south has been repeatedly included in the program guidelines and objectives indicated by the Coops nationally. Thus far, however, the results have been limited, and the strategy of providing assistance to the small co-operatives of the south has not been sufficient. On the other hand, the regional co-operatives are not highly motivated to pursue the expansion of the network in difficult areas far from their locations. In 1994, a direct growth strategy in the south will be initiated by the northern co-operatives with the opening of two hypermarkets in Apulia by Coop Estense, based in Emilia.'

MARKETING APPROACHES

Interrogation continued and a journalist took up the issue of marketing, asking, 'what are your marketing policies? Do you really have a policy or is it just everyone doing what they want?'

'Right, let me explain', replied the marketing manager trying to be restrained, 'the format from which the Coops derive the lion's share of their turnover (around 70 per cent) is the supermarket. The supermarkets vary widely in size and commercial strategy according to the region and the co-operative.'

'Just as I said – you've no real policy' retorted the journalist.

'Wait and listen,' responded the manager. 'Supermarkets are of two types. *Integrated supermarkets* are retail outlets with an average size of 1,500 m² which carry a broad, deep product assortment and a large share of non-food product items. They are located primarily in suburban areas, and their price positioning is generally good but varies according to the region. *Neighbourhood supermarkets* have an average size of 600 m² are most often located in small or medium-sized communities or in urban neighbourhoods and are characterized by a medium average price level and good product quality.

Hypermarkets have been introduced more recently, and the point of reference was the French hypermarkets, although that model has been adapted to the specific opportunities and constraints of the Italian market and the internal organization of the Coops. The average size of these outlets is therefore smaller than that of the major French groups and some leading Italian chains, for example Euromercato and Finiper. They therefore have fewer non-food products, are less discount-oriented and are located preferably in shopping centres, along with a couple of specialized superstores and a few dozen small specialized shops.'

At this point, the editor of *Mark Up* requested the floor, as he felt a clarification was in order. 'Based on our research,' Luigi Rubinelli observed, 'Coop's price positioning and breadth and depth of assortment differ not only according to the format (super or hyper) but also according to the type of product (branded or private-label).

Regarding private-label products, Ipercoop is, in our view, in a position of leadership in both pricing (more competitive than that of the competitors' private-label products) and breadth of selection, measured as the number of items. In the supermarkets, the Coop-brand products also have lower prices than those of the own brands of the other leading chains in the sector (GS,

PAM, SMA, Sidis), which also have a more limited assortment. Only Esselunga has a deeper assortment than Coop.

The positioning of Coop in branded products is different, however. Here, in both the hypers and supers, the depth of the assortment is the lowest in the sector, due both to the wide selection of own brands and the smaller average size of the outlets (hypers). Coop's pricing (supermarkets) of branded products is in line with the sector average and close to that of the associated group supermarkets (as well as A&O, Conad and Crai). Ipercoop, for its part, has a pricing level one percentage point higher than the average hypermarket prices and more than two points higher than the leader.'

'Thank you. These figures are interesting,' responded the marketing manager. 'It is certainly true that over the years the competitive positioning of the Coops has been gradually clarified. While originally it was characterized by a quest for price leadership, it explicitly differentiated its offering during the expansion phase begun in the 1980s. Differentiation was chiefly through the gradual introduction of more private-label products, an area in which Coop is a leader in Italy, and greater enhancement and communication of its "social" and "environmentalist" orientation.

Regarding the image of the Coop-brand products, it might be said that customers' satisfaction is definitely high, as is their appraisal versus other brands. As for this latter aspect, an in-house survey conducted in 1993 revealed that, in terms of price, 54 per cent of the consumers considered Coop products slightly better than the similar products of other brands, 20 per cent much better, 24 per cent the same and 2 per cent a bit worse. With reference to quality, 59 per cent considered them equal, 26 per cent slightly better and only 11 per cent slightly worse.

Another survey that compared Coop products with the private-label products of competing chains (Esselunga, Sidis and Generale Supermercati-GS) registered a definitely better judgement of Coop products in all the variables tested, with the exception of price, which was viewed as higher than that of some competitors. On the whole, however, consumers regarded the presence of branded products as an important factor in selecting the store where they shop. From the data furnished by *Mark Up*, Coop it seems has made progress with reference to the cost-effectiveness of its private-label products.'

At this point, in response to a question from Mr Carmignano, editor of a magazine specializing in private-label products, a Coop Italia manager began to present Coop's policy regarding relations with suppliers and the characteristics of its private-label products.

'The Coop's large national market share and strong regional roots give it a strong bargaining power with suppliers. Another factor in this respect is the availability of a broad assortment of private-label products. On the other hand, Coop's participatory approach limits the results that can be obtained in purchasing negotiations. As a consequence, the purchasing conditions Coop is able to obtain on branded products are better than the average but not as good as those of its more aggressive competitors. Especially not as good as those it could obtain if it were more integrated,' the speaker mused, long convinced that the incomplete organizational integration of the co-operatives partially limited their aggressiveness in purchasing activity. He continued his report, however, without dwelling on this point. 'Coop brand products were introduced from the outset for the purpose of defending the purchasing power of consumers and giving good quality. The products are thus characterized by a high quality level, the absence of colouring agents, a controlled use of additives and excellent informative labelling. There were about 600 at the end of 1993, and their market share of total turnover was 5.6 per cent. Special attention has been directed recently at perishables, for which the slogan "products with love", accompanied by the Coop trademark, was coined.

The quality of Coop products is assured by an acceptance screening process. First, suppliers are selected by the purchasing function on the basis of an evaluation of their ability to comply with the specifications of product characteristics. Then the Coop quality control structure performs prior checks on all the so-called high-risk products, which it later checks on a sample basis. For "products with love", the production process is controlled: for produce, for example, field inspections are conducted to ensure that the established levels of agro-chemical use are not exceeded. The animals that provide meat are selected at birth, marked and checked periodically to ensure the absence of steroids and growth hormones.

It is estimated that these controls of produce and meat cost a total of L. 2 billion for less than L. 1,000 billion of total sales. In the past, the farm co-operatives were favoured as suppliers and were often selected even when their prices were higher than other non-co-operatives. The situation has changed today, because the agro-industrial co-operatives, if they wish to supply Coop, must have a quality level at least as high as their competitors. In effect, the percentage share of the agro-industrial co-operatives in Coop purchases has declined over the past decade, from 22 per cent to around 15 per cent.'

'Where does advertising fit into this marketing policy?' asked a journalist from the back of the room.

The Marketing Manager continued, 'The traditional promotional campaigns of the 1980s were based on special price discounts and were conveyed through local newspapers. In addition to these, there was advertising communication focusing primarily on the themes of pricing and the nearness of Coop to the consumer.

The new institutional communication has sought to accompany and sustain Coop's product position differentiation, aimed at an ever-broader audience of consumers with higher characteristics (education, income and occupation). To achieve this result, it focused on the themes of its social action and its specific institutional characteristics.

The new advertising campaigns of the 1990s are based on themes, claims and testimonials consistent with this objective: significant examples are the advertising campaigns produced with Lt. Colombo (Peter Falk) and with Woody Allen. The former is extremely popular and is presented as a simple but intelligent person, profound and highly authoritative. "Coop is you. Who can give you more?" is the promise of quality service based on the specific nature of the co-operatives' organization. With Woody Allen the idea was to speak to a more urbane consumer, relatively younger and intellectually more refined.'

◇

FINANCIAL STRENGTH

At this point, a financial analyst from Mediobanca decided to ask about the group's financial strategies and its sources of capital for expanding its network. 'The share capital of the Coops is limited,' responded the Coop finance expert, 'for reasons associated with their special juridical nature. In fact, there is a series of legislative restrictions on the amount of share capital, the freedom to sell shares, the percentage of profits to allocate to the legal reserve and to distribute to the shareholders. Given these limits, it is difficult to increase capital through new share issues.

The Coops have circumvented this obstacle and raised the enormous financial resources necessary to implement their development plans primarily by reinvesting profits in the company operation (self-financing) and by using the member loans. These are loans that each member can grant to the co-operatives and that are remunerated at a rate competitive with what the banks pay on demand deposits. Since the interest paid on account balances is rather low in Italy, the Coops are able to procure low-cost financing even though they pay higher rates. These loans, in effect, reach impressive totals, even exceeding company turnover in some co-operatives. At least 20 per cent of their total (but no more than three times share capital) may be used for investments, thus representing a fundamental source of financial equilibrium for the Coops.'

Table 13.5 Main operators of hard discount stores in Italy

	Number of stores July 1994	July 1995
Vegé (Sosty-Ecu)	231	298
Crai (Eurospin, Europa Europa, others)	186	190
Lidl	146	135
Lombardini (LD)	81	117
Italmec (Tuo, others)	75	76
Gea (EGA)	41	50
Pam (In's discount)	40	48
A&O Selex (Topdì, others)	37	52
Sigma	42	41
Franchini	41	n.a.
Conad	n.a.	36
Others	292	528
Total	1,212	1,571

Source: Nielsen

THE SPECTRE OF HARD DISCOUNT

The meeting seemed to be drawing to a close when a journalist from *Mark Up* took the floor again: 'The responses furnished so far have been highly interesting, but now we would all like to know the Coop group's assessment of hard discount and whether you intend to diversify into this sector. Your group, in fact, has been one of the few to maintain its distance from this sector so far. Look at these figures [see table 13.5]. What are your plans for the future?'

The question was expected, and all turned to Barberini for a response. The chairman of the group then began his reply thinking back to the report he had read several months before: 'Coop does not believe that hard discount is just a transient phenomenon ...'

────── QUESTIONS ──────

(1) In the light of the discussion and debate do you consider that Coop have been leaders of change or have they been followers reacting to the changes external to them?

(2) Will Coop's general marketing strategy be affected if they move seriously into hard discount retailing?

(3) What are the key success factors for hard discount grocery retailing?

(4) What are the strengths and weakneses of Coop in entering the hard discount market?

Further reading

Barberini, I. 1995: *Competere per cosa*. Roma: Liocorno Editori.

Butera, F. 1991: *La Métamorphose de l'organisation*. Paris: Edition d'Organisation.

Chandler, A.D. 1962: *Strategy and Structure*. Cambridge: M.I.T. Press.

Colla, E. 1994a: *I Discount. Le nuove forme distributive con prezzi bassi in USA e in Europa*. Milano: Etas Libri.

—— 1994b: Discount developments in France: the introduction of the format and the competitive response. *Journal of Marketing Management*, 10, 645–54.

—— 1995: *La Grande Distribuzione in Europa. Evoluzione delle formule distributive, strategie e strutture aziendali, rapporti con l'industria*. Milano: Etas Libri.

—— 1996: The development of hard discount in Italy. Foreign penetration and evolution in the competitive situation. *The European Retail Digest*, Winter 1995–6, 22–6.

Détrie, J.P. and Ramanantsoa, B. 1983: *Stratégie de l'entreprise et diversification*. Paris: Nathan.

Knee, D. and Walters, D. 1985: *Strategy in Retailing*. Oxford: Philip Allan.

Miles, R.E. and Snow, C. 1978: *Organisational Strategy, Structure and Process*. New York: McGraw-Hill.

Porter, M. 1985: *The Competitive Advantage*. New York: The Free Press.

Rumelt, R.P. 1974: *Strategy, Structure, and Economic Performance*. Boston: Harvard University Press.

14

When Logistics Threaten to Become a Source of 'Competitive Disadvantage': The Intermarché Co-operative Case

GILLES PACHÉ

OVERVIEW

The Intermarché retailer co-operative is one of the four most powerful food retailers in France, well-known for its discounter positioning. It has implemented from its foundation, in 1969, an integrated physical distribution system which kept strengthening itself as the years went by. This system allows Intermarché to carry on with successful policies of centralization of supply and of speculative inventory. However, some threats started to emerge in the 1990s. These were linked to the availability of an important storage capacity which might very well increase logistical costs and, consequently, question the discounter positioning. This case study analyses the mechanisms that led to such a situation. It then expounds alternative solutions so as to avoid logistics becoming a source of 'competitive disadvantage'.

KEY WORDS

France, Logistics, Purchasing policy, Retailer co-operative.

INTERMARCHÉ IN BRIEF

Founded in September 1969 by Jean-Pierre Le Roch, a personality as charismatic as Sam Walton in the USA, the Intermarché retailer co-operative is one of the four most powerful French food retailers, with sales of nearly US$26 billion, not including its manufacturing and foreign activities. The spectacular progression of Intermarché may be explained by the application of strict principles of management. It is also the result of its members' dynamism; 2,200 independent entrepreneurs owned 3,100 outlets in 1995. Members have a responsibility to take part in the management of the co-operative by dedicating on a voluntary basis one-third of their time to coordinating activities at national or regional level.

Together with the Leclerc retailer co-operative, from which it originated, Intermarché appears to be one of the precursors of modern discounting and firmly belongs to the conventional retailing model of low price/low cost associated with low service (Rosenbloom and Dupuis, 1994). In fact, at a time when France is experiencing the end of an era of unprecedented economic growth, Jean-Pierre Le Roch believes that, in the future, the consumer of convenience goods will be far more aware of lower costs than of service in outlets, as exemplified by many sales staff and high-quality physical facilities from buildings to fixtures, etc. How can sales prices be kept low? He believes the answer is by reducing overheads, but mainly by centralizing purchasing and logistical operations.

During the first ten years of its existence, Intermarché specialized in a single formula: the supermarket. Unlike its major competitors who preferred the adventure of the hypermarket, Intermarché remained a supermarket operator. Even today, the company remains the supermarket leader in France, owning about one-third of the total sales area. This strong national presence in this field was even strengthened in 1991 with the launching of new outlets (*Comptoir des Marchandises*) in the hard-discount sector. The objective was to take a significant market share in the face of the German leaders such as Aldi and Lidl, while confirming its primary discounter positioning.

But this single-minded policy has been questioned since the early 1980s. The Intermarché management team decided to build up a portfolio of different formats with the objective of satisfying the customers' various needs, from grocery to household supplies. The company thus diversified successively toward DIY (*Bricomarché*), fashion (*Vêtimarché*), the catering trade (*Restaumarché* and *Bistrot du Marché*), service stations (*Stationmarché*), convenience stores (*Relais des Mousquetaires*) and even cash-and-carry

Table 14.1 Intermarché's various distribution formats in France

	Number of outlets in December 1995	Sales in 1995 (in millions of US$)	Number of outlets in June 1990
Supermarkets	1,891	23,200	1,525
Convenience stores	385	(*)	–
DIY	334	1,180	240
Hard-discounting	192	500	–
Service stations	95	400	90
Fashion outlets	117	190	70
Cash-and-carry outlets	34	190	7
Catering trade	53	32	30
TOTAL	3,101	25,692	1,962

(*) The sales are included in the supermarket formula sales turnover.
Source: Intermarché co-operative, 1996

(*Procomarché*). However, supermarkets account for 85 per cent of the sales turnover (see table 14.1).

The second advance taken by Intermarché involved internationalization, but only in respect of supermarkets. The phenomenon is relatively recent, with the opening in 1988 of an Intermerca store in Spain. Since then, the Iberian Peninsula has become a major market offering the most interesting possibilities for development with Intermarché becoming one of the five leading multiple retailers in Portugal. Internationalization is continuing in Italy, Germany and Belgium. The management team has in fact laid out an ambitious project: make Intermarché the leader of the 'Europe of the co-op'.

But the greatest innovation of the company is undoubtedly its unique policy of manufacturing concentration in Europe, whereas the other food retailers have progressively sold their former plants. For about 15 years, Intermarché has built or acquired 24 production units and several shipping companies whose sales were more than US$ 2 billion in 1996. The production units acquired mainly belonged to small businesses in the agri-food industry (mineral water, meat, beer, seafood, etc.) with a well-known corporate brand name and distributing quality products.

Until the end of the 1980s, the acquisition of manufacturers was not the result of an intentional aim at diversification, but rather of opportunities, for example taking over a family business without a successor (Secher, 1995). This is no longer the case. The company has a deliberate strategy of creating an 'industrial heritage' for two main reasons. First, the company wants to secure safe sources of supply for its own brands, which represent 25 per cent of supermarket inventories. Secondly, the company wants a counter force to multinationals during commercial negotiations (Paché, 1997) believing that owning factories gives more freedom to act.

In brief, Intermarché is in favour of vertical integration to allow the co-operative members to be less dependent on their environment. It is unquestionably a contrary policy as other multiple retailers are concentrating on core skills and are abandoning manufacturing activities. This will to directly control the supply chain is also quite obvious at the level of planning and of physical distribution.

◇

CONTROLLING THE SUPPLY OF PRODUCT

For Jean-Pierre Le Roch, controlling the supply processes of the branch network has been, since the founding of the co-operative, a *critical dimension* so as to challenge the competition of powerful chains of hypermarkets. The reasoning is simple: if the chains of hypermarkets such as Carrefour and Auchan succeed in selling at low prices, it is among other things because they buy at cheaper prices from suppliers through their buyers' capacity to negotiate and, above all, on the volumes bought. A co-operative of independent retailers wishing a strategy of cost leadership must consequently acquire structures that reach the same level of buying performance, and even an higher level through a optimization of logistics (Secher, 1995).

The creation of Intermarché thus resulted from the desire to implement a supply policy which was daring at the time, but which was later widely imitated by other multiple retailers: the centralization of purchase and logistics operations. Characteristically, the Deputy Chief Operating Officer of the Promodès group readily admits that in 1996 'concentrating volumes by large geographical areas is a *key tool* in optimizing flows at the national or regional level' (Salto, 1996, p. XIV). Furthermore, by guaranteeing the most efficient supply conditions to its members, a co-operative ensures their loyalty and consequently its own durability. For more than 25 years, Intermarché has never abandoned this 'philosophy' which may be summed up as follows.

First, purchase of large quantities of goods makes it possible to get attractive differential prices from suppliers. So that the members do not bear prohibitive storage costs in each of their outlets, inventories must be kept at the regional distribution centres (RDCs). This also helps increase the space in outlets dedicated to sales by reducing both storeroom and delivery bay congestion. Secondly, these RDCs are systematically located out-of-town, where the ground rent is low. 70 per cent of Intermarché's logistical sites are currently located in local communities of less than 10,000 inhabitants, close to motorways. In order to avoid bureaucracy and reduce distances in reaching sales outlets, the size of the RDCs is deliberately reduced, but not their numbers. Thus, each RDC has to supply from 80 to 100 outlets within a radius of 130 miles and employs a maximum of 400 salaried staff. Thirdly, and consequently, none of the co-operative members must feel remote from the logistical facilities, which could encourage them to negotiate with geographically closer suppliers, or even with wholesalers, to obtain better delivery conditions. Thus, the development of the sales front of supermarkets and diversification to new formats systematically go together with a quantitative expansion of the depot network.

Based on these three major principles, the Intermarché logistics organization is characterized by the extreme simplicity of the supply modes to the outlets, since 85 per cent of products go through the RDCs before order picking and final delivery. From this point of view, the company closely resembles the 'British model' (Fernie and McKinnon, 1991). This choice concentrates transportation from the factories and helps in making significant economies of scale. It also has the advantage of simplifying operations of order processing and invoicing for the co-operative members while eliminating wholesalers. In other words, logistics play an active part in Intermarché's strategy of cost leadership.

Only a few categories of products do not go through an RDC. These are, among others, household appliance supplies, directly delivered by the manufacturers since it is only a minor activity for the supermarkets. In the same way, perishable products such as fruit, vegetables and poultry, mostly supplied by local producers, are taken in charge by specialized middlemen specifically skilled in purchasing and logistics.

Each RDC has a transportation management service whose mission is to organize routes, not only for replenishing the outlets, but also for picking up products from suppliers and from the co-operative factories. Once the products have been collected, they are sent to other RDCs for delivery to the sales outlet. Most of the RDCs have both a collection and a redistribution function. (Aurifeille et al., 1997).

INTEGRATING WAREHOUSING AND TRANSPORTATION ACTIVITIES

Giving up direct supply and eliminating wholesalers to replace them by deliveries via RDCs does not necessarily mean that the retailer personally

Table 14.2 Intermarché's depot network in France at the end of 1996

	Number of RDCs	Storage capacity ('000 m^2)
RDCs for fresh and deep-frozen products	19	594
RDCs for grocery and household products	17	396
RDCs for household appliance supplies	3	165
RDC for cash & carry outlets	1	8.5
RDC for hard-discounting outlets	1	7.5
Total	41	1,171

Source: Intermarché co-operative, 1996

takes over the operations of physical distribution. Logistics may be contracted to a third party while keeping control over the design. This is not the case of Intermarché, whose main characteristic is the strong integration of warehousing and transportation activities upstream of the shop.

Logistics is a source of competitive advantage. Jean-Pierre Le Roch has consequently chosen to control the function without wholesalers by building new RDCs, specialized by categories of products, as the branch network has developed (see table 14.2). At the end of 1996, Intermarché thus had 41 RDCs spread over seven economic regions (compared to only 11 RDCs in 1984). The storage capacity was 1.2 million m^2 compared to about 3.3 million m^2 of sales space, which represents the largest for a food retailer in France – 65 per cent higher than the storage capacity of the major rival co-operative, Leclerc (Duong et al., 1994).

This model is also applied outside France. In Portugal, Spain and Italy, RDCs were built as soon as the sales volumes were sufficient. The same occurred in Belgium where about 30 outlets located in the French-speaking part of the country justified the opening of a 34,000 m^2 RDC in June 1995. Intermarché chose to abandon the transitional logistical organization based on replenishment from French RDCs, which is still the case for Germany.

The same logic of integration appears in the other essential activity of the logistics chain – transportation. Intermarché, which uses road haulage only, is an own-account operator owning and renting about 2,000 articulated vehicles. This is an exceptional case in France, where other food retailers, for example Casino and Promodès, disinvested in transportation in the 1990s, and increasingly resorted to independent carriers. Of course, some RDCs resort to chartering occasionally, but this remains a marginal phenomenon. In fact, Intermarché wants to completely control transportation in so far as the volume of delivered goods is large and stable enough to amortize the capital cost in good conditions.

The implementation of integrated logistics is explained by the objective to create, then consolidate, the economies of scale and the experience generated by supply centralization. Obtaining the lowest costs depends on two factors. First, there is the ability to spread fixed expenses over an important volume of production or distribution. Secondly, there is the cumulative learning resulting from increased dexterity in repetitive activities and the discovery of better ways of organizing work (Day, 1984). This analysis is well-known in the field of purchasing, since the experience curve partly explains the favourable prices obtained by the multiple retailers during negotiations with suppliers. This is also true for physical distribution. Cumulative learning leads to a better organization of the handling, order picking, delivery, etc. activities, while the quantities of goods handled by the RDCs make it possible to get significant economies of scale. But what would happen if the level of activity of these RDCs was significantly reduced?

THE MOVE TOWARDS A NEW PURCHASING POLICY

The Intermarché retailer co-operative is indubitably one of the precursors of the 'French-style' discount. Even today, Intermarché maintains its low price policy by passing on to the consumer the greater part of its increasing productivity, notably in logistics. Its gross margin thus ranges between 13 per cent and 15 per cent, that is seven points less than other firms, for example Comptoirs Modernes, which also specialize in the supermarket format.

As was previously said, the low price policy is the result of a rigorous organization of purchasing, entirely dedicated to the search for better price conditions with suppliers. Intermarché has a central purchasing office in charge of commercial contacts with powerful multinationals at European level. It has a justified reputation for aggressive negotiation. To this central purchasing office are associated about 15 regional purchasing offices whose mission is to complete assortments with local products.

The driving idea behind the purchasing policy is that only by increasing the volumes supplied to each outlet is it possible to demand quantity discounts high enough to benefit from lower costs than the other retailers. The logistical tools are thus used for a 'volume logic' which has been regularly progressing. As it owns a very large storage capacity, the company has well understood that it was easy to buy very large quantities of products to benefit instantly from promotional offers proposed by a particular supplier, but also

Table 14.3 Logistic capacities of Intermarché's major competitors

	Warehousing organization (*)	Storage capacity (SC) in '000 m²	Sales areas (SA) in '000 m²	SC/SA ratio
Auchan	C/I	170	580	0.29
Carrefour	C	276	1,200	0.23
Casino	C/I	550	1,585	0.34
Comptoirs Modernes	C/I	212	610	0.35
Cora	C	64	475	0.13
Leclerc	I	625	1,650	0.38
Promodès/ Logidis	C/I	440	1,300	0.34
Système U	I	390	1,020	0.38

(*) Contracted (C) or integrated (I) logistics.
Source: Personal survey, 1995

to anticipate price increases. These speculative inventory practices (or 'forward buying'), also current in the United States for dry groceries, deep-frozen food and personal-care products, were the backbone of Intermarché's purchasing policy in the 1980s. Almost half the products were then bought on special offers and covered the needs of the outlets for several weeks or even months of sales. This may explain why the RDCs built during that decade were *systematically and deliberately overdimensioned*. It was essential to buy in very large quantities, then stock in very large quantities. It is possible to measure objectively the extent of the phenomenon with the ratio of storage capacity in RDCs to sales areas in retail outlets. Estimated at 0.45 for Intermarché supermarkets (450 m² of storage capacity for 1000 m² of sales areas), it is only of 0.38 for Leclerc, 0.29 for Auchan and even 0.13 for Cora (see table 14.3).

It was not until the 1990s that a profound change took place, leading to a complete reformulation of the purchasing policy. Now, priority is given to accelerating the stock turnover by, if possible, relying on a replenishment triggered by actual sales in the outlets. As a result, between 1989 and 1996, the level of forward buying collapsed because, although the basic inventory was still seven days, the speculative inventory decreased from 13 to six days.

How can such a change be explained? Two reasons are mentioned by Intermarché's management team. First, suppliers now work with the multiple retailers, and are more ready to accept spreading their promotion campaigns over the whole year. Secondly, with the improvement in cost accounting, and more particularly since the introduction of the Direct Product Profit (DPP), it has been found that the savings made in purchasing are no greater than the increased logistical expenses induced (Paché, 1995). This second reason is particularly interesting to examine since it shows the impact that a new management tool may have on decision-making. Schematically, the DPP subtracts the costs of physical distribution from the gross margin obtained by marketing a product (selling price *minus* purchase price). With its forward buying, Intermarché had entirely focused on good purchasing bargains. The introduction of the DPP made it possible to see that the actual profit from these practices was smaller than expected, because warehousing and inventory costs were previously underestimated.

IS INTERMARCHÉ THE PRISONER OF ITS LOGISTICAL INVESTMENT?

With the reformulation of its purchasing policy, the Intermarché retailer co-operative is today confronted with a recurring problem: the increased availability of a storage capacity previously used for the speculative inventory. This storage capacity induces fixed expenses which will have to be reflected either in the selling price to the consumer, or in the buying price from the suppliers during commercial negotiations. Here is the major limitation of the Intermarché model whose success rested, until the end of the 1980s, on aggressive buying using integrated logistics as the preferred weapon.

If this model is threatened, it is because the company seems to be prisoner of its logistical investment. Indeed, the efficiency of the organization that has been set up depends on the maintenance, and if possible the growth, of the volume of activities. This volume depends of course on outside factors, like the stability of the branch network. But a retailer co-operative is an association of independent entrepreneurs who are free to join a competing co-operative or to sell to chain stores. Jean-Pierre Le Roch no longer hides his worries on the subject (*Enjeux–Les Echos*, 1995).

The redirection of the choices of physical distribution by suppliers is another outside factor which could have a significant influence on the volume of activities of the RDCs. Numerous manufacturers have become aware that by giving up logistics management, they were likely to lose the physical contact with the consumers and to suffer from jolts in the final demand depending on the multiple retailers' strategies. Some of these manufacturers have thus shown a desire to once more control the distribution channel. Specifically, their objective is to regain control over the direct supply of the outlets, for example Coca-Cola France, since 1993, has been delivering to its large accounts from its own seven regional warehouses.

It is easy to imagine the disastrous impact of the spread of such a behavior on Intermarché's logistical organization. With the volumes handled being constantly reduced, the goods which still go through the RDCs would suffer increasingly higher fixed expenses. Confronted with the increase of the invoiced logistical costs, members of the co-operative would leave, which would reduce again the volume of activities, and so on. In fact, this *snowball effect* is virtual only, but it shows how vulnerable Intermarché appears in its environment, when it was convinced previously that it was controlling it.

◇

WHAT THE FUTURE HOLDS

What is to be done so that logistics do not become a source of 'competitive disadvantage'? Several options may be envisaged, but are of varying feasibility. Some advise a reduction in the logistical facilities to progressively adjust capacities to needs. Others focus on the expansion of the volume of activities by developing the supermarket format or currently marginal distribution formats.

Restricting logistical facilities

The contraction of forward buying, the return to direct supply and the potential departure of a large number of co-operative members may result in an enormous storage overcapacity. Is it possible to let RDCs go? Or more accurately, can one schedule the closing of one or several RDCs? Leaving aside the employment implications of such a decision, it has to be admitted that the French warehousing market has been experiencing a recession for several years which makes a massive divestment difficult, for lack of financially sound acquirers. For example, the Intermarché RDC located near Marseilles and closed in 1991 following a several months-long strike (it has been replaced by an RDC built near Toulon) has still not found a purchaser five years later.

The immediate closing of RDCs is made difficult by another technical problem. The logistical pattern was designed for the replenishment of outlets in a maximum radius of 130 miles so as to optimize transportation activities.

The loss of one or several RDCs would have the consequence of creating 'dark areas' in the depot network, which would be unacceptable in terms of costs and consumer service.

There remains the solution of a transfer of logistics to a third party, who, in exchange, would work both for Intermarché and other shippers. Examples are numerous in industry, such as SATEM, the logistical subsidiary of the Unilever group sold to Danzas in 1985. This type of strategic move seems, however, far from the co-operative culture, so strongly opposed to outsourcing. Yet, integrated multiple retailers up to now resorting to contractors often have the opportunity of restructuring the circulation of goods and of proceeding to a much needed rationalization (Quarmby, 1990).

Developing the commercial activity

If the adjustment of the depot network to changes in the branch network is not feasible through a divestment policy, the other solution is to work on the expansion of the volume of activity to amortize the capital cost. This means developing the basic distribution format, the traditional supermarket, and also developing other distribution formats which are for the time being still marginal in the sales, for example small size convenience stores and the hard-discount stores. This solution, chosen by the management team, meets with two difficulties:

1   To develop significantly the commercial activity requires finding new members, unless it is accepted that some of the current members are allowed to own more than three outlets – which is the rule today. The democratic running of the co-operative obviously seems threatened. Members more powerful than others might take advantage of their position and impose their own vision of the future. It is therefore essential to create a new generation of independent entrepreneurs, despite the rather negative image of Intermarché, through, among other things, advertising campaigns in the general public press. This was undertaken in the summer of 1996.

2   French regulations authorizing the setting up of large self-service stores have become particularly restrictive, which means that the expansion of commercial activity can only involve outlets of less than 350 m^2 sales area. This could give rise to accounting problems for logistical procedures between distribution formats. Order picking and delivery modes are in fact very different between the traditional supermarket on the one hand, and the convenience and hard-discounting

stores on the other. In these conditions, a common logistics system based on the handling of mixed volumes of flows, and allowing economies of scope, seems hardly likely. Paradoxically, the development of new distribution formats should even require additional RDCs.

The Intermarché retailer co-operative now finds itself at a crucial moment of its history. After being instrumental in its rise, will the physical distribution system be the cause of its fall? The next five years will be particularly interesting to follow. We should then know if, after Jean-Pierre Le Roch's retirement in December 1993, the management team will be able to put aside his inheritance and make the logistics organization flexible.

———— QUESTIONS ————

(1) How does managing the logistics operation affect the feasibility of operating a chain of discount stores?

(2) What cost considerations are there in deciding the balance between direct store delivery and using regional distribution depots?

(3) Is Intermarché a prisoner of its own logistical investment?

References

Aurifeille, J.-M., Colin, J., Fabbe-Costes, N., Jaffeux, C. and Paché, G. 1997: *Management Logistique: une approche transversale*. Paris: LITEC.

Day, G. 1984: *Analysis for Strategic Market Decisions*. St Paul: West Publishing.

Duong, P., Mattiuzzo, N. and Paché, G. 1994: *La Logistique de la Grande Distribution*. Paris: Editions Eurostaf.

Enjeux–Les Echos 1995: Indépendants: la fin de l'âge d'or, No 108, 100–3.

Fernie, J. and McKinnon, A. 1991: The impact of changes in retail distribution on a peripheral region: the case of Scotland. *International Journal of Retail & Distribution Management*, 19(7), 25–32.

Paché, G. 1995: Speculative inventories in the food retailing industry: a comment on French practices. *International Journal of Retail & Distribution Management*, 23(12), 36–42

——— 1997: La sélection des PME par les détaillants français: une perspective stratégique et logistique. *Gestion 2000 – Management & Prospective*, 13(5), 147–60.

Quarmby, D. 1990: Changes in the physical distribution of food to retail outlets. In Fernie, J. (ed.), *Retail Distribution Management*, London: Kogan Page, 173–83.

Rosenbloom, B. and Dupuis, M. 1994: Low price, low cost, high service: a new paradigm for global retailing? *International Review of Retail, Distribution and Consumer Research*, 4(2), 149–58.

Salto, L. 1996: Toward a global retailing: the Promodès case. In Dupuis, M. (ed.), *Proceedings of the 4th EAERCD Conference*, Paris: ESCP, pp. XI–XXII.

Secher, R. 1995: *Jean-Pierre Le Roch, de l'exil aux Mousquetaires*. Noyal-sur-Vilaine, Editions ERS.

15

Finding the Right Location: A Case Study in the Ethics of Retail Location

PAUL WHYSALL

OVERVIEW

This case study focuses on a proposed superstore development in the city of Nottingham. The background to the proposed development is summarized and this highlights conflicts between different perceptions of the 'right' location between the retailer, residents, local shopkeepers, planners, and the health authorities who owned the site. It is argued that this constitutes an ethical problem rather than a technical one, and some ethical theoretical approaches are briefly introduced to suggest some ways in which it might be handled as such.

KEY WORDS

Retailing, Location, Planning, Ethics, UK

THE ISSUES

In the literature of retailing, few topics have received more attention than location, and the notion that finding the right location is essential for retail success is rarely challenged. But what do we mean when we talk of the *right* location? Right for who? Traditionally, techniques for locating stores have assumed that the answers to these questions are straightforward: right in terms of maximizing turnover, and right for the retailer. The underlying assumption is that those answers also imply that the location is right for the shoppers, since an optimal location is defined as one which the greatest number of customers will use. The assumption that right for the retailer is the same as right for the consumer is, however, questionable. For example, most formulations of central place theory aim to maximize consumer accessibility and convenience, by minimizing excess profits, and that clearly implies that the right locational solution for the shoppers is *not* the same as the most profitable solution of the retailer.

In the practical realm of retail location, more intuitive and less quasi-scientific methods such as checklists and analogues are often used by retailers. In moving to this more practical realm, it becomes clear that the retail location decision cannot be isolated from a wide range of other issues: competitors' locations, traffic flows, public transport provision, non-retail uses, and so forth. Also, it becomes apparent that planning policies and controls are an important concern. That is to say that the concept of a 'right' decision is not capable of being determined solely in terms of the interests of the retailer and potential customers. This means that the notion of a 'right' decision will often involve a trade-off between many interests, implying effectively that the problem becomes an ethical problem rather than a technical one.

THE CASE

Sainsbury's in Sherwood

In 1994, Nottingham City Council received an application for planning permission to build a 6,500 m² superstore in the suburb of Sherwood. The site for the store was to be on land in the grounds of the Nottingham City Hospital. The public debate which ensued over the proposal was prolonged and wide ranging, and was extensively reported in the local newspaper, the *Nottingham Evening Post* (NEP henceforth), and on local radio. Much of the public criticism of the scheme focused around adverse impacts on Sherwood's traditional shopping centre. According to a retail consultants' report presented to the county council in 1988, Sherwood 'is a linear centre on a busy main road. It enjoys rather more success than this location would suggest. It . . . does not have a major modern foodstore. There would appear to be scope to improve convenience facilities but due to the length of the centre and the presence of the main road its potential is limited.' At that time, the shopping centre was estimated as having a total sales area of 44,400 m^2., of which about one third was convenience goods retailing.

The initial proposal for a store on the 3.9 ha site was opposed strongly by local shopkeepers through the activities of the Sherwood Shopkeepers' Association (SSA). In September 1994, more than 50 shopkeepers launched a petition against the store, claiming support from local residents who feared traffic congestion in the vicinity of the site and disturbance to patients in a nearby hospital. Eventually 2,500 signatures were obtained. The chairman of the SSA was quoted as saying:

> If these plans get the go-ahead, half the shops in Sherwood will shut because Sainsbury's will pinch our customers. We deal with a lot of elderly people who view the local shops as part of the community. They are the ones who will suffer if Sherwood closes down, because they don't have the cars to get to a superstore. (NEP, 1.9.94, p. 12)

Opponents also suggested that the opening of the new Sainsbury's store might precipitate the closure of the company's outlet in Arnold, a few miles north of Sherwood. Previously, when the company had opened a new store at Castle Marina, Nottingham, an undertaking had been given to keep the company's then city centre store open for three years but at the end of the three years the city centre store was closed. Here, the company gave a commitment to keep the Arnold store open for one year after the Sherwood store opened, after which they said they would review the position.

City council planners appeared sympathetic to the opponents' claims, although impacts on Sherwood were seen as lesser concerns than those on three other nearby centres. They also perceived possible problems of traffic congestion (NEP, 11.1.95, p. 7). A study was undertaken into this and four other potential store developments in the northern part of the city which suggested that three of these, including the Sherwood site, might have adverse impacts on neighbouring centres, notably the Hyson Green centre in one of the poorer parts of Nottingham's inner city. The importance of jobs in the

Hyson Green superstore was a further area of concern for some. Conflict with revised government advice on out-of-town retailing was also claimed as a basis for rejecting the proposed development.

In January 1995, when it appeared likely that the city council would refuse planning permission for the store, Sainsbury's withdrew the application 'at the last minute' (NEP, 12.1.95, p. 5). A month later the company confirmed its intention to submit a new scheme. Again the SSA proclaimed their opposition:

> This scheme could ruin Sherwood shopping area. It would take our customers and the place would resemble a ghost town. The people who would suffer are the elderly and people with children. We are not just shopkeepers after their money, we are part of the community. (NEP, 14.2.95, p. 5)

The report went on to suggest that a buyer had been found for Sainsbury's Arnold store, but the company denied that.

In March 1995 a new application was made, this time on a 4.5 ha. site. The plan envisaged a 5,896 m^2 food store with parking for 538 cars, together with a restaurant and petrol station. The health authorities were said to be gaining £15m for the sale of the site. The City Hospital Trust argued that without this money developments such as a new medical centre would be delayed. The store would create 350 new jobs, it was claimed. The new proposal had been amended in the light of previous criticisms of highway access, and offered landscaping to screen the store from the hospital. Sainsbury's development surveyor was quoted as saying that the City Hospital site was the only available site in the vicinity, and that the company had 'been looking for years and we have been frustrated with our Arnold store. It has a limited range of goods and inadequate car parking', although initially they would see how the two stores traded side-by-side (NEP, 31.3.95, p. 16).

Opponents of the development claimed 200 people attended a protest meeting, where another petition was launched. Both Labour and Conservative candidates in local government elections expressed opposition to the development. The Conservative councillor was quoted as wishing to retain open space while the Labour candidate expressed sympathy for local opponents to the scheme (NEP, 3.5.95, p. 4). Both candidates expressed concern over traffic and impacts on Sherwood and Arnold.

The company had sent brochures to 40,000 homes of local residents, as well as councillors, which stressed the benefits to the hospital from the sale of the land. A company spokesman was quoted as saying this was part of Sainsbury's policy of community awareness and involvement: 'Sainsbury's does this for every site. It has a corporate policy of community care and being community-conscious.... It's not just a planning issue. It's about health-care and the people who live there' (NEP, 4.5.95, p. 16). The supporters of the proposal argued that the land was surplus to healthcare needs and the development would create more surplus land after empty buildings were demolished. Apart from the income to the health authorities, the scheme would also include a deal to redesign a congested road junction nearby.

In seeking to counter the opposition of Sherwood traders, the company publicized research findings that claimed that of the target shoppers for the store, who were described as weekly shoppers using a car, less than one-fifth did their main household shopping in Sherwood. Sherwood shoppers were said to be predominantly pedestrians (60 per cent), and 70 per cent of those surveyed said the convenience of shopping near to home was the main reason for shopping there. Hence, the company claimed, the new store 'will not compete with shops in Sherwood but with other large supermarkets in north Nottingham' (NEP, 25.5.95, p. 12).

The health authority tried to distance itself from the details of the debate beyond saying the land was surplus to health service requirements and that any proceeds would be reinvested into developing and improving local health services (NEP, 21.6.95). Further details of Sainsbury's survey data suggested that 57 per cent of 930 people surveyed within a five-minute drive time radius of the site favoured the store, suggesting 'there is a silent majority behind the proposal'. However, the Chairman of the SSA was unimpressed, arguing that this was a wide area, but local opposition was still strong as evidenced by a second petition, now with 2,750 signatures (NEP, 26.6.95, p. 5).

Planning department officers produced a report to the city council recommending rejection of the scheme in September 1995. The rejection was to be based on the store ruining the 'vitality and viability' of shops in Arnold, Hyson Green and Top Valley, and being likely to undermine prospects for upgrading facilities in Sherwood, where permission had been granted to redevelop and upgrade a Kwik Save discount store (Report of Director of Development, 14.9.95). The city's planning committee voted unanimously to reject the proposal, although Sainsbury's were said to be disappointed and contemplating an appeal to the Secretary of State. One councillor argued that the land should be safeguarded for future hospital development, ignoring the health authority's assertions that it was surplus to requirements, and that they wanted the income from the land sale. Councillor Taylor went on to say: 'It is a sorry state of affairs when we have to fund hip replacements by selling off hospital playing fields' (NEP, 15.9.95, p. 3). Shortly after this, Asda were reported to be interested in another site in the north of the city, with a city council officer suggesting that although few suitable sites existed in the north of the city, several other retailers had been awaiting the outcome of the Sainsbury's application (NEP, 19.9.95).

ETHICAL APPROACHES AND RETAIL LOCATION

Alternative ethical frameworks

If we interpret the problems deriving from the proposed Sherwood store as ethical in nature, then the problem becomes one of applying an acceptable ethical model to the case. Of course, even a passing familiarity with ethical theory suggests that many contrasting approaches *could* be invoked, so it is perhaps legitimate to consider a number of approaches.

Deontology, or the science of duty, suggests that moral agents have a duty to act in certain ways, usually in response to some fundamental belief. The report by the Director of Development to the City Planning Committee notes objections from the Open Space Society seeking to keep the site reserved as open space, and the Nottinghamshire Wildlife Trust on similar grounds as well as the severance of a wildlife link. However, whilst some might perceive fundamental principles to be involved here, such objectives do sometimes have to be infringed by retail planning, suggesting that the alternative approach of *teleology* or *consequentialism* seems the more appropriate route to follow. Indeed, generally this seems to be appropriate:

> Applying these ethical distinctions to urban planning, it is clear that the prescriptive nature of the planning process makes it concerned with normative ends or goals; and thus it is a teleological activity in which issues like the inherent or resultant social justice should rightly be questioned. (McConnell, 1981, p. 143)

None the less, before leaving deontology, we might consider some basic ethical concepts and their relevance to the case. It might be asked if any fundamental *rights* are at issue here; traders might feel a right to trade 'fairly' is at stake, or residents may feel property rights are at issue. There are those who would contend that ethical arguments based on rights are more appropriately pitched at the individual level, whereas this case raises several communal issues.

If a rights-based framework is inappropriate or insufficient, perhaps there may be guidance from concepts such as *justice* or *welfare*. Such considerations tend to move us into a consequentialist approach, however, requiring estimation of relative gains and losses, and an evaluation of outcomes.

Perhaps the most elementary form of consequentialism is *egoism*, meaning putting one's own interests at the forefront, but the main parties in this case have all set their arguments out in terms of wider community interests.

Utilitarianism is probably the most familiar consequentialist framework, built around a Benthamite concept of the balance of human happiness, or the maximization of 'utility' after Mill. To seek something approaching the greatest good for the greatest number could well invoke parallels with such as cost-benefit analysis, but here problems of quantifying such as the loss of open space or negative visual impacts pose daunting problems of measurement. Another problem is how to define the 'community' within which to undertake the appraisal. Sainsbury's were able to claim general benefits and approval across a wide catchment, whereas the SSA pointed to negative impacts at a more localized level of analysis; the catchment area problem is not merely a technical challenge, but also seemingly impinges upon our ethical analyses. More generally, the view that through some variant on the stakeholder model we can gain a framework for resolving ethical problems is also potentially dangerous. A single individual may be a member of many relevant stakeholder groups (local shopper, resident, company shareholder, retail employee, conservationist, etc.), and if stakeholders include all those who are potentially affected by the decision, is there any limit to the population to be considered in an era of global environmental awareness? Then, even if we do identify stakeholder groups, who is to prioritize them?

The British planning process almost inevitably raises questions of paternalism. Is it right for those in key political or professional roles to prevent some enjoying better shopping facilities in order to protect other vulnerable groups? Or, should Sherwood be a place where one takes from the rich to give to the poor in the style of Robin Hood? A related issue here is the nature of the utilitarian framework to be employed: should the process provide what most people want (*preference utilitarianism*), or what is in the interest of the majority (*interest utilitarianism*)?

Then there are those who would contend that rather than maximizing benefits to the majority, we should focus our efforts on minimizing disadvantage to minorities, or more basically opting for the least harm to the fewest number (*negative utilitarianism*).

Clearly, then, to portray the problem as one with ethical connotations is one thing, but it would be quite another to assume that this then meant a simple resolution by applying any single ethical 'rule'. The inherent tension between several such rules may even lead us to reject that avenue of inquiry in favour of some other approach, perhaps akin to Aristotelian virtue theory.

REFLECTIONS ON THE CASE

It would be quite unreasonable to portray any of the key actors in the case study as having acted with anything but the best of motives, virtuously one might argue. Hence the problem of whether or not the development should be allowed is more a matter of the interpretation of information than any fundamental principles.

Sainsbury's Development Surveyor offered the following views on the company's behalf:

> We believe locating the store in the right place to satisfy our own commercial interests directly satisfies the requirement to locate the store in the best possible place for the customer. In identifying a suitable location for a foodstore and developing the concept of that store, we are clearly seeking to target a particular sector of the food retail market. We accept that our stores are predominantly aimed at the 'once a week' or 'once a fortnight' bulk food shopper who wishes to shop by car. . . . That is not to say that such stores are not also accessible to other sectors of the market and without doubt, they will be used by people without cars . . . Other sectors of the market are served by other retailers with different formats of store that cater more specifically for the sector of market they are seeking to serve. (Personal communication, 15 November 1995)

Can this be portrayed as a utilitarian approach of seeking the greatest benefits to the greatest number?

The Sherwood shopkeepers, however, were most concerned that any loss of trade to them would have adverse impacts on their remaining customers who were seen to be elderly or disadvantaged. Might this loosely be termed a negative utilitarian stance of seeking to have minimal adverse impacts on minorities?

The city council's Director of Development took a view stressing negative retail impacts on existing centres, adverse environmental impacts through transport and highway implications, a need to safeguard the city's health provision needs and local visual and environmental impacts. This too might be seen as a utilitarian stance, but based on a different constituency of interested parties by comparison with Sainsbury's perhaps? The Director's report also addressed equality of opportunity, leading to the statement that:

> Out of centre stores are generally not as accessible to people suffering disadvantage and any detrimental impact on existing centres would be particularly detrimental to these groups. (Report, 14.9.95)

And then, through considerations of local residents, the health authorities, and so forth we can trace different interpretations of the same information leading to different judgements of the public good.

Acknowledgement

While this case study is based on the author's own findings and opinions, I am grateful for the assistance afforded me in preparing it, especially by employees of Sainsbury's and Nottingham City Council.

─────── QUESTIONS ───────

(1) Who are the stakeholders and what are their interests in the 'right' location for a supermarket?

(2) Should the store development process provide what most people want, or what is in the interest of the majority?

(3) How, as a local authority decision-maker, would you seek to balance the range of conflicting claims and interests?

Reference

McConnell, S. 1981: *Theories for Planning. An Introduction.* London: Heinemann.

16

The Early Socialization of Graduates into the Retail Industry

JACQUI GUSH

OVERVIEW

Using three different case histories, this case study tracks the development of three graduates over their first 18 months of permanent employment in a retail organization, with a view to discussing the factors which lead to successful socialization into a company, and an early contribution to company objectives. By implication the study addresses the issue of longer-term graduate retention in an industry without a tradition of employing large numbers of high calibre, formally qualified young people. The process of socialization is underpinned by the full range of personnel systems and practices, thus the case study has a wider applicability in the context of Human Resource Management.

KEY WORDS

Graduates, Retailing, UK, Socialization, Training, Management development

SANDRA

Background

Sandra joined the company after completing a vocational degree course chosen in order to equip her for a career in retailing. She sees herself as having a positive outlook on life, with a high degree of confidence, motivation and valuing high standards, and believes her upbringing promoted these values and attitudes. Her expectations of the company and the job were based on previous working experience with the company and thus she feels she knew what to expect.

She chose the company for the training she would gain and to strengthen her CV for future marketability.

She feels that knowledge of the company helped her significantly in the rigorous selection procedure, 'I got in because I knew what they wanted me to be', and in the assessment centre she made sure that she gave them what they wanted. Thus she was not surprised to have been selected and felt relatively prepared/attuned as she entered the company's employment.

Early job experience

On joining the store management trainee scheme, she had initial feelings of apprehension and felt 'like a spare part' where 'everything is so big and so new'. An initial one-week induction was structured, but confusing and overwhelming because there was so much to learn. Then followed a further seven weeks of structured learning on the shop floor as well as gaining early experience of some of the back-room functions. The on-the-job approach to training meant that in this short time she was expected to deliver in a managerial capacity at the same time as learning. She was soon participating in management decision-making and taking early responsibility for people.

She was surprised at such early responsibility and liked the immediate involvement. After the initial eight weeks, she was placed in the role of deputy supervisor. This produced a discernible step-up in her managerial responsibility and she found that the main challenge now was 'getting on with people'. One particular aspect of this challenge was having to manage individuals significantly older than herself. In previous group work and leadership roles undertaken this challenge had not arisen.

She did not feel that the technical skills needed for the job presented a problem, and felt she had learnt fast. However, the personal skills of time management and the ability to prioritize her own and others' tasks were a challenge.

As well as on-the-job training there were one day or half-day formal training sessions arranged for the trainees of a particular division, designed to cover relevant aspects of their learning and development, e.g. P&L accounts, presentation skills, objective setting and customer service.

An important aspect she had to adjust to was the hierarchical nature of the management reporting and communication structures. Coming from years of education, hierarchies were meaningless, thus responding to orders did not come easily, and it was a shock to discover that no longer was she in charge of her own time, that someone else was controlling her activities. Learning the nature of communication channels and how to use them effectively, informing upwards and as well as downwards was a learning experience. This handling of communication was integrally linked to learning the culture of the company: 'you have got to say the right thing at the right time'.

The culture

An impression of the company's values or culture was formed early on: 'I find the culture quite restricting. There is not much room for creativity, there is room for good ideas, within constraints'. She felt she wanted to challenge the culture, but realized that you 'do as you are told'.

The need to communicate upwards to create an impression and develop a profile with senior management was an important aspect of learning self-management. 'Your personality has to change to suit each individual. Relaxing with senior management is unheard of.'

Relationships

She was grateful for the support from colleagues, particularly other trainees, during these early weeks. Learning who to trust and thus on whom to unburden oneself was seen as a vital lifeline in turbulent, uncharted and potentially hostile waters. 'The environment is hostile ... you must assert yourself and communicate upwards. At the end of the day the only person who is really going to give an accurate description of what you have been doing and all the good things you have achieved, is you. Until you tell people who are perceiving your performance they don't have solid evidence.'

Sandra found the formal mentor system very supportive and felt able to trust her mentor, gaining a lot of emotional and moral support, as well as guidance on 'how to do things'. 'It's working for me', although she knew it did not work for others. In particular, she valued the regular contact or get togethers with all the other graduate trainees in the division through formal training sessions, meetings and presentations or informal gatherings.

Challenges regarding formal relationships seemed to focus on learning to manage upward, and there appeared to be significant focus on 'managing the manager', as well as subordinates. There is little contact with senior management who do not get involved with the trainees. However, it was seen as vital that trainees develop and nurture a profile to senior management, particularly with high profile visitors.

Skills learnt and employed

Sandra felt that she had been able to use a wide range of the technical skills which she had learnt at university. As part of day-to-day management she did not feel she employed her ability to analyse and reflect and evaluate alternatives as she had learnt to do in higher education, but the separate project work that trainees were set in addition to their ongoing responsibilities on the floor, gave her the opportunity and the satisfaction of continuing to use many of the skills associated with student days. She felt that her university experience continued to serve her well, 'I'm always pulling from it', both in terms of the understanding of commercial concepts and technical skills, as well as activities related to team work and managing others. She also felt that university 'prepared her mentally' and developed a 'strength of personality'. 'Toughness', resilience and assertiveness were traits needed for the job.

When asked about areas of satisfaction, aspects associated with managing self were mentioned, e.g. time management, planning and organizing, feeling totally in control. Her biggest area of challenge remained the effective use of interpersonal skills. In this connection negotiation skills were mentioned as well as leadership and the ability to listen in order to gain the respect of staff. She had been criticized for not delegating and remaining 'too involved'. Three months into the job, areas of 'stickiness' included: communication, the ability to manage hierarchy and 'politics' and developing the ability to approach senior management.

Feedback

Did she know how she was doing at this stage? Formal reviews were part of the system but they often did not happen automatically. It was necessary to push for them, to be assertive. She found positive feedback very motivating. She knew implicitly that the company expected very high standards, and found that she was becoming very self-critical, imposing even higher standards on herself than she thought the company would expect.

At this stage, despite the pressures of Christmas, where she felt she had been unable to meet her own standards, feedback helped her to realize that she was doing a good job. She got a buzz from the sales floor, found that she went to sleep and dreamt of the company, felt in control and had the much needed stamina, energy and enthusiasm to handle the pressure and expectations.

Expectations

She felt that the company expected a lot from the trainees. A good level of commercial information, knowledge and understanding, as a result of being on top of the job, despite being less than three months into employment; good communication upwards and downwards, good quality of work, from projects as well as day-to-day duties, and to make a good impression on head office visitors. She knew that she and the others were being pushed through the training rapidly, and that the challenge was 'to get to grips quickly', or risk being judged as a failure. There was undisguised competition between the trainees which seemed to be encouraged by management.

She was pleased that she had anticipated the long hours and the tough physical work. She kept stressing that retail is a special type of business, it could not be seen as just another company in terms of its demands and pressures. She had not expected to be part of the management team and to carry as much responsibility so early, but clearly this was a source of challenge and early job satisfaction.

First move

After eight months Sandra entered her second stage of training in a new store. She had elected to pursue a personnel specialism within the company and now she started this more focused, on-the-job training stage for the first time.

The first three months here were very difficult for her, several factors contributed to this. First, she was learning from the start once again, and felt like 'a fish out of water'. Secondly, a major contributory factor to this was the lack of training, 'I wasn't getting the training I needed'. In turn she found it difficult to manage her supervisor. All three factors resulted in a bad three-month review. She faced criticism of her communication, poor administration and an inability to manage her supervisor.

Critical incident

This presented her with a management challenge which had to be overcome if she was to succeed in going forward. She had to learn the job, and with only training guides, or manuals, available to her, on-the-job training meant working more effectively with her supervisor.

The reporting structure meant that the faster and better Sandra learnt the job, the greater the threat to the supervisor's position and status, as once Sandra was appointed as assistant to the personnel manager, the supervisor would then be reporting to her. It was not in the supervisor's interest to train someone who was to usurp her position once competent. Sandra felt that the supervisor did not have the experience to be in the position she was in. She was young and had been pushed through her training programme to meet the needs of the organization.

How could Sandra have dealt with this situation? 'I was too passive, I didn't know what I didn't know, it was difficult to learn because she was pushing me into the ground.'

Feedback re-visited

At a later stage, she emphasized more strongly how difficult it was to gain structured feedback very often, but how important it was in gaining a balanced and objective understanding of how you were progressing. 'You don't know to what, or whose standards you are performing.' She felt she had become so self-critical that her own judgement was unbalanced. Not helped by the fact that spontaneous feedback tended to be criticism. This can be very disheartening when it is not balanced with more positive comments, and less assertive trainees were known to suffer greatly from the lack of structured feedback.

Sandra seemed to be suffering from self-doubt. She knew the company expected a lot from her, but wondered, 'am I really going to be that good'.

'They push you as far as you can go.' It is easy to internalize the criticism and thus develop unrealistically high personal standards. The company becomes all-pervading, 'driving, driving till you are ill'.

Re-visiting the culture

How has she adapted to the culture over time? She went through a 'confusing stage', but came out of it stronger and believes she is still the same person deep inside. 'You get used to it, or you don't get used to it.' It is difficult to know who to trust, opinions are to be guarded and couched, 'I say what they want me to say.' She admits to dishonesty, or at least a lack of honesty in her formal relationships within the company. This is the 'underpinning for all formal relationships'. 'The art is to develop a dual personality and to ensure there are opportunities outside work to be oneself, while in work the qualities and characteristics demanded by the culture are demonstrated.' 'Learning the rules of the game' was seen as added pressure on the trainee. 'You have to understand the culture to do the job well.'

The future

She is certain that she will not be with the company in the long term. She sees no barrier to her career opportunities within the company, 'doors will open if you want them to, ... as much as you put in, you get out', but her choice at the moment would be to move on. She will know when the time is right to leave.

Her values had changed to the extent that she now appreciates the need for a balance between work and personal life and has learnt to value family and friends more, realizing the important role they play. 'There are more things to life than work.' In this respect she has learnt to manage herself and her life better and is learning to re-assess what she wants out of life. Therefore, apart from everything else, she feels that the requirement for infinite mobility may not suit her expectations in the future.

Figure 16.1 shows Sandra's assessment of her happiness on a scale of 1–10 at any point in time over the 18-month period she has been with the company. Sandra feels that her expectations have been well met and indeed exceeded. She has grown up and learnt a lot about herself and others. She has developed resilience and self-sufficiency and a confidence to cope with any situation. She realizes that she will continue to learn and is confident about her ability to contribute effectively to any company that employs her.

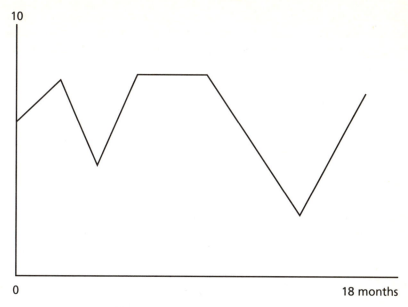

Figure 16.1 'Happy Chart' – Sandra

Through her ability to understand and manage herself and the knowledge and skills gained, she is confident that she will be able to achieve whatever she wants out of life.

JANE

Background

Jane joined her company after completing a languages degree at university. Despite not having a vocational educational background, she felt that she was prepared for what to expect from her organizational entry. Her father was a buyer for a retail company and she herself had worked abroad for a year in a small shop during her time out from university. In addition, her sister had worked for the company several years previously. She had an interest in retailing, particularly in dealing with merchandise.

Pay was apparently an issue amongst the graduates of this company as it was seen to be lower than other retailers. However, its reputation for training was what enticed Jane to accept the offer.

She sees herself as 'dogged', level headed and patient, as well as a little

timid and quiet. Her upbringing was supportive, and challenge and high performance were encouraged. Her school bred pride in achievement. Because
of her interest in merchandise, she had originally applied to head office for a
merchandise position. They had felt her commercial instincts were not sufficient and had recommended her for a store management trainee position. A
current relationship at that time had induced her to request a specific location, which had been agreed.

Introduction to the company

She had an initial induction week during which she felt she was well supported and 'felt at home'. Following this week she went onto three weeks as
a sales assistant undertaking 'little projects' as well as learning company
systems and procedures with the help of the resources of her supervisor and
training workbooks. In this initial period she received 'a lot more support
than she expected' and was pleased that she was in a department 'where
people really wanted to see you develop'.

She appreciated the early involvement of senior management in her training, 'they come to see you' and how they took an interest in the trainees. She
admits that she 'thrives on encouragement', and found they were 'not short
of praise'.

The job

In the early weeks she was a stage 1 trainee manager and worked closely
with her supervisor, preparing estimates for the department, attending meetings and getting involved with contact with head office. She felt the graduates were 'treated as potential', as 'something special'. 'The company makes
you feel they need you.' She learnt that her career progression was up to her,
and as the training was predominantly on-the-job accompanied by training
workbooks, she was able to set her own pace and progress at the speed that
she and her manager felt appropriate to her needs. They also tried to match
the personality and the development needs of the trainees to the branch and
its management, which she considered worked well. She had thought that it
would be 'more regimented', but found that she was given a lot of responsibility and a free reign, and was 'treated as part of the management team'.

Was her non-vocational background a problem to her? She said that she
had been supported in her learning and that 'much of the basic technical
knowledge is taught', while some she was expected to pick up herself

through reading and asking. She felt 'comfortable' with the development of her technical skills and she was able to 'probe' for commercial knowledge. Understanding the business and its commercial priorities 'needs to be constantly worked at to build', but she did not think it is a 'particular problem'. She believes that a vocational background would have helped 'to some extent' but, 'I haven't found it a problem. I had an interest in working in retailing.'

She believes the training is 'second to none'. However, in discussion she admitted that she sometimes felt a little isolated, as she was the only graduate trainee in the store and opportunities for meeting up with other graduates seemed limited. She would also have appreciated a broader experience of the company, as her training programme was limited to stores.

Critical incident

One problem was that six weeks into her employment her manager went off sick and as a result Jane was jettisoned into a supervisory role to do her job. As a result her formal training system was shelved and Jane was left to learn by experience. She received a lot of moral support but no one had time to spend with her and the onus was on her to ask and seek help when it was needed. She found the absence of her immediate boss to be a particular challenge over a three-week period at a critical stage in her development. The company appeared to have no fall-back plan and the general under-resourcing of the store meant that she was expected to shoulder the extra responsibility and automatically assume a great deal of accountability.

Her biggest challenges had been: first, the managerial responsibilities of dealing with people, learning how to phrase things and how to be tactful, and, secondly, learning to manage time when under so much pressure. Unlike at university where she could decide how her time would be divided and allocated, here she felt out of control, and felt as if she was constantly reacting and fire-fighting. As a 'perfectionist', she had to learn how to compromise and 'do the best you can'. However, she experienced frustration, 'you feel you haven't done well – haven't had the time to do a good job'. This was very different from her previous working experience, which had given her 'time to think and time to deliver'. 'You want to be involved in as much as possible' but she found that she could not do everything and had to prioritize.

Although she obviously learnt a lot over this period, she believes that it had not been the best way, as she made too many mistakes, especially in the handling of customers and their complaints. 'You don't want to step out of line, you must know company policy.' She recounts her manager saying ' "unless you are making mistakes you are not actually learning," but it doesn't make it any easier'. On reflection she found this period to be 'enjoyable, tiring but rewarding'. She enjoyed working with the staff and the merchandise, 'there is a buzz around the place'.

Needs and expectations

On leaving university, primarily she sought enjoyment in her job. One where 'I look forward to getting up in the morning and going to work.' Challenge in her work and responsibilities was seen to give her that enjoyment. Although she emphasizes that she tries to carry no expectations into a situation prior to experience, from what she had learnt about the company she had expected to achieve what she sought. The stamina and physical energy needed had not been expected, and she was suffering from tiredness which she believes affected her mental performance.

What did they expect of her? They expected her to be able to make her own decisions and use initiative, they expected 'to guide you, but not to lead you, you had to be your own person'. They expected total commitment, and here Jane had not expected the time commitment. She cited how management trainees were expected to do overtime without extra pay. After working a whole weekend in her early months, the only recognition she received was a thank you in person from the area manager. However, she considered that this was 'worth its weight in gold'.

Have her expectations been met? She felt that she had progressed well in the company and felt that she was doing a good job. She was pleased that she could develop at her own speed, but she had an element of doubt about whether she should be further in her career progression by this time and whether she should have pushed herself harder and whether the management have taken enough responsibility for her progression. She expects to be a manager of her own store within three years, but she is not clear about this.

First move

After 11 months, and a formal performance appraisal, she was moved to another store and onto stage 3 management. The movement between the stages of management training appeared to be quite fluid and flexible. A trainee can go straight onto stage 3, responsibility for a department, or in her case she became customer services manager for a larger store. The personality of this branch was quite different and she believes was chosen to meet her development needs at that time.

She was grateful for the support and friendship of another trainee in the branch and sharing accommodation with her helped her to settle into a new and unknown part of the country. The manager was less approachable and communicative. 'I need praise, and now I'm only told when I'm doing a bad job, not when I'm doing a good one. If I need an opinion, I don't get it. I could say the company is letting me down, but it's one person, not the company.' However, she knows that 'its up to you to make the most of it'. 'Its up to me to decide what my needs are and do something about it.'

She also had to face confrontation for the first time in her handling of staff. 'I don't like confrontation', but recognizes that 'I have to learn to deal with it' and she felt that she could 'work it out' from her past experience. She had been told by her manager that she was 'too nice'. She found discipline 'quite hard'. She missed the team spirit of her previous branch, which had a 'brilliant atmosphere'. 'So much depends on your branch manager. You learn to play to the manager at that time.'

At each stage the necessary formal training is 'pulled in' to answer individual needs, 'you tell them what you want'. She talked with enthusiasm and praise for the head office graduate training manager, who always kept in touch and listened to problems and supported trainees in their development.

University influence

She learnt self-discipline, self-motivation and confidence during her formative years in education. She also believes that her year out was an important experience in the context of her present position. She wanted to go into business when she left university and was ready to move on by the end of her course. She prefers 'doing' to theory, but now does miss the opportunity to reflect, discuss and think about issues. She comments that academic norms hold no value in the company.

Culture

Overall she finds the culture to be supportive and informal, but has learnt that this has changed dramatically over the last few years. She refers to the 'old boys network' and the residual traditional management styles still in the company. Hierarchical structures and autocratic decision-making are being overturned, and the company was seen to be making an enormous effort to change the culture and bring in new young managers. Recently, there has been a large number of management redundancies and at the same time the graduate intake increased. She is very grateful to have been in branches with a young management team.

However, in this store she now finds the 'buck is passed a lot' and within a hierarchical management structure, responsibility tends to get passed down the line. As an honest person who values fairness and integrity it is often hard to face and deal with 'injustice'. She kept stressing the ability to be yourself as a plus point of the culture.

She also commented that you cannot take the attitude that you are a graduate and therefore should be treated differently. It was important to show that you are 'willing to give as well as take'. In her previous branch it had 'amazed me and pleased me that they had thought of me as a human being, and not a graduate upstart'.

The future

She is happy in the company and does not plan to move on. She has a lot more to learn. 'If I stick with it they will make me a good manager.' She sees no barriers to her progression within the company. The perceived lack of opportunity to move to head office and pursue her original career choice was a regret.

However, although her relationship has now ended, she recognizes that there is more to life than just work, and that expected mobility may be a problem in the future. She recognizes that this is likely to be more of a problem being female. She wants to be able to stay for long enough in one place so she can build a life outside work, but feels she has no control over locational decisions.

Figure 16.2 shows Jane's 'Happy Chart' for the period under consideration.

CHAS

Leaving university

Chas completed a vocational degree course before joining his retail organization. His father owns his own retail business and Chas is a committed

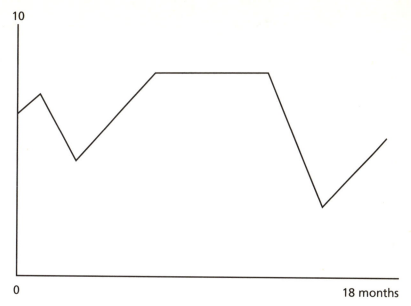

Figure 16.2 Happy Chart – Jane

retailer. He was the first of his family to go to university and did this in order to improve his career prospects and to get a good and a broad retail grounding. He considers himself to be ambitious, stubborn, hard headed, conscientious and independent.

On leaving university he applied to major blue chip retailers seeking good training and a good name to add value to his CV. Through the knowledge and confidence that his course had given him, on leaving university he felt that he 'could do anything'. Although he applied to graduate training schemes he decided he wanted 'an actual position' as a starting point to his career. He had completed a year's placement with a retail company as part of his course, and now 'wanted to do an actual job ... didn't want to be someone's dogsbody for another year'. He achieved more success with applications for actual job positions as opposed to training schemes, and found himself with four offers from which to choose.

Location and salary played a part in his final decision, as well as the reputation of the company and the actual job. He joined the head office marketing promotions team and was responsible for point-of-sale promotional material for the branches. He was particularly interested in product marketing and considered that down the road his ideal job would be in this area. However, he felt this was a good starting point and expected to be able to achieve his ideal job in a year's time.

The early experience

He considered that he had achieved a highly responsible and worthwhile position straight from university and felt confident that he could do the job and was satisfied that he was making a real contribution to the success of the company at such an early stage in his career. One aspect of this was being responsible for a team of people straight away, and it was obvious that he considered that this put him above his university peers.

The 'downside' to the job was that it was seen as 'a very specialist' position, and his aim was to try to get into a more generalist role within the company. At an early stage, he perceived that there was a lack of opportunity now within the organization as traditional generalist roles were being divided into increasingly specialist functions, 'no-one is a generalist', 'there are no traditional general roles for retailers'. He realizes that he needs to get a broader exposure to different parts of the business, but, 'it doesn't happen'.

Relationships

Chas felt a little isolated in his job, which was due to a combination of factors. First, he was five floors down from his immediate boss, whom he also judged knew little about the job Chas was doing and therefore was of little help and support to him. In addition, he felt his boss was inexperienced generally and this gave Chas a sense of insecurity. Because it was a specialist role, he did not feel part of a team, and felt a heavy responsibility for the group of young women who constituted his subordinates. He considered the management of people was 'a job in itself'.

He saw the company as 'greatly under-resourced' and that no one had time to help and guide him, 'everyone is rushing around'. He started to realize the disadvantage of not being considered a graduate trainee, in that he did not participate in any formal training and development programme and as a result never got to meet any of the other graduate recruits. He recounted an experience at the coffee machine on a recent occasion when he started speaking to another employee and discovered he was also a graduate who had joined the company at the same time as him.

A large company tends to be impersonal, he thought. This led him to feel like 'a little bit in a large machine'. Beyond relationships formed within his own department, there was little contact and mixing within the company, and a 'cold atmosphere'.

Training and development

The company did not have an official graduate trainee scheme, and only appointed graduates into specific positions. They offered little or no structured training programme, there is 'no special treatment for graduates to integrate'. You are 'treated like everyone else'. He had discovered that 90 per cent of the managers in head office in the company were graduates, so there was a graduate culture to the organization, but no trainee scheme. 'You're not special, everyone's a graduate', and as such you are expected to cope and contribute.

Chas had a one–two-day induction before being placed in his position. He had a two-week handover period during which he was expected to learn the job from the previous incumbent. What about training courses? 'You have to ask for training.' Another problem was seen to be that training courses were available according to grade, so despite his need (specially mentioned were the managing people aspects), if he was not the right grade, he was not eligible. He felt personnel and training functions in the company were remote from line management.

Appraisals were viewed rather cynically, and seen as a 'personnel pushed idea'. It seemed as if he had adopted this view based on the experience of others, as he felt these offer an opportunity to discuss and identify training needs. He feels that the company has no interest in developing him, rather they judge his performance in a specific job.

The knowledge and skills which he learnt at university have served him well, pointing particularly to the development of commercial awareness, rather than theory. 'You can't expect to leave university and use all the stuff you learnt.' But from university he considers that he understands 'why we are doing what we are doing and who we are doing it to'. He considers that he has a big advantage over 'everyone else' because he did a vocational course.

The culture

'You learn to work with others and respect hierarchy. You learn when to open your mouth and when to shut up. A lot of back-stabbing goes on. Everyone round here covers their back. Its an "I'm alright Jack" attitude.' This was seen to be because no one knew what was going on in the company, on an ongoing basis, and gossip and rumours had been rife concerning major changes and restructuring.

There have been recent attempts to change the culture when senior management held open meetings and conferences and spoke openly and positively about future plans. This led to a noticeably more positive atmosphere for a short time and everyone was a lot more friendly and open towards each other. However, it has now receded and things are the same as they were previously.

The job

To start with he tried to please, you 'do everything to please everyone'. Because he was remote from a boss who did not know his job, he learnt a lot from trial and error. He has learnt not to be such a perfectionist and compromise, 'it can't be 100 per cent'. This upset him to start with as he has always taken pride in his work and is conscientious. 'You learn to prioritize and manage your time more effectively.'

He has been criticized for not delegating more and thus not developing his staff. His previous experience of 'man-management', e.g. team work at university, Duke of Edinburgh Award Scheme etc. has helped him to manage his team. He points to the need to understand other people from their point of view, like how boring their jobs are and to understand the limits to their capabilities, and to work within this. To motivate them can be difficult. However, he now feels 'I have developed the team'.

Dealing with people generally has been a learning experience for him, particularly learning to handle people of different ages. His subordinates are young, but managers are represented across the age range. However, he feels that his confidence has helped him to present himself professionally and to 'argue his case'.

He is generally satisfied with his chosen career route to date, and considers his current job to be giving him invaluable experience to help him move on and up rapidly. This is an 'ideal job for the first year'. He now feels that he has outgrown the job and learnt all there is to know. He does not see the job providing the satisfaction he seeks in terms of 'a decision-making role' and 'high involvement in the running of the company'. There is 'little decision-making responsibility in the job. The job now lacks stimulation and challenge, it doesn't need much intelligence. I know I can do better.'

Expectations

He thinks that the company also is expecting him to use his current position 'as a learning, progressive role', as a 'training bed'. They expect him 'to do

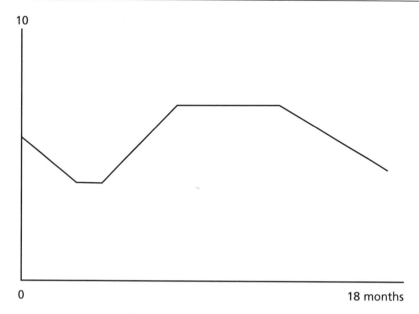

Figure 16.3 Happy Chart – Chas

the job to the best of his ability' and within a year to 18 months to progress on from there.

Is he confident? He has no concerns about being able to meet the needs of the company and still 'feels he can do anything'. Is the job and the company what he expected, is it how it was painted? He knew enough of the company, 'it wasn't oversold'.

He points out that the job on paper is often very different to the day-to-day experience. He did not expect as much paperwork and administration, and the people management side of the job was new to him. 'I'm not doing 100 per cent of the job in the job description ... Difference between what a job sounds like on paper and what it is in real life.'

Future prospects

Chas is waiting. The company appear to accept and agree that he needs to move on and keep 'using carrots' to reassure him that his case is being considered. However, Chas is unclear about where the opportunities lie and at the moment can not see any career path open to him within the company. Restructuring is muddying the waters and he feels it may be some time before a suitable vacancy occurs. Will he be prepared to wait as long as it takes? He knows his preferred career direction is product marketing and if it is not possible to pursue this in his present company, he will search elsewhere. He is already having interviews.

Figure 16.3 shows Chas's 'Happy Chart'.

————— QUESTIONS —————

(1) To what extent were the aspirations of the three workers met in their first job experiences?

(2) How might the training and development activity have been improved for each of the three people?

(3) For each of the three individuals what are the key upsides and downsides of their experience from the point of view of themselves and of the company for whom they are working?

Further reading

Hackman, J. and Oldham, G. 1980: *Work Redesign*. Addison Wesley.

Kolb, D. 1984: *Experiential Learning*. Prentice Hall.

Kotter, J. 1975: The psychological contract. *California Management Review*, 15(3), 91–9.

Porter, L., Lawler, I. and Hackman, J. 1975: *Behaviour in Organisations*. McGraw-Hill.

Porter, L. and Steers, R. 1973: Organizational work and personal factors in employee turnover and absenteeism. *Psychological Bulletin*, 80, 151–76.

Schein, E. 1964: How to break in the college graduate. *Harvard Business Review*, 42, 68–76.

—— 1968: Organizational socialization and the profession of management. *Industrial Management Review*, 9, 1–16.

—— 1978: *Career Dynamics*. Addison Wesley.

Spurling, A. 1992: *Investing in Talent*. The Council for Industry and Higher Education.

Van Maanen, J. 1973: Breaking in: socialization to work. In: *Handbook of Work, Organization and Society*, Chicago.

Vroom, V. 1964: *Work and Motivation*. Wiley.

Wanous, J. 1980: *Organizational Entry*. Addison Wesley.

Wanous, J. et al. 1992: The effects of met expectations on newcomer attitudes and behaviours: A review and meta-analysis. *The Journal of Applied Psychology*, 77(3), 288–97.

17

'A Christmas Fit for a Princes' Square': The Role of Design in Shopping Centre Positioning

MALCOLM LOCHHEAD AND CHRISTOPHER M. MOORE

——— OVERVIEW ———

This case study examines the role and contribution of design and visual merchandising in specialty shopping centre positioning. Using an actual design situation, the case examines both the shopping centre's design requirements, as well as the design management process, as followed by the commissioned designer. The case serves to highlight the significant contribution of design and visual merchandising to the generation of shopping centre identity and the wider customer communications mix. By understanding better the information and resource requirements of the commissioned designer, it is anticipated that the case will enable retail managers to maximize the potential benefits of design and visual merchandising within their business.

——— KEY WORDS ———

Retail design, Visual merchandising, Specialty shopping centres, Market positioning, Communications mix.

CONTEXT

A shopping centre to compare with the great of Paris, Milan and New York was the original intention for the new infill shopping centre to be constructed in Glasgow's Buchanan Street, the most fashionable shopping area of the city. And so it came to be. In 1987 the Princes' Square shopping centre opened, and instantly won national and international acclaim as a space of elegance, borne from its fine architecture, the use of the best quality materials and the skills of expert craftspeople.

Situated in Glasgow's most prestigious retailing area, and coupled with the elegance of the centre itself, Princes' Square was very soon established and positioned as a centre for the discerning shopper, and this was replicated in the tenant mix of the centre which included the most 'up-to-the-minute' fashion companies, specialty retailers and an assortment of bars and restaurants with an 'up-market' image.

This market positioning for Princes' Square was supported and endorsed by a carefully managed marketing communications programme, which included television advertising, quality press advertisements and radio coverage. But perhaps the most significant dimension of the Square's promotional armoury was the development of events within the Square, such as music recitals, fashion shows and art exhibitions, all of which sought to present Princes' Square as an integral element of the cultural life of Glasgow, as well as an important retail/commercial concern.

MARKET RESEARCH FINDINGS

Market research, commissioned by the Square's owners in 1993, and with the centre now well established, sought to inform of the profile of their customers and visitors. In particular, the research sought to understand customer motivation for visiting Princes' Square, as well as their perception of what the centre had to offer. Perhaps, not surprisingly, the research identified the following characteristics of Princes Square customers:

- a mature, affluent and discerning customer;
- a customer with high expectations of service;
- visiting the Square is seen as a leisure experience, either in a retailing or socializing capacity;

- high expectations of 'added value' from the Square, in the form of promotional events and visual merchandising;
- an expectation to see 'something different, sophisticated and interesting' from the retail tenant mix, the products on sale and the overall environment of the centre.

The managers of Princes' Square had succeeded in their aspirations for the positioning of the centre. However, by Autumn 1995, one important aspect of the Square's identity, that of the decoration and styling for the Christmas period, came under intense scrutiny both from the Centre Management Team and the retail and hospitality tenants housed within. Princes' Square customers expected the centre to be magical and exciting and to fit with the established image of the place. The tenants, in particular, no longer felt that Princes Square was satisfying this important customer expectation, at a crucial period in the trading year.

Independent research of the Square's customers found that they felt the Christmas decorations to be predictable and uninspired and, overall, a disappointment, considering the reputation of Princes' Square.

$$\Diamond$$

THE PROBLEM

From the time of its opening in 1987, Princes' Square was decorated in a traditional manner with a large Christmas tree and swags with gold decorations. This approach, having been well received by the public, was repeated for a number of years. In 1991, the traditional scheme was replaced with a 'futuristic' sculptural design. This sharp departure received adverse public reaction and was withdrawn after a very short lifespan. In subsequent years, Princes' Square's decorations centred around a set of textile banners illustrating the story of Cinderella. These were hung at the west end of the centre which was not an ideal positioning given that the best vantage point is directly opposite, and as a result the majority of customers were unable to see them to full effect.

The tenants of the centre have a committee which negotiates with Princes' Square management about events and seasonal promotions such as Christmas decorations. In August 1995, the committee had informed the management, in no uncertain terms, that they were unhappy with the decorations as they felt that they were inappropriate in style to the various audiences who visit the centre during the festive season. The various retail units house predominantly up-market fashion orientated shops and the general feeling was that the 'Fairy Story' theme did not reflect accurately the quality of the various stores. In addition, the decorations were held to be dull, too traditional and were looking exhausted. It was against this background that the commission for a new Christmas decoration scheme was received.

THE SOLUTION

The commissioned manufacturing company who had had previous experience of mounting exhibitions in Princes' Square were well appraised of the technical problems of the decoration of such a large and complex space but had no design competency. Consequently, a Glasgow designer with an international reputation in the designing of large-scale textile instal-lations was commissioned to undertake the design of the project.

The first meeting in late August was held on a day when the temperature was in the high eighties and most people's attention was focused on barbe-cues rather than on Christmas fare. The designer, two representatives of the manufacturing company and the centre manager met at Princes' Square. The manager explained the background to the project and stressed particularly the widely held dissatisfaction of the tenants of the centre. The designer did not receive a written brief (which is obviously not best practice) but instead received the instruction to 'design Christmas decorations which would be an improvement on what has gone before'. Only two stipulations were made. The first was that the decorations should not impede the view of visitors in respect of other retail outlets. The second was that there should be a Christ-mas tree, probably at the mid-point of the ground floor. Vague reference was made to having decorations which would be 'a bit more grown up'.

In the light of such minimal direction, the designer sketched some ideas to help the manager and the manufacturing company's representative to understand the embryonic ideas. These sketches could be described as the designer's private language or shorthand and would only be seen by the designer or by a very small audience in order to explain a concept visually.

A fee was then agreed for the production of concept drawings. Concept drawings are highly developed and could best be described as public lan-guage and are intended for a wider audience. Drawings of this nature are often described as 'artists' impressions'. A separate fee for these drawings was negotiated in order to cover the cost of time and materials should it be decided that the project would not go ahead.

The design and development process is potentially a difficult activity not only for the designer to complete but for the client to comprehend. A problem which is often faced by clients is that they do not understand or cannot accurately interpret the visual information being presented. To overcome this problem the Princes' Square designer used the medium of photography to establish context and impressions of the decorations were superimposed using both drawings and computer aided design techniques. As a result the proposed images were as accurate as possible and very easily understandable. It should be borne in mind that design has been described as a 'complex act of faith' and that a design is only a representation of a plan and that reality can often be disappointingly different, particularly if managers are not sufficiently informed and aware at the design stage. Normally, when a designer presents the designs, the clients can use the brief as a form of checklist to ensure that all of the requirements have been met. Sometimes, however, the designer may stray from the brief to follow a highly creative path which reaches a highly innovative answer. If the client is happy with the result then the project may go forward. If not, the designer is normally given the opportunity to modify the designs until an acceptable solution or compromise is reached.

The designer was given one week to produce the concept drawings. This is a very short space of time, since most designers require a period of 'navel contemplation' and research before putting pen to paper. The luxury of time was not available. A further pressure lay in the fact that no formal brief was available to the designer and he, in turn, had to construct his own system of constraints to check his creative thinking. The brief can be regarded as a set of constraints placed round the designer like a corral. The constraints might be, for example, a clearly defined target market, safety requirements, method of manufacture, capabilities of the manufacturer, costs, legal requirements etc. All of the potential constraints help to confine the designer's activities within what is possible. Designers almost always need constraints as they are highly creative individuals who can stray from the point without these accurate guidelines.

Imagine the designer's problem: 'design Christmas decorations which would be an improvement on what has gone before and that the public can view what is going on at the other side of the centre'. The problem assumes that the designer both knows what has gone before and that he has a good knowledge of the setting.

It must be stressed that the everyday users of buildings become blind to them, its possibilities and its shortcomings. For this reason, it is important that the designer becomes intimately knowledgeable about the building. This can be done by conducting 'user research'. This involved the designer becoming a customer, i.e. a user of the centre and finding out as much as possible about the way in which the building is used.

Princes' Square can best be described as a glazed atrium surrounded by retail units on four levels three of which are fronted by balconies. The centre is entered from its principal frontage on Buchanan Street by three possible routes: two at street level to the left and right and the third by means of an escalator which brings the customer into the centre on the top level. There is also a fourth entrance to the rear which brings the visitor in at street level. Within the centre the visitor then has three choices of accessing the various levels. First, by escalator, secondly, by glass lift and, finally, by a staircase. The grand staircase faces the three principal entrances and can be considered to be the focal point of the centre.

These considerations, when taken as part of the user research, became guiding principles for the decorations. It was considered to be very important that no matter how the visitor entered the square that there should be something festive visible. It should be borne in mind that because of the nature of customer flow their levels and points of view will change constantly. Having followed all of the conceivable routes which the customer might take, the designer was able to determine a number of major concepts for the design:

1 that there should be something large and eye-catching in the large void in the middle of the centre;
2 that the shapes involved should be curvaceous to echo the sinuous style of the architecture;
3 that the grand staircase and the walls and windows above it should be given a 'big' treatment.

Princes' Square is not a 24-hour centre, but does open in the evening to give access to the various restaurants and bars located there. For this reason, it was imperative to consider the impact of the decorations on the viewer under different light conditions. Having a glass roof and a south aspect, the building can be very sunny and bright, even in winter. The more regular grey winter light creates different problems and night yet more. Princes' Square has a number of lighting plots designed to cope with the changes mentioned above and to ensure that the centre, its tenants and their clients look their best at all times. Much of the lighting is very subtle and the light sources would not normally be noticed by the visitor. Others are included as part of the interior scheme to be a major element in the decoration of the centre. The most important decorative light fittings are installed at regular intervals on the balustrades of the three upper levels. They comprise wrought iron frames with art glass globes 30cm in diameter. Each level is a different colour, ranging from pink on the first level then blue and finally green on the top floor. These colours coupled with the predominant ambient honey colour, which comes from the pale sandstone walls and limed oak woodwork, prompted the designer to consider developing a pink, blue and green scheme. Many people would argue that these are not, perhaps, Christmas colours but the overall pallid colour scheme of the centre would make 'traditional' reds and greens look garish and prominent. It must be stressed that while seasonal decorations are vitally important in creating festive ambiance these should not interfere with the principal aim of a retail environment which is to sell goods.

The other principal instruction from the centre manager was that the customer should be able to see across the centre to other retail outlets. This, in turn, suggested the idea of creating transparent, softly coloured decorations which would be subtle yet eye-catching. The designer created a concept which included a giant, symbolic, tulle (transparent nylon net) tree, with each of the three levels echoing the colours of the light fittings previously mentioned. The festive element was introduced by the addition of silver tissue and net stars. The apex of the suspended construction was some 27 m from the floor. The scheme was carried through to the balustrades by creating metre-wide bows of tulle, silver net and tissue which were highlighted with 2 cm mother of pearl paillettes (sequins). The desired effect was to be magical, perhaps fairy wings? In the centre of the well of the atrium a 6 m grey/blue artificial Christmas tree filled with white lights and swagged round with a spiral of tulle pointed up to the symbolic tree above. The grand staircase which is dominated by a symmetrical group of doors and windows was punctuated by four 2 m trees which echoed the style of the central tree. The windows were enlivened by window boxes filled with artificial greenery wired with twinkling white lights and decorated with tulle bows.

The final problem was to create an eye-catching effect for the top level which is predominantly occupied by the food court. The centre roof is supported by huge steel arch constructions the shapes of which the designer opted to echo with semi-circular swags in tones of blue decorated with silver stars to suggest the night sky.

The concept drawings were presented to the centre manager by the designer. It must be stressed that the designer or design team should be given the opportunity to present their own ideas to the management in any design project. This gives both sides the opportunity to question, explain, defend and reach a final agreement. The manager of Princes' Square, who is a woman of few words, was delighted with the designs and pronounced the concept to be 'brilliant!'. Subsequent discussions centred around technical matters, such as fire safety, since decorations of this nature must meet with the approval of the fire department. It is the responsibility of the centre management to ensure that such approval is received. Nylon tulle, the principal material, is inherently fire retardant as it melts rather than burns with a flame. It was assumed, therefore, that the decorations would meet the approval of the authorities. It was also agreed that one of the lighting plots would be modified to include star shaped filters to light the atrium well with star shapes. The choice of stars as the overall decorative theme was fortuitous since a civic marketing campaign, 'Shine on Glasgow' which seeks to promote Glasgow as a centre for excellence in Christmas shopping was announced at the same time. The central image of this campaign was a star. The festival was launched in Princes' Square at the end of November.

Having received the approval of the centre manager, the final design problem was to convince the tenants that the scheme was appropriate for Princes' Square. It was initially decided that the designer would present his ideas to the centre's tenants' committee In the intervening period, between the two meetings, the manager decided to 'test the water'. She dispatched her secretary with the concept drawings to gauge the reactions of a cross-section of the tenants. This group included the tenant who had been most vociferous in condemning the decorations from the previous years. The reaction was unanimous (even here), they loved it and the project could go ahead!

FROM DESIGN TO REALITY

Needless to say, this is not the end, but the beginning of the next stage, which can best be described as technical, i.e. the bringing of the concept to life. The decorations were to be installed overnight on 12/13 November, which meant that there were only three months in which to manufacture them, a very short space of time. For the designer the technical stage had been reached. This is the stage of producing technical drawings which are measured to scale and accurate and ought to be easily understood and interpreted by the manufacturers. It is also the stage of specifying the exact materials and methods of construction. Given the scale of a project such as this, it is essential that full-scale samples are produced which can be seen in situ and context by all of the interested parties. The sample stage helps to avoid expensive mistakes and also gives the designer the opportunity to refine the concept. At this stage, the concept moves from design (a plan) to reality. In the Princes' Square project the bows were found to be too small and were radically enlarged to look more important within the vast space. The swags in the food court needed enlivening and it was decided that they should be peppered with twinkling lights to increase the feeling of a starry sky – particularly at night.

For the manufacturer, this is the stage of ironing out the technical problems and streamlining the processes to make them as economic as possible. Accurate timings of the processes allows for process costing to be calculated. They also have the task of locating the materials in bulk and sourcing trees, lights etc. It should be borne in mind that owing to the cyclic nature of such work, in some cases it may be almost too late to access exactly the materials and accessories necessary. In the Princes' Square case the very short time span severely restricted the choice of materials available.

With the technical difficulties resolved, manufacture went ahead. At the end of October the manufacturers had a meeting with the civic fire inspector who immediately placed an injunction on the installation of the decorations in their existing form! His concern was that, in a fire, the nylon material would drip onto customers below. With only two weeks to go, a quick compromise had to be reached. All of the relevant decorations were lined with fireproofed cotton muslin which, in theory, would catch any melting material. The bows on the lightfittings were repositioned closer to the balustrade, again to catch potential drips. This was a period of high anxiety for all parties involved! Eventually, the civic fire inspector was satisfied.

With this hurdle surmounted, manufacture was completed on 12 November and the decorations were glamorously delivered in two large estate cars. (An important point to note is that most retail organizations use their decorations more than once, not necessarily in the same location. Storage and care are vitally important.) The fact that decorations for such a large area of space could be safely confined in such a small area was well received by Princes' Square. The materials are easy to clean and virtually impossible to crush so a year of storage will do minimal damage.

At six o'clock on Sunday 12 November a team of four professional display artists and six others including the designer and manufacturers met two of Princes' Square's technical staff to begin the installation. Fourteen hours later, a ragged little group stood swaying with exhaustion on the floor looking up at the final effect. Two cleaners wandered in. The first said 'it's lovely, but what's the theme?', her colleague replied 'it's for grown ups . . . it's what you'd call sophisticated!'

THE DÉNOUEMENT

It had worked. The complex act of faith had become reality. The more traditional elderly shoppers were unsure but the tenants loved it and there were many positive comments from customers. Not all customers are as well behaved as they might be. There were anxieties that as two of the colours were those of the local rival football teams there might be vandalism. This did not happen but some people did throw things such as coins, wrappers etc. on to the large swathes of fabric. An illustration, perhaps, that designers can never fully anticipate the uses or misuse to which the consumer will put their work.

——— QUESTIONS ———

(1) Explain the significance of Christmas decorations to a shopping centre such as Princes' Square from both a retailers' and consumers' perspective.

(2) Analyse the various stages of the case and identify the factors which made the successful completion of the exercise so uncertain.

(3) Assume the role of manager of Princes' Square and explain what you would do differently in similar circumstances.

(4) Visit your favourite local shopping centre and identify the particular problems and requirements for the installation of effective seasonal decorations.

18

The Caisse d'Épargne: Towards Optimal Distribution

FRÉDÉRIC JALLAT & ÉLISABETH TISSIER-
DESBORDES

OVERVIEW

The 'Caisse d'Épargne' (Savings Bank) is one of the main French banks which have had to face new competitors. This new situation has involved a whole new reorganization of the bank, with the creation of balanced work areas, new agency design with a new approach to welcoming customers and the implementation of databases to improve services and increase sales.

KEY WORDS

Marketing services, Branch design, Network administration, Geomarketing, Banking deregulation

French savings banks ('Caisse d'Épargne') are special cases in European banking. Generally speaking, these institutions have a long-running history (the Paris 'Caisse d'Épargne' for example was founded in 1818) and they serve a social welfare function, by attracting modest savings. In France, part of the funds collected by the 'Livret A' are used to finance social housing. (A type of savings account allowing the French saver to deposit up to FF 100,000 and earn a tax-free interest of 3.5 per cent. This social welfare function endows the Caisse d'Épargne with a special status.

For a long time, the Caisse d'Épargne was granted a monopoly on savings accounts. Some critics zealously underlined the amazing privileges bestowed upon the institution.[1] In any case, the Caisse d'Épargne was special and the 'Livret A', 'a symbol of republicanism and a sacred cow'.[2]

A new law passed in July 1983 set out the first reforms for the Caisse d'Épargne. This action was furthered by a deregulation law passed in January 1984 with a broader legal scope extending to the French banking community at large. Since then, the Caisses d'Épargne have become banks whose traditionally protected commerce now has succumbed to the throes of competition. A case in point, several financial products such as the CODEVI, were quickly offered to the public by all banks. Even today these substitutes continue to threaten the Livret A. Once the monopoly was abolished, competition got tougher. At the same time, the Caisse d'Épargne was finally able to shake itself free from the shackles of its previous restrictions and took advantage of the new horizons.

The socio-cultural environment and opinion change have been undercurrents in promoting the reorganization of the interface between financial institutions and the public. Both the fact that local branches of the Caisses focused on managing a few simple products and their equipment infrastructure showcasing the prevalence of teller operations underlined the lengthy procedures and lacklustre image of this institution. All of these points were detrimental to the bank in its new context. In order to promote its long-term ambition of shaping a modern corporate image the Caisse had to change. Change required very concrete actions in each branch as well as setting up a network at large.

Until 1986, branch design involved two distinct operations in the front-office: counsel and financial operations on the one hand, and deposits and withdrawals on the other.

The zone reserved for counsel was in reality very limited (at best 30 per cent of the total work area) showing the double difficulty of serving a general public and offering a wide range of services defined in 'technical' terms.

Deprived of checking accounts until 1978 and stock-linked accounts until 1980, the bank's main business was basically focused on linear 'paying' teller windows.

Bank activity was primarily composed of deposits and withdrawals on savings accounts carried out by low-motivated bank staff. In the back-office, loans were handled by a specialized department that received clients in a cubicle at the back of the branch office. This organization created a 'geographic' ditch, a psychological gap between tellers obliged to carry out repetitive and low-value tasks compared with 'privileged' advisers who were stimulated both by the type and nature of their financial advice.

In the middle of the 1980s, the institution's challenges were threefold:

1   to move away from product management to client management, fully aware that the clientele was now better informed, more demanding and better able to perceive and make decisions in a highly aggressive and competitive environment, whose reach was nation-wide and well-prepared;
2   to cater to this clientele with a staff which was busy building on its knowledge, learning to understand the whole gamut of new products and keen to enhance its pedagogical role and image. Yet, the staff could not fully exploit its know-how and develop its skills, since it was overburdened with repetitive and operational tasks that for some reason did not reduce waiting lines;
3   to enhance obsolete structures which no longer corresponded to the requirements of a computer-based market, which regardless of its degree of automation, were paradoxically more personalized, since operations were redistributed within its banking activities by streamlining institutions and its network of bank branches.

Building on these facts, a new area was designed called 'Espace Ecureuil' (the thrifty squirrel is the bank's mascot and emblem). The 'Espace Ecureuil' merged new banking distribution concepts (creating small and personalized branches) with new technologies.

Branch layout is divided between a personalized services zone and an automated service area for Livret A operations. The 'Espace Ecureuil' spearheaded the company's strategic options, symbolizing its corporate ambitions (a modern and recognized institution, 'fully acknowledged' competition of product/services offering, professional motivation and enhanced employee satisfaction).

But reviewing branch blueprints was not limited to reviewing the dismantling and re-installation of physical dividers, of aesthetics or automated banking operations. The new branch design streamlined the network (paying close attention to service areas, carrying out an analysis of competition by geographic sector, closing unprofitable branches) with an immense effort made on in-house training and keeping personnel informed. Revamping the concept of work and branch conception was indeed part of a new organizational definition and hierarchical aspirations: between 1983 and 1990 the level of network concentration and structure streamlining was amazing with the number of branches dropping from 467 to 186.[3]

The 'Centre National des Caisses d'Épargne', CENCEP (National Centre of Savings Banks) was the overseer of streamlining network management and presented the branch agency revamping plan in 1992. As CENCEP Chairman, Jean-Pierre Thiolon, pursued and reinforced this policy, basing change on the findings of a McKinsey survey. The CENCEP project imposed merger, thereby defining 31 geographic units in addition to the Caisses d'Épargne in French overseas departments (Guadeloupe, Martinique, New Caledonia and the Réunion Islands).

After somewhat difficult negotiations (spiked by, for example, local specificity and personal conflicts), the network was finally ready to confront direct banking competition, regardless of numerous attacks on the Caisse d'Épargne's main weapon, the Livret A, which had 'conquered' 26 million clients and held a solid and long-standing reputation.

This wide revamping sought to stimulate responsibility and autonomy of each branch, by reinforcing its financial aspect and by delegating account management to each local branch director. At the same time, the scope of product lines offered was broadened (corporate loans, municipal loans, collective management products) to enhance the institution's clientele positioning. Finally, the staff were trained to market these performing products.

The new network was now more homogenous. Before this reform, the range between the smallest and largest Caisse d'Épargne was 1 to 1,000. That difference has currently come down to a 1 to 6 spread, opposing the Paris and Adour branches. The weight of all these savings institutions is comparable to regional banks. On average their equity tops FF 1 billion, boasting a network of 180 branches with approximately 1,100 employees.

In 1991, Paris' Caisse d'Épargne merged with neighbouring Caisses taking on a broader geographic status, and consequently renaming itself Caisse d'Épargne Ile de France-Paris. The Caisse Midi-Pyrénées stemmed from the merger of 12 regional Caisses and the Caisse d'Épargne Rhône-Alpes-Lyon merged the Lyon, Aix En Provence, Rhône Nord-Beaujolais and the Vienne Nord-Dauphiné institutions.

Once the reform was underway, the banks had to merge clientele files and find a compromise to set up different services on a local level. Creating a decision-making tool was the crux of this modernization programme. The tool helps strike a balance between branch performance and market potential.

At the end of 1992, the group embarked on a programme to optimize sales. One year after the creation of 31 new institutions and after carrying out operations for the required reorganization, an in-depth analysis of the distribution network was conducted.

Teaming up with Line Data Coref, one of France's leading geomarketing companies, the Caisse d'Épargne set up optimization tools including Geobase, a powerful and innovative program providing quick results. The software helps optimize sales by visualizing likely prospect areas, a sector's potential, competitive tension and a network's links. Market analysis and internal data specific to each sales point help set up a thorough audit of the network and suggest corrective action.

The action plan includes a number of operations aiming to enhance production processes and to increase branch sales. The main points focus on:

1 reallocating personnel and equipment provided to branches (for computerized stations, automatic tellers) to enhance market sales;
2 reorganizing sales outlets into sales units more capable of responding to the clients' specific needs. These units also housed estate planning and management of corporate accounts. Each sales outlet redefined its role within each sales unit, based on market specificity and its own business;
3 the modifications to carry out, such as creating new branches for potential markets, transferring sales points and pursuing modernization and setting up sales outlets.

Today, seven institutions use this software tool and 12 others subcontract their work to the CENCEP which operates two computer stations.

The Flandres institution, for example, has its own geographic information system, Sigma, which is the fruit of three years of work on client databases. The institution can pilot its direct marketing and local communication actions within a zone including 610 sales outlets divided into 14 sales divisions. Sigma is used both as a tool to elaborate business strategies on the field and to organize the network.

The territory covered by the Flandres Caisse was built up from the INSEE blocks up through the commune, township, neighbourhood and clusters (approximately 5,000 inhabitants). A town like Roubaix for example breaks down into 19 neighbourhoods, 40 clusters and 700 blocks. Information technology provides zooms for a more-detailed analysis of the territory covered and the database. The geographic information system then uses mathematical models to obtain penetration rates by clientele, attraction profile by branch and signs of 'branch cannibalism'.

This system is a powerful weapon to counter both downtown banks and other distributors cropping up just outside towns.

——— QUESTIONS ———

(1) Why was the Caisse d'Épargne's reorganization necessary? What motivated this reorganization in relation to the evolution of bank marketing.

(2) What possibilities does geomarketing offer? What are the subsequent consequences on branch reorganization?

(3) What are the functions of a banking agency? What are the consequences at an operational level and in terms of branch design?

Notes

[1] De Closets, F. 1982: *Toujours Plus*. Grasset.

[2] Plassart, P. 1996: Matignon reluctantly reviews the Livret A financing. *Le Nouvel Economiste*, no 1032, 26 January, p. 29.

[3] Caisse does not mean branch. In reality, the overall network of the Caisse d'Épargne network at large currently represents 4,274 sales outlets and 3,228 cash dispensers. Generally speaking, and akin to the French postal services, the group upholds its neighbourhood status, frequently reaffirming the branch's aspiration to maintain a privileged relationship between the client and the institution. The Caisses are consequently more synonymous with fully fledged field activities rather than sales outlets.

19

The Olympic Museum Shop

LLUÍS MARTÍNEZ-RIBES AND MARÍA DOLORES DE
JUAN VIGARAY

OVERVIEW

The case of The Olympic Museum Shop demonstrates how the retail
business operates, but as of yet the marketing department has not made
any definitive decisions relating to the marketing strategies. In this case
study we will analyse the necessary information for two objectives. The
first objective is to gain an understanding of the present marketing situation of the shop, and the second objective is related to the design of
alternative strategies in order to improve the shop's profitability. The
approach is to consider The Olympic Museum Shop as a *selling machine*.
That is, making profit is the main goal, but always keeping in mind the
importance of communicating the Olympic values and ideals, which is the
theme of the shop. Considering the above-mentioned objectives, it will be
possible to implement various plans based on repositioning as well as on
merchandising techniques and a better management of the retailing mix.

KEY WORDS

Retail marketing, Museum shop, Positioning, Merchandising, Retailing
mix, The Olympic Museum, Shop design and layout

THE MUSEUM

On 23 June 1993, the dream of Mr Juan Antonio Samaranch, President of the International Olympic Committee (IOC), came true when The Olympic Museum opened its doors to the public. The goal of the museum was to be something more than just a building containing Olympic memorabilia. It had to be a place where visitors could immerse themselves in the Olympic atmosphere. That goal has been achieved.

The Olympic Museum is located in the heart of Lausanne (Switzerland), next to Lake Leman. The building, of contemporary architecture, is surrounded by wonderful gardens which are complemented with many attractive statues. This combination of elements provides the visitor with an atmosphere of serenity but at the same time is very stimulating.

The museum takes one back through the history of the Olympics, all the way back to ancient Olympic Greece, whose values are encouraged as much today as they were then. This philosophy has been summarized by Père Henri Dion, friend of Pierre de Coubertin in this quotation: 'In order to discover the best of oneself, one must set a goal higher than ever thought possible. Altius, citius, fortius.'

The visitor encounters room after room of sporting memorabilia. There are the champions' awards including laural wreathes, the interactive information points, objects from both the Summer and Winter Olympic Games, the collection of Olympic stamps and coins, Olympic videos and other miscellaneous items. In 1995, this modern and dynamic museum was given the European Museum of the Year Award. This indicates the acknowledgement of the museum's world-class status.

SHOP DEVELOPMENT

As with most major museums, shops with souvenirs are part of the visit. The Olympic Museum is no exception and included in the building's design was space for a museum shop where the visitor could browse through the shop's items. We all know that when we experience something very pleasurable, we like to bring something back home that will later remind us of that experience.

Keeping this in mind, the museum's directors realized immediately that their know-how did not include the issues relating to retail management. Therefore, in order to fill the 130 m of selling space, they contracted some well-known sporting goods retailers of Lausanne to manage the shop. Between the IOC and the local partners the duties were divided: the search for products, wholesale purchasing, recruiting and training of salespeople, bookkeeping, stock management, sales management, etc.

Very soon a collection of products relating to the Olympics was developed. These products were organized in six departments:

1   gadgets, pins, watches and the like;
2   clothes and accessories;
3   stationery;
4   games, puzzles and confectionery;
5   posters;
6   stamps and coins.

From the very beginning it was clear that a specific computer program would be needed to manage the shop's retail operations (total sales, unit sales, total promotion sales, unit promotion sales, value of the inventory, costs, selling prices, gross sales, net sales, profit margins, etc.) not only for all the items *as a whole* but also for *each specific item*. Because of this, each item is coded and can be easily identified. This system of tracking the inventory and cost control allows for the constant monitoring of the facts and figures of the business.

THE SHOP'S CUSTOMER BASE

After a period of preparation, the shop opened to the public and started to fulfil its customers' wishes of taking home a souvenir of the visit to the museum. The types of people who visit the museum could be classified in the following categories:

1   sports enthusiasts;
2   tourists coming from post- or pre-Olympic sites;
3   students from the surrounding area (maximum travel time three hours by car or bus);
4   adults that come with organized daily tours;
5   Lausanne residents.

However, due to their proximity, the Lausanne residents tend to visit the museum more frequently and use the shop to buy gifts. This is because many of the other types of visitors live far from the museum and repeated visits are unlikely. Adults who come individually comprise the segment with the highest buying power, and it is estimated that they account for 76 per cent of the visitors. The rest are divided as follows: 11 per cent are groups of students, and the remaining 13 per cent are senior citizens and children. In general, most of the visitors come in the summer. Approximately 13 per cent of the annual visitors come in July, making this the busiest month.

The number of visitors to the museum in the years 1993–5 was as follows:

1993   (six months)   108,838
1994   200,005 (it was the ninth most visited museum in Switzerland)
1995   (until 10.12.95) 158,219 (the goal for 1995 was to reach 215,000)

◇

THE SHOP'S EXPANSION

In the middle of 1995, it was decided to expand the selling area by 40 m². With this expansion, the marketing director of The Olympic Museum realized the need for a European expert on retailing who could give a professional opinion about the shop's operations.

As the visitors of the museum increased so did the sales, but the figures were not very encouraging. Up until the middle of 1995 the shop's average sale per customer was only 45 SFr, and the average sale calculated on the basis of total visitors to the museum was only 5.9 SFr (from 23.6.94 to 3.10.95). In the last quarter of 1995 the average sale per visitor increased slightly to 9 SFr on week days and 8 SFr on the weekends. As an additional reference, in 1990 the average sale per visitor to the Tower of London's shop was £1 (£1 = 2 SFr). Taking into account the type of customers that visited The Olympic Museum, their buying power and their enthusiasm for the Olympics, the average sale per visitor should have been higher.

After visiting The Olympic Museum, the newly hired retailing expert was as impressed as the majority of the visitors. He entered the shop, observed the environment carefully for a long period of time, paid close attention to the buying behaviour of the customers and finally decided to interview the customers as they left the shop.

The conclusions from the interviews of the customers and museum visitors plus the quantitative results of a previous survey conducted a few months earlier were the following:

Table 19.1 Relative contributions of product departments

	Shelf space %	Sales in unit %	Sales in volume %	Contribution margin %
Gadgets, pins, watches	7.90	26.70	35.95	30.67
Clothes, accessories	56.33	16.08	43.39	49.18
Stationery	29.76	45.30	16.01	14.47
Games, puzzles	3.39	1.12	1.88	1.90
Art reproduction	1.49	0.01	0.84	0.84
Stamps and coins	1.14	10.78	1.93	2.94

- the general impression of The Olympic Museum was very favourable (76 per cent);
- 42 per cent of the visitors decided to go to the museum on the recommendation of family or friends;
- 82 per cent stated that the interactive computer terminals were easy to use;
- 76 per cent would like to return to the museum;
- the shop's merchandise was generally perceived as being of good quality;
- the maintenance and organization of the shop was considered very good;
- the most common complaint was that the prices of the merchandise were too high;
- there was a lack of merchandise at the medium-price range;
- there was practically nothing for children;
- there was a great variety of clothes, but a shortage of other exclusive products;
- there was no sale merchandise or promotional items;
- one visitor said he would like the shop to be 'more fun and have more personality'.

THE SHOP'S MERCHANDISE BASE

The assortment of products in the shop is organized in six different departments. Their percentages are measured in shelf space, sales in unit, sales in volume and contribution margins and are shown in the table 19.1.

Table 19.2 Contributions by product category

	Shelf space %	Sales in unit %	Sales in volume %	Contribution margin %
Postcards	9.21	32.85	1.74	1.68
Stamps	1.13	10.72	1.33	1.88
T-shirts	22.57	10.48	19.50	22.73
Keyrings	0.45	7.18	4.19	3.84
Books	15.80	5.84	7.30	6.55
Pens and pencils	0.14	5.79	1.56	1.47
Watches	1.81	4.36	21.35	15.70
Pins	0.68	3.49	2.99	3.15
Posters	1.35	3.07	3.40	3.94
Caps	1.81	1.69	3.19	3.75
Sweatshirts	5.42	1.33	7.46	8.30
Umbrellas	0.23	0.67	1.85	2.30
Total	60.60	87.47	75.86	75.29

There are 12 categories of products that make up almost 90 per cent of the shop's sales in SKUs:

1 postcards (33 per cent);
2 stamps (11 per cent);
3 T-shirts (10.5 per cent);
4 keyrings and similar products (7 per cent);
5 books (6 per cent);
6 pens and pencils (6 per cent);
7 watches (4 per cent);
8 pins and insignias (3 per cent);
9 posters (3 per cent);
10 caps (2 per cent);
11 sweatshirts and pullovers (1 per cent);
12 umbrellas (1 per cent).

The current situation for these twelve categories is shown in table 19.2.

Here are some examples of prices in the shop: The average price per miscellaneous gadget is 23 SFr, but we must consider that the most commonly sold gadgets have a psychological threshold of 10 SFr. The average prices of

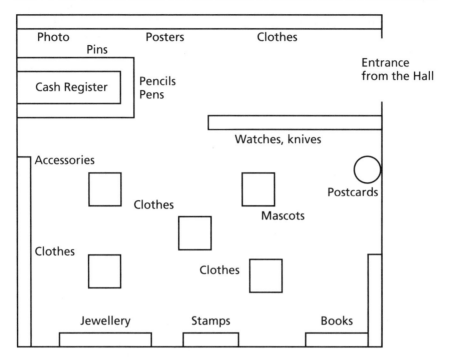

Figure 19.1 The current layout of the shop

the different products in this department are as follows: 3.5 SFr for the pins, 10 SFr for the keyrings, 5 SFr for the pens and pencils, 84 SFr for the watches (Swatch watches 100 SFr) and umbrellas at 48 SFr. As for clothing, the average price is 32 SFr for T-shirts, 96 SFr for the sweatshirts, and 32 SFr for the caps. The *star products* are the T-shirts.

THE SHOP'S DESIGN AND LAYOUT

The museum shop's interior design and layout reflects the trends of most European clothing shops from the early 1990s. The displays and fixtures are basically modular with two types of materials predominating: chrome metal and glass. The fixtures can be converted into freestanding units which can create small square islands, as well as shelves along the wall. These islands can have a maximum height of 120 cm. The shop is 130 m², distributed approximately as shown in figure 19.1

The shop has a dark marble floor and a ceiling made from different materials depending on the area. There is a false square cell ceiling with hidden halogen spotlights. There are also sections where the ceiling is made of a metallic material and the light fixtures are visible, exceeding 700 lux when the light is measured one metre from the floor. Moreover, the light comes from various sources with the fixtures focused at different angles illuminating the areas unevenly.

The presentation of the merchandise is that of fashion boutiques, with the garments carefully hung on the fixtures, leaving plenty of space among the merchandise. The *facings* are not repeated even when the product is small, and the price and product characteristics are not shown on the shelf space. These data are reserved for tags which are stuck to the products or hung on their label.

The system for arranging the products is not very clear to the visitor. For instance, T-shirts may be displayed in several different areas of the shop. They can form part of an Olympic theme, some in the winter section, others in the summer section, and may even be grouped with display T-shirts from a specific supplier. In general, T-shirts are arranged by size, with the larger sizes on the bottom rack and the smaller sizes on the top. However, there are no signs or graphics to indicate this. The agendas, posters and postcards have their own displays which are positioned so that the customers can easily see them. Some merchandise, like home accessories and miscellaneous gadgets, are displayed close to floor level.

Outside the shop there is a mailbox. Next to this are two mannequins dressed elegantly with clothes that have The Olympic Museum logo on them. They are also outfitted with accessories such as purses and caps. The prices are not displayed on this merchandise.

The counter for the cash register is white and stands 120 cm high. It is located directly in front of the shop's entrance and is the first thing the visitor sees upon entering. A multitude of gadgets are also displayed on the counter.

Because the shop has practically no graphics or signs to distinguish different sections, the customer is forced to wander through the shop, browsing among the products. Therefore, the type of sales practised here can be classified as *assisted sales*. The visitors are free to circulate through the shop and have access to the majority of the merchandise. As mentioned above, all the merchandise has tags indicating the price and internal shop codes. For example, visitors interested in T-shirts can choose the colour they prefer, take a garment from the rack or the shelf and examine the tag for size, material and other information. If it is what they want, they can take the garment straight to cash register and pay for

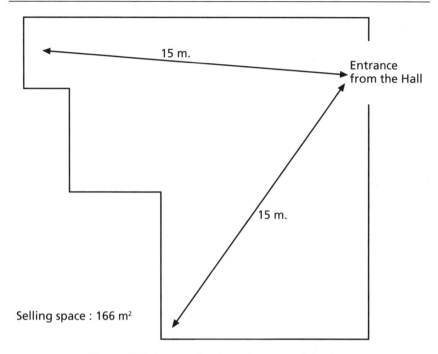

15 m.

Entrance
from the Hall

15 m.

Selling space : 166 m²

Figure 19.2 Layout showing sales space of the shop

it, but if it is not, they can continue looking or else ask for assistance. There are several friendly salespeople to help the customers. They speak several languages, which facilitates their dealings with customers from all five continents.

The gross margin for the shop's products is 50 per cent or more, and, as of now, the sales space will be 166 m², with the layout as shown in figure 19.2.

In conclusion, increasing the sales space of the shop by about 40 m² is more than just a simple matter of expansion. The plan is to use this sales space as an opportunity to move in a new and different direction to improve the shop's productivity and personality as opposed to simply acquiring more space for the same operations as before.

Acknowledgement

We would like to express our gratitude to all the managers at The Olympic Museum in Lausanne for their collaboration and support for this case study.

—————— QUESTIONS ——————

(1) The directors of The Olympic Museum would like to know how to increase the shop performance since the shop should be an important source of income. What do you suggest?

(2) Given the floor plan of the new shop what might be an appropriate layout of departments and categories?

Index

Page numbers in *italic* refer to tables and figures.